Mercyhurst College Learning Resource Center

Presented By:

Mary Royer '52 Rodgers

ethics

ethics:

alternatives
and
issues

by

NORMAN L. GEISLER, Ph.D.

Foreword by Harold B. Kuhn

ZONDERVAN PUBLISHING HOUSE
GRAND RAPIDS, MICHIGAN

ETHICS: ALTERNATIVES AND ISSUES
Copyright © 1971 by Zondervan Publishing House
Grand Rapids, Michigan

Library of Congress Catalog Card Number 79-156247

Printed in the United States of America

Affectionately dedicated to my children
RUTH, DAVID, DANIEL, RHODA,
PAUL, AND RACHEL

Contents

Foreword

PART ONE: ETHICAL ALTERNATIVES

PART TWO: ETHICAL ISSUES

Foreword

He who undertakes to write a textbook in Christian Ethics in our time faces a formidable set of challenges and problems. It is fashionable today to speak of "doing ethics"; the term suggests a kind of detachment of the writer from his subject. The Christian writer must, however, not only survey data, but also give to them some framework which will be meaningful for the individual seeking to live the Christian life in today's context, including the writer himself.

Professor Norman L. Geisler has undertaken to steer the precarious course between an abstract principial ethic on the one hand, and situationism on the other. His method is basically inductive, in that he seeks to move from the investigation of systems which present themselves as options for human adherence, to a system which will do justice to the mandate of the Lord of the Church and at the same time incorporate the valid insights secular systems may possess.

The second part of the volume comes to grips with some of the thorny issues of our time — issues which are often selected as radical samples to support situationism. Dr. Geisler undertakes the difficult task of analyzing cases in terms of principles, and seems to this commentator to have done it well. His volume not only surveys, from Christian perspectives, alternative systems, but proposes one which commends itself to the Evangelical conscience.

Ethics: Alternatives and Issues embodies careful surveys, restrained evaluations, and modest proposals. It is a textbook without being bookish, a scholarly work without being pedantic.

HAROLD B. KUHN

PART ONE
ETHICAL ALTERNATIVES

This section of the book deals with the basic options available in ethics. Most fundamentally, it opts for a normative or deontological approach to ethics as opposed to a utilitarian or teleological approach.

Within normative ethics there are six basic options; each of these will be examined in turn. The special problem treated throughout is threefold: Are there any universal norms? How many are there? If there are more than one, what ought one to do if they conflict?

Chapter seven is the view defended in this book. It becomes the basis on which an approach is made to some of the major contemporary ethic issues of Part Two. The first chapter provides an overview of the entire first section of the book.

1 / Introduction: Basic Ethical Approaches and Alternatives

Is it ever right to lie in order to save a life? The question poses a conflict in ethical norms. Is truth-telling more important than life-saving? What would you do? The various answers to this question can be used to illustrate six basic approaches to ethics and to introduce the first section of this book. All of the ethical views have to do with fundamental ethical questions, viz., are there any valid ethical norms? If so, how many? And if there are many ethical norms, then what does one do when two of them conflict? Does one tell a lie to save a life or sacrifice a life to save the truth?

I. THE BASIC ALTERNATIVES IN NORMATIVE ETHICS

The basic positions which may be taken on the question of ethical norms may be illustrated from a recent case involving U.S. Commander Lloyd Bucher of the spy ship Pueblo, who, with his crew of 23 men, was captured by the North Koreans. When the interrogators threatened to kill his crew, Bucher signed confessions, untruthfully admitting to the guilt of spying in North Korean territorial waters. These false confessions became the grounds for sparing the lives of the crew and led to their ultimate release. The question, then, is this: was Bucher's lie to save these lives morally justified? Or, more broadly, is lying to save a life ever morally right? One way to answer this is to reject the notion of morality altogether.

A. *Lying Is Neither Right Nor Wrong: There Are No Norms*[1]

One alternative to this question is to deny that there are any meaningful ethical norms whatsoever. This position is called antinomianism

---

[1] Antinomianism will not be taken here in the strict sense of *against* law but in the loose sense of *without* law. Chapter two is devoted to a discussion of the antinomian position.

(literally, against law). It affirms that there are no moral principles (such as "one ought not lie") which may be validly applied to Bucher's case and by which one could pronounce his action right or wrong. And if there are no moral standards, there can be no moral judgments. Hence, Bucher was neither right nor wrong ethically. What he did may have been personally, militarily, or nationally satisfying, but it cannot be declared morally good or bad.

There are various ways by which an act of lying might be "justified," but there is no way that it can be objectively *judged*. For, on the antinomian view, there are no objective norms by which the judgment can be made. Bucher's lie, for example, might be "justified" by appealing to its results on his crew or for his country. Or, it might be "justified" subjectively as an authentic decision he chose to make. But in no case would these pragmatic consequences or personal choices be objectively valid moral criteria for concluding the correctness of his choice. Indeed, the subjective considerations which were "good" for Bucher's crew and country were thereby "bad" for the enemy country, that is, insofar as the confession was known to be false. When there are no objective moral standards which transcend the subjectivity of individuals and nations, then there is no objective way to declare an act morally good or bad in an objective sense.

In other words, lacking any objective moral norms, Bucher's actions could be considered either good or bad, depending on one's perspective. And from an overall point of view his lie was neither good nor bad. Indeed, there is no overall or objective point of view. If there were such an overall perspective, then one could make an objective pronouncement on the action as to whether it was really right or wrong. But since there are no objective standards, Bucher's lie cannot be said to be either right or wrong.

B. *Lying Is Generally Wrong: There Are No Universal Norms* [2]

Most ethical positions avoid the antinomian stand against all objective norms. One way of doing this without condemning Bucher's lie is to hold that lying is generally but not always wrong. This view will be called generalism. That is, lying is wrong as a rule, but there are times when the rule should be broken, viz., when a greater good is served, and saving a life is certainly such a time. That one ought not tell a lie is objectively meaningful but it is not universal. In some circumstances one ought to lie. Hence, this moral principle (and others too) is generally but not universally valid. That is, as far as ethical principles go, they are objectively valid. But ethical norms are not universal; there are exceptions.

There are many possible reasons for holding to generalism, i.e., that

[2] This view is discussed in chapter three.

ethical norms are not universal but, rather, admit of some exceptions. One basic reason is that if there are two or more general norms which come into conflict (such as truth-telling and life-saving), then it would seem that both cannot be universal. It would seem that there must be an exception to at least one of them, since both of them cannot be followed. And if there are exceptions to all of them (or even all but one), then there are not many universal norms. At best, all (or all but one) of the objective ethical norms must be general, but they cannot all be universal principles.

If truth-telling is only a general norm, then when is it right to lie? The generalist may answer this in a number of ways. A common answer is to suggest that it is right to lie when lying will accomplish a greater good than not lying. This approach is utilitarian. Lying is utilized to bring about a greater good for a greater number of people. Another reason one might consider truth-telling only a general but not a universal norm is that there is one overriding principle the keeping of which sometimes necessitates telling a lie. However, if there is at least one universally objective norm, then this is no longer a complete generalism. Rather, it is a one-norm universalism, which leads to the next position.

C. *Lying Is Sometimes Right: There Is One Universal Norm* [3]

The view that there is one universal norm in view of which it is sometimes right to lie is really an absolutism, but for circumstantial reasons it will be called situationism. It is called situationism not only to distinguish it from other forms of absolutism (which hold that there are many universal norms, in contrast to only one) but also because proponents of the view so label it. The name situationism is somewhat descriptive. It reminds us that since circumstances are so radically different there can be only one universal norm capable of adapting to all of them. For it argues that only one thing can be truly universal to all situations. If there were more than one universal norm, there would be a conflict, and an exception would have to be made to resolve the conflict. And if there can be an exception made to all but one norm, then no more than one norm can be truly universal.

As applied to Bucher's lie to save lives, the situationist affirms that it is right because Commander Bucher was acting in accord with the highest and only truly universal norm. This is often, though not necessarily, said to be an absolute love norm. On this statement of the norm, Bucher is justified for lying in love. Lying was the loving thing to do in order to save these lives. His lie is judged right because it accords with the only absolute ethical norm there is, viz., love. A lie could be wrong if it were done unlovingly, i.e., selfishly (e.g., to cover up

[3] See chapter four which expounds this view more fully.

for one's wrong). But if the lie is told selflessly for the sake of others, then it is morally right, according to the love norm.

According to this view, the end does justify the means, if by "end" is meant the love norm. In fact, only the end justifies the means. For nothing but the absolute norm of love makes an act morally right. And nothing but the lack of love makes an act morally wrong.

D. *Lying Is Always Wrong: There Are Many Non-Conflicting Norms* [4]

Holding to one universal norm is not the only position possible with regard to absolute principles. There is the view that there are many valid universal norms which never really conflict. This position will be called non-conflicting absolutism. There may be an apparent conflict between two ethical norms but never a real conflict of duties. There is always a third alternative or a way of doing one without disobeying the other. The domain of each ethical norm has been ideally or providentially allotted to it so that it never actually overlaps with that of another universal norm. This means, for instance, that lying and killing never really conflict. One can always tell the truth without really taking the life of another innocent person. Both lying and killing are always wrong.

If this is so, then what should Commander Bucher have done? If he was not supposed to lie under any circumstance, then what course of action should he have followed? [5] There are several things Bucher could have done consistent with this position, but under no circumstance should he have told a lie to save the lives of his crew. He could have remained silent. That is, he could have refused to make any false confessions whatsoever. Or, he could have told the truth (viz., that he was spying) but not the lie that his boat was in the Korean territorial waters when it was not really there at all. If this confession were not acceptable to the interrogators, then Bucher and his men would have to suffer the consequences of telling the truth and pray for mercy.

But are not the consequences of telling the truth a worse evil, viz., the killing of innocent people? A direct answer to this dilemma which is perfectly consistent with this position (that there are many non-conflicting universal norms) is that killing is wrong but telling the truth which leads someone else to kill on the basis of that truth is not wrong. That is, Bucher had no real moral dilemma. His choice was not "Shall I tell a lie *or* shall I kill?" Rather, his choice was, "Shall I tell a

---

[4] See a more complete discussion of this view in chapter five.

[5] It is possible, according to a non-conflicting absolutism, to argue that Bucher's falsification was not a lie (i.e., was not morally wrong), on the grounds that *in that context* it was not a lie. In other words, by an extension of the meaning of truth to include situations like Bucher's, one could still hold that "lying is always wrong" and yet that Bucher's false confession was morally right. Chapter five has more on this alternative.

lie or shall I allow the possibility that someone else may be killed?" And since Bucher could not be absolutely sure that the North Koreans would kill his crew and since he himself would not be doing the killing, he would be absolved of moral responsibility. On this view, Bucher could not be considered morally blameworthy for the evil other men would do because he told the truth. Indeed, the proponents of this view may appeal to some kind of teleology or providence which says that a greater evil will never come (at least ultimately, if not immediately) from keeping a universal norm. In theistic terms, God will always provide a way of escape so that one will either not have to lie or else a greater evil will not come from truth-telling.

E. *Lying Is Never Right: There Are Many Conflicting Norms* [6]

Another way out of the apparent dilemma of holding that there are many universal norms which sometimes conflict is to declare a violation of any of them to be wrong. That is to say, it is always wrong to lie and it is also wrong to take an innocent life (or it is even wrong not to try to prevent another from doing either), and if one is caught in a real dilemma between these two, he should do the lesser of two evils. Which is the lesser of two evils can be judged by which would result in the fewer bad consequences, i.e., in a utilitarian way. However, both acts (lying and killing) are intrinsically evil; neither one is right, according to their universal norms. And even if there were some way to judge which act is intrinsically (and not merely instrumentally) better, nevertheless, both would still be wrong. However, one will probably be a lesser wrong or evil than the other.

On this view, Bucher would have been wrong no matter which of the only two possible alternatives he took. However, even though evil was unavoidable for him it was also *excusable,* particularly so since he chose the lesser of the two evils. A Christian theist might say that for Bucher sin was inevitable but pardonable. He should commit the lesser sin (whether this be judged intrinsically or extrinsically) and then get on his knees and confess it.

Ideally, if no one broke any of the universal norms, there would be no conflict between any of them. Many moral dilemmas are set up because someone is sinfully forcing someone else into a position where the latter will have to choose between two universal norms. And perhaps all of the rest of the cases of real conflict can be explained by antecedent evil choices, i.e., previous evil actions of oneself or others which bring about such dilemmas. In Christian terminology, if this were not a fallen and depraved world, then there would not be any conflict between these universal norms. But since the world is fallen and there is a conflict, only the atonement or forgiveness of God can resolve the problem.

[6] This position is the subject of chapter six.

It is difficult to give this view a descriptive name. It will be called ideal absolutism because it believes in many absolutes which ideally do not conflict but actually (because of the sins of others or other sins of one's own) do sometimes come into conflict. But because of its connection with sin and its ultimate resolution in forgiveness, this view might also be called harmatological absolutism (relating to the doctrine of sin) or soteriological absolutism (relating to the doctrine of salvation).

F. *Lying Is Sometimes Right: There Are Higher Norms* [7]

Another way of responding to this sample ethical problem may be called hierarchicalism. It might be contended, e.g., that there are many universal ethical norms but they are not equal in intrinsic importance so that when two come into conflict one is obliged to obey the higher of the two commands. So then, in the choice between killing and lying, both of which are universally wrong in the absence of any conflict between them, one ought to choose to save the life because it is an intrinsically higher value. Telling the truth is good but not at the expense of sacrificing a life.

On this view Bucher's lie was right, even though lying in itself is universally wrong, because there is a higher ethical norm than truth-telling, viz., life-saving. Bucher followed the norm which was intrinsically higher when he found two universal norms in conflict. The good action is always the one which is intrinsically better.

This view is similar but different from several other views already mentioned. First, it differs from the immediately preceding view called ideal absolutism. Ideal absolutism holds that both alternatives are wrong when they come into conflict, whereas hierarchicalism contends that one is right, viz., the one which is intrinsically higher. In the former view both alternatives are wrong, but a man ought to do the lesser evil. According to the latter position, at least one alternative is right and a man ought to do the greater good.

Furthermore, hierarchicalism should be distinguished from situationism, for the former holds that there are many universal norms (even though the lower must sometimes be suspended for higher ones) and situationism holds that there is only one universal norm. These many norms, according to the hierarchical view, are universal *in their area*, as long as they do not conflict with another area. They are universal *as far as that relationship goes*, unless there is a conflict of relationships. Hierarchicalism holds that lying *as such* is always wrong but that lying *as transcended* by life-saving is not wrong. In fact, in the latter case it is not really lying at all (in the sense of being something wrong); it is justifiable falsifying for the sake of life-saving.

[7] A more complete discussion of this position is found in chapter seven.

In Bucher's circumstance, giving the wrong information was the right thing to do because it was acting according to a higher ethical norm.

Finally, hierarchicalism differs from generalism in that the former contends that there are many (i.e., at least two) universal ethical norms which are not merely general principles. There are *exemptions* from keeping lower norms (viz., when they come into conflict with higher norms), but there are no *exceptions* to the lower norms. To borrow an illustration from the natural realm, there are no exceptions to the law of gravity for physical bodies but a nail may be exempt from "obeying" the law of gravity by its "obedience" to the higher physical force of a magnet.

G. Summary and Comparison of the Alternatives

There is another possible view, viz., "Lying is always right," but it will not be considered at any length for two basic reasons. First, because it is not seriously set forth by any significant contemporary ethical philosopher known to this writer. Second, the position is self-defeating. For if everyone lied, there would be no more truth to lie about, in which case it would no longer be possible to fulfill the command to lie. Furthermore, if one ought *always* to lie, then presumably the author of that statement is following his own advice, in which case we should take the reverse of it to be the truth of the matter. But if the reverse is true, then one ought not always lie. Then we are back to the question of when one should lie and when one should not, which is what the other views are addressing. Finally, if the author of the ethical universal "One ought always to lie" were giving the statement the way it really ought to be given (i.e., truthfully) then he would not be following his own principle, and he would therefore be inconsistent. So in either event, whether the norm is followed or not, it is self-defeating.

These six views may be summarized by the following comparison. The antinomian sets forth a view to the *exclusion* of all ethical norms whether they be universal or general. The generalist says there are objective norms but they all have *exceptions*. The situationist holds out for one *exclusive* universal norm, readily conceding that all of the rest are at best only general. On the other hand, the non-conflicting absolutist contends for many universal norms which never really overlap, always leaving a way of *escape* from the supposed moral dilemma. Holding to many universal norms which do in reality conflict (though ideally they would not), the ideal absolutist says that doing evil is inevitable but *excusable,* especially if one does the lesser of the evils. Finally, the hierarchicalist accepts many conflicting universal norms which are arranged according to intrinsic value and in view of which a man has an *exemption* from keeping the lower norm by virtue of his acting in accord with the higher norm. The following six chapters will be devoted to a more complete discussion of these ethical alternatives.

These alternatives all revolve around ethical norms. Actually, there is another approach to ethics which does not stress norms but ends.

II. The Basic Approaches: Ethical Norms or Ethical Ends?

The distinction between these two approaches can be expressed by the words teleological and deontological. The first of these stresses ethical *ends* or results of actions; the other emphasizes ethical *norms* or principles for action. A better understanding of these is necessary before the normative approach taken in this book can be adequately understood.

A. Rules Versus Results

The basic difference between teleological and deontological ethics can be explained from the root meaning of the words. Teleology comes from the Greek word *telos,* meaning end or purpose. Deontology comes from the Greek word *deon* which means what is due. As applied to ethics, then, a teleological approach is one which stresses the end or *result* of action and a deontological approach looks to basic *rules* by which one can determine what is due in any given case regardless of the results. That is, the former is a *pragmatic* or utilitarian ethic, being concerned with whether an action will in the end work for the good of most men. The latter is an ethic of *principle* which is concerned with one's duty to do what is inherently right apart from the foreseeable consequences.

In other words, teleological ethics is concerned with the *extrinsic* good of acts insofar as they produce good or evil. Deontological ethics, on the other hand, looks to an *intrinsic* good in the act itself, independent of the alleged good or evil it may produce. The former is concerned with duty for the sake of good results; the latter, with duty for duty's sake. This does not mean, of course, that duty ethics is not concerned with results. Indeed, the deontologists may believe that doing one's duty will bring the greatest good in the long run. However, this is not the *reason* for one to do his duty (i.e., because it will bring the greatest good); rather, he does his duty because it is intrinsically good to do what one ought to do. He does not follow a rule primarily because it will *bring* good but because it *is* good to do so.

This does not mean, on the other hand, that utilitarian ethics is not concerned with rules. It is to say that there is a root difference in theory and that the teleological approach bases the good of human actions only on their utility or usefulness to men in general. The deontological ethic bases the good of human actions on the intrinsic value of following certain norms or rules because these actions are intrinsically right. In fact, the "rule-utilitarians" hold that some rules should never be broken, even if there are legitimate individual exceptions, simply because rule-keeping (even in the exceptional cases) brings about a greater good than rule-breaking. But these never-to-be-broken rules do not qualify as universal norms under our discussion, since they are not duty norms concerned with intrinsic value nor are they really universal. Their "universality" is justified only by an appeal to results (i.e., extrinsically). So actually they are not universal. There are some exceptions, such as when two rules conflict. Furthermore, the reason for not breaking them is only that *as a whole* rule-breaking is bad, even though in a given case it may be justified. In the discussion which follows, both intrinsic and utilitarian norms will be included. But the question for which an answer will be sought there is this: Are there any meaningful deontological norms which are universal? In other words, are there any moral prescriptions which should never be broken?

B. *Prescriptive Versus Descriptive and Emotive*

A normative ethic is one which is prescriptive rather than merely descriptive. It is an ethic which commands certain courses of action as opposed to others. A normative ethic does not merely describe how men *do* act; rather, it prescribes how they *ought* to act. It is not an ethic of the "is" but an ethic of the "ought." In a normative approach to ethics, one is primarily concerned with discovering meaningful norms for prescribing what men should do as opposed to mere scientific or statistical descriptions of what men in fact are doing.

Not only is a normative ethic prescriptive as opposed to descriptive, but it is also opposed to a purely emotive ethic which is centered in the way men feel about certain human actions. The purely emotive approach contends that all alleged ethical statements (i.e., statements which contain ethical symbols like "ought not" and "should") are no more than expressions of how the individual feels about certain matters. That is, what is right varies from one individual's feelings to another's. For example, the command, "You *ought* not lie," really means "I *dislike* lying." The emotivist argues that ethical statements are neither prescriptive nor descriptive. That is, they are not "ought" statements and they are not "is" statements. They are merely individual "feeling" statements. The normative ethic, on the other hand, stands opposed to the emotive ethic in that the former holds that there are at least some ethical statements which are not purely emotive and subjective but imperative for all men. Normative ethics contends that besides declarative statements (descriptive or "is" statements) and ejaculative statements (emotive or "feeling" statements), there are distinctly ethical statements (i.e., prescriptive or "ought" statements). It holds that there are certain things men *ought* to do whether or not any men in fact *do* them and whether or not any men *feel* that they should be done. Normative ethics argues for prescriptive norms which take precedence over both feeling and fact.

C. *Categorical Versus Hypothetical*

Another way to stress what is meant here by normative ethics is to distinguish it as categorical, as opposed to hypothetical. It is the ethic of *commands,* not of conditions. Normative ethics say, "Thou shalt do this," not "*If* you do this, good will result, etc." It is the ethic of the imperative and not the subjunctive mood. In brief, a norm is provided which commands a given course or way of acting which is intrinsically good as opposed to one which is merely the condition or grounds for producing a good.

The difference may be clarified by an illustration. The categorical approach holds that the act of attempting to save a drowning man is an intrinsically good act whether the attempt is successful or not. The hypothetical view, on the other hand, contends that the act of trying to save him is not intrinsically good but is good only *if* it brings about good results, such as actually saving the man. [8] The reason for the difference is that the one is built on a categorical command to do an intrinsic good and the other is based on a hypothetical condition which leads to an extrinsic good.

D. *Principles, Norms, and Rules*

There are many and sometimes subtle distinctions made between principles, norms, and rules. None will be attempted at this juncture. For the sake of inclusiveness (within a normative context), these and like terms (e.g., axioms, postulates) will be used as roughly synonymous. However, in order not to be so all-inclusive as to be ambiguous, a normative approach may be defined as one which posits one or more moral precepts possessing *at least* formal (if not some contentful) meaning by which human actions ought to be controlled.

In the end, of course, one must decide whether whatever norms there may be (universal or not) are meaningful enough to base ethical decisions upon. For, a purely formal norm (without any real experiential content) may be little better than no norm at all. In accordance with a common usage of the terms "principle," "norm," and "rule" (which are roughly synonymous, although the last two have more content), we are ultimately seeking to discover whether there are any contentful "principles" or any universal "rules." But since for the

---

[8] Of course, a hypothetical approach could call an unsuccessful attempt at saving a drowning man good on the ground that the act did bring about other good results such as inspiring bravery in others, developing character in the rescuer, or occasioning appreciation in the friends of the drowned man. But even in this sense the unsuccessful act is not considered good in itself but only because of the good results it brings, intangible as they are.

time being these terms will be used synonymously, the question is simply: Are there any meaningful norms which should never be broken?

E. *Universal Versus General*

So, the concern here is not only with the question: Are there any meaningful ethical norms? The real question is: Are there any *universal* ethical norms? If so, how many are there? Therefore, it is necessary to discuss just what is meant by the word "universal" as applied to ethical norms.

By a universal norm is meant one which applies to all men in all places under the same circumstances. There are no unspecifiable or indefinable exceptions to a universal norm. In fact, since a definable exception is really no exception at all but really part of the definition of what kind of act is being prescribed, a universal norm really has no exceptions at all. For example, *if* (and this may or may not be the case) one sets forth the norm that "lying ought never be done, *except* in a context where the truth is not expected," then this would qualify as a universal norm. [9] It would qualify as a universal norm because it specifies the contextual exception as part of what is meant by a lie. The so called "exception" or circumstance under which the act may be performed qualifies the act so that it is really not a lie but is actually a good form of falsification. Falsifying to get a friend to a surprise birthday party might be given as an illustration. Since the friends are only "fooling" and since this kind of activity is expected in this circumstance, one would not say that the false information is really a lie (i.e., morally wrong). Surprise parties are not a context in which the truth can be expected. Spying for one's country is also used to explain this same point. But more on this later.

Whether or not one accepts these illustrations or even whether or not there are ever any so-called "exceptions" to intentionally giving only correct information, nevertheless, the basic point is the same. A universal norm is one which applies to all morally responsible creatures in any given situation. For whatever definable "exceptions" there are become part of the general rule which then does really apply to all men in that particular circumstance *without exception.* The problem, of course, is whether or not there are any such ethical norms which can be meaningfully defined so as to admit of no *more exception.* Or, the problem is to find a norm which, when qualified by all the exceptions, has a meaning left. [10] But before the discussion moves in the direction of searching for universal norms, a word is in

---

[9] This point will be discussed more fully in chapter five.

[10] The question as to whether the rule-utilitarian norms are really universal or only general, or whether a norm can be really universal, if it is based on utilitarian rather than intrinsic values, will be reserved for the end of chapter three.

order as to why a normative approach is taken in contrast to a non-normative or utilitarian approach.

III. WHY A NORMATIVE APPROACH?

There are several reasons for studying ethics from the vantage point of "norms" rather than merely from the standpoint of "ends." As the discussion unfolds, the reasons, given here in summary, should become more evident. Two basic reasons may be stated: norms are inescapable and they are necessary.

A. *Norms Are Inescapable*

Norms are inescapable for several reasons. This becomes obvious when it is seen how the non-normative or ultilitarian ethics actually depends on norms in several significant ways.

1. *The Need for Norms to Foresee Consequences* — Perhaps the most basic criticism of the approach to ethics by way of "ends" or results of action is the fact that the whole practical value of this system depends on the ability to foresee the long-range consequences of decisions. Surely the individual cannot see what will happen in the long run. And he cannot wait for the results before he has some assurance that his decision is the right one. The future can be a helpful guide only if there is some way of knowing now what the future will bring in the way of good or evil results of one's decisions. But since the individual as such does not have that kind of foreknowledge, he has no way of knowing which course of action will bring the greatest good to the greatest number of men *over the long haul.*

In other words, acting solely on the basis of utilitarian ends would be workable only for an all-knowing God. Finite man simply cannot foreknow the final and total results of his choices. Some who have adopted a utilitarian approach have been frank to confess, "So much of the time we are making, at best, 'educated guesses.' " [11] The classical utilitarians were not unaware of this problem. Their answer to it was by way of an appeal to the "fund" of human experience as a guide for determining which course of action would probably bring about the best for the most people. [12] That is, one can draw from the experiences of what most men in the past have found to work toward the greater good. But this concession to using the "fund" of past experience for a guide involves norms in several ways which will be revealed in the following criticisms. In fact, the very "fund" itself becomes normative in determining which consequences will probably be best. But even more basic than this is the fact that norms are needed to establish the "fund" in the first place.

[11] Fletcher, *Situation Ethics: The New Morality,* Westminster Press, 1966, p. 154, cf. p. 136.
[12] The utilitarian view will be discussed in chapter three under "generalism."

2. *The Need for Norms to Determine the "Fund"* — A factor often overlooked is that the very origin of the "fund" of experience itself presupposes some kinds of guidelines or norms. That is, the first moral creatures no doubt had some kind of guidelines which were prior to the "fund" and by which the very "fund" itself was established. For experiences cannot be evaluated as "good" or "better" and, hence, qualify to be part of the "fund" for future guidance unless some standard of value apart from the experiences is brought to bear on the experiences. Either one would have to admit that experiences come with intrinsic value (which is contrary to utilitarianism, which says they have only extrinsic value) or else there must be some standard outside of experience by which they can be evaluated. Whatever this standard might be, it is obviously normative for the "fund." One has no way of knowing that he possesses a "good" set of guidelines for determining the "better" results unless he has some standard of good by which he can judge them to be "good." This standard would, then, be normative, and it would be prior to the "fund" which it establishes.

3. *The Need for Norms in Order to Determine the Consequences* — Regardless of how the "fund" was established in the first place, it is obvious that the "fund" itself has a normative function. It serves as the utilitarian's guidelines for determining what course of action will probably yield the greatest good for the most men. The individual alone does not usually (if ever) possess the foresight to choose that which will maximize good. He must lean upon the wisdom of the past to guide him in the present in regard to what will be best in the future. This wisdom, however it may have originated, serves as a norm for ethical choices.

To be sure, these norms from the "fund" of human experience are not held to be really universal or absolute. They are not infallible guides, but they are a necessary part of the utilitarian's decision-making procedure. Nevertheless, some kind of norm is needed to make the utilitarian ethic work with any decent degree of probability. Indeed, the need for norms is such that some utilitarians have suggested that the norms or rules should never be broken, not because they are really universally valid, but because rule-breaking brings worse results than rule-keeping. For example, even though telling a lie might bring a greater good in a special case, nonetheless, a greater good would result from keeping the rule of truth-telling in all cases, simply because breaking the rule in *any* case tends to undermine it in *all* cases. Rule-keeping in all cases results in a greater good (even with the bad consequences in some few cases) than rule-breaking does.

Without passing judgment on the rightness or wrongness of the rule-utilitarian position, it is sufficient to conclude here that both kinds of utilitarianism illustrate the need for rules or norms, whether or not there are any occasions when one ought to break them.

4. *The Need for Norms to Evaluate Consequences* — In addition to the need for norms to help determine which result will be the best for the most people, there is also a need for a normative *evaluation* of whether or not the result is better for most once it has happened. There is no way to know if the result is really "better" unless there is a standard of "best" by which it can be judged. In other words, there must be some norm by which one is able to evaluate the consequences *once they have occurred* (apart from the question of the need for norms to guide one in making the best results occur). So the utilitarian needs norms not only to guide his choices about the future consequences but he also needs norms to determine whether or not those consequences are really *better* and not merely *different*, if and when they do occur.

In brief, norms are inescapable, even for the utilitarian whose position is supposedly centered in ends or results. Even the allegedly non-normative approach demands norms to make it function properly. Norms are inescapable, whether they are desirable or not. So the question in ethics is not *whether* there are norms but *which* norms one will use.

B. *Norms Are Necessary*

Norms are not only inescapable, they are *necessary*. They are necessary, that is, if one is to have a meaningful guide for life's decisions. For without some kind of thinkable or statable guidelines there is no way for one to make reasonable or meaningful decisions about alternate courses of action. So if ethics is to be meaningful, it must be normative. That normative ethical statements are meaningful implies several things.

First, normative statements are *rational*. That is, they are statements subject to the law of non-contradiction. This means that the opposite of what is right is wrong. If one ought always to be loving, then it follows that to be unloving is wrong. If opposite courses of action are not opposed as right and wrong, then it is impossible for one to make a meaningful ethical decision between them.

Second, normative statements can be more than formally rational; they can be *contentful*. [13] They are not only speakable, they are ex-

---

[13] Just *how* contentful norms must be to be meaningful and how they get their content is a question to be settled later (see critique at end of chapter four). All that is being contended here is that a norm must be at least rational (i.e., formally meaningful) and also it must be at least capable of being experientially or contentfully meaningful as well. For if norms could not be filled with experiential content, they would be unusable or *useless* as norms.

periential. There is a basis in human experience for their meaning. One is able not only to conceptualize them; he can also give concrete examples of them. If a norm can have no more than thinkable form, it cannot have any meaningful experiential content for the individual who wishes to understand it in terms of his own experience.

Further, a norm can be *practical*. Not only can norms be apprehended in meaningful ways by the mind, they can also be *applied* in a practical way to one's life. Their meaning must not only be based in experience but it must also be applicable to experience. This leads to another characteristic of norms which makes them indispensable for a meaningful ethic.

Finally, norms are *objective*. They constitute a standard outside an individual's subjective experience by which he can determine if his ethical experiences are good or bad. If norms were purely subjective, they would not really be norms at all. For something to stand in judgment over an experience it cannot at the same time be an intrinsic part of that experience. There must be standards or norms outside of individual, subjective experience in order to measure it as good or bad.

In summary, norms are both inescapable and essential for a meaningful ethic. They are inescapable because they are needed to establish and evaluate what is meant by "good" or "better." They are essential because there is no meaningful way to make ethical decisions (or even to speak ethical sentences) without some non-contradictory, and/or contentful way of understanding or expression. The "good" may be *caught* without the use of norms, but it cannot be *taught* or even *thought* without some kind of cognitively meaningful ethical statements. And what is more, the "good" cannot be meaningfully *wrought* without some meaningful ethic norm to determine what is the "good" thing to do.

2 / Antinomianism: There Are No Norms

The first alternative with respect to ethical norms is that there are no norms whatsoever, at least no *objective* ones. That is, we are literally without law *(anti-nomos)* to guide meaningful ethical actions. The alleged ethical norms men use are either without objective value or else without empirical meaning. They are either purely subjective or completely emotive. Two positions which have representative antinomian views are existentialism and emotivism.

I. ANTINOMIANISM EXPLAINED

The first three representatives of existential ethics which will be used here are Sören Kierkegaard, Friedrich Nietzsche, and Jean-Paul Sartre. Not all of these are technically antinomians, but they manifest an ascending tendency in that direction, culminating in Sartre. The fourth representative, A. J. Ayer, is from the school of logical positivism whose ethic is known as emotivism.

A. *Kierkegaard: Transcending the Ethical*

Properly speaking, Kierkegaard was not an antinomian. He believed sincerely in the moral law, and he held even that it is universally binding in an ethical sense. However, for Kierkegaard when the ethical and the religious conflict, the ethical ought to be suspended in view of a man's religious duty of direct obedience to God. So in this sense Kierkegaard is a precursor of a kind of antinomian transcending of the ethical.

1. *The Ethical as Universal* — Kierkegaard believed that "the ethical as such is the universal, and as the universal it applies to everyone,

which may be expressed from another point of view by saying that it applies every instant." [1] Or, "the ethical as such is the universal, again, as the universal it is the manifest, the revealed." [2] In fact, he says, "The ethical is the universal, and as such it is again the divine." And in view of this, "one has therefore a right to say that fundamentally every duty is a duty toward God." [3] This should leave no question that Kierkegaard believed sincerely in universal moral obligations, even to the point of calling moral duty a divine obligation.

However, this is only part of the picture. Kierkegaard writes, "But if one cannot say more, then one affirms at the same time that properly I have no duty toward God." That is, "duty becomes duty by being referred to God, but in duty itself I do not come into relation with God." For example, "it is a duty to love one's neighbor, but in performing this duty I do not come into relation with God but with the neighbor whom I love." [4] Indeed, "the paradox of faith is this, that the individual is higher than the universal. . . . The paradox can also be expressed by saying that there is an absolute duty toward God, for in this relationship of duty the individual as an individual stands related absolutely to the absolute." [5] In other words, even though the ethical as such is universal, it is not always binding. The individual in absolute duty to God can and ought to transcend the ethical.

2. *The Religious Individual Over the Ethical Universal* — There are times when an individual's direct duty to God comes into conflict with his universal duty to other men. At such times the ethical as universal ought to be transcended by the individual as religious. "Faith is precisely this paradox, that the individual as the particular is higher than the universal, is justified over against it, is not subordinate but superior. . . . It is and remains to all eternity a paradox, inaccessible to thought." [6]

This paradox of the individual's religious responsibility over his ethical duty is brought to focus in the account of Abraham and Isaac. When God commanded Abraham to kill his son whom he dearly loved and in whom rested his hopes for future blessing, Abraham had to *suspend* his ethical responsibility in order to express his duty to God. "In Abraham's life there is no higher expression for the ethical than this, that the father shall love his son. . . . Why then did Abraham do it? For God's sake and (in complete identity with this) for his own sake." [7] So despite the universal moral imperative about killing

[1] See *Fear and Trembling*, New York: Doubleday and Company, Inc., 1954, p. 64.
[2] *Ibid.*, p. 91.
[3] *Ibid.*, p. 78.
[4] *Ibid.*
[5] *Ibid.*, p. 80.
[6] *Ibid.*, p. 66.
[7] *Ibid.*, p. 70.

and for the sake of his faith in God, Abraham overstepped the ethical altogether. He showed that the religious individual is higher than the ethical universal.

3. *The Teleological Suspension of the Ethical* — When the ethical is transcended by the religious, the universal by the individual, it is not suspended by virtue of a higher *ethical* norm. There is no higher ethical *telos* or purpose which justifies the religious act. In Kierkegaard's way of expressing it, the knight of faith is not a tragic hero. The tragic hero assures himself that there is a higher ethical duty which he fulfills by breaking a lower, as when Jephthah sacrificed his daughter for the whole nation. [8] In Abraham's case there is no such higher ethical rationale. "He acts by virtue of the absurd, for it is precisely absurd that he as the particular is higher than the universal. . . . Abraham is therefore at no instant a tragic hero but something quite different, either a murderer or a believer." [9]

The difference between the tragic hero and Abraham is clear. The tragic hero "lets one expression of the ethical find its *telos* in a higher expression of the ethical" but "with Abraham the situation was different. By his act he overstepped the ethical entirely and possessed a higher *telos* outside of it, in relation to which he suspended the former." [10] The ethical is suspended for the religious, but there is no higher ethical purpose or principle which would justify this suspension. As a matter of fact, the way in which the religious transcends the ethical may mean a "reversal" of the ethical.

4. *Religious "Reversal" of Ethical Norms* — When a man like Abraham acts in faith by virtue of his absolute duty to God, "the ethical is reduced to a position of relativity." For example, "love to God may cause the knight of faith to give his love to his neighbor the opposite expression to that which, ethically speaking, is required by duty." [11] This is quite obvious in Abraham's case. In fact, Kierkegaard admits that *so far as the moral law is concerned* Abraham was a murderer, not a believer. But faith "is capable of transforming a murder into a holy act well-pleasing to God. . . ." [12] Even Abraham's closest friends and loved ones were incapable of justifying Abraham's act in any ethical sense. [13]

Further, it would follow from this that were Abraham to be tried before a court for murder, his own loved ones would have to admit to his guilt before the moral law! Indeed, even Abraham could not justify his own act morally. "He believed by virtue of the absurd;

[8] *Ibid.*, p. 88, n. cf. Judges 11:31ff.
[9] *Ibid.*, p. 67.
[10] *Ibid.*, p. 69.
[11] *Ibid.*, p. 80.
[12] *Ibid.*, p. 64.
[13] *Ibid.*, p. 91f.

for there could be no question of human calculation, and it was indeed absurd that God who required it of him should the next instant recall the requirement." In fact, "the distress and dread in this paradox is that, humanly speaking, he is entirely unable to make himself intelligible."[14] The ethical is meaningful and rational in that it can be put in an intelligible, universal propositional statement. Not so with the religious, which is passional, subjective, and radically individual.[15] In brief, there are no universal ethical statements which ought not be "reversed" by the individual religious experience of absolute duty to God such as Abraham faced.

5. *Ethical Is Dethroned But Not Destroyed* — However, lest Kierkegaard be misrepresented, it should be noted that in no way is the ethical discarded simply because it is sometimes disenfranchised by the religious. The ethical *as such* remains universally binding. Just because the ethical is considered relative *as related to* the religious does not mean that it does not remain absolute *in itself*. The ethical can be suspended but must not be discarded.[16] "From this, however, it does not follow that the ethical is to be abolished, but it acquires an entirely different expression, the paradoxical expression. . . ."[17] In fact, the ethical is an essential ingredient in setting up the dialectical tension which occasions the paradox. Without great respect for the moral law the religious man would have no "fear and trembling" in transcending it. Apart from the belief in the rational there would be no merit in the "irrational" act of faith, and so on. To repeat, no one can be religious who does not first believe deeply in the ethical. The religious dethrones but never destroys the ethical.

It is for this reason that Kierkegaard does not fear any abuse of the ethical by the religious man. "He who has learned that to exist as the individual is the most terrible thing of all . . . will scarcely be a snare for the bewildered man, but rather will help him into the universal. . . ." For "the man who lives under his own supervision, alone in the whole world, lives more strictly and more secluded than a maiden in her lady's bower." That there are some who without compulsion would be freefooted and selfish Kierkegaard does not doubt, "but a man must prove precisely that he is not of this number by the fact that he knows how to speak with dread and trembling."[18]

[14] *Ibid.*, pp. 46, 84.

[15] Kierkegaard does say that a religious experience, which transcends the ethical, can be understood, but it cannot be understood in terms of rational universals. It can be understood only "paradoxically," i.e., dialectically by a desultory illumination of the subject from all sides so as to break its overall intelligibility down into understandable parts. *Fear and Trembling*, pp. 121, 84 (with editor's note).

[16] *Ibid.*, pp. 77, 131, and *passim*.

[17] *Ibid.*, p. 80.

[18] *Ibid.*, p. 85.

In brief, the ethical is a prerequisite for the religious, and the ethical remains intact even when it is transcended by the religious.

6. *The Soil for Incipient Antinomianism* — Even though the ethical is not destroyed while it is suspended by the religious, there are at least two ways in which Kierkegaard's teaching is the soil for incipient antinomianism. First, Kierkegaard posits as higher the duty to break these "universal" ethical norms without having a higher *ethical* or *rational* reason for doing so. In other words, no ethical norms are really universal; they can and should be broken for non-ethical reasons (or, non-reasons). Thus, Kierkegaard has taken a stand against any unbreakable ethical norms — there is always the religious duty to disobey the so-called "universal" ethical norms when a man is called upon by a religious consideration to do so.

Second, the realm of a man's ultimate duty is described by Kierkegaard as "absurd," "paradoxical," and beyond all rational "understanding." There is no way to state one's religious duty in a universal proposition. It is not known propositionally or rationally; it is known only passionally by an act (or "leap") of faith. And this "irrational" act of faith can even "reverse" the ethical principle.

Kierkegaard, of course, did not identify this realm of the "irrational" or "paradoxical" as ethical. He did say, however, that it was the realm of a man's ultimate duty, even though he dubbed this duty as religious instead of ethical. It is not difficult to understand how someone else might conclude that ethics itself should be placed in this realm beyond the categories of good and evil. Such an approach is implied in the works of Friedrich Nietzsche. [19]

B. *Nietzsche: Transvaluating the Ethical*

Kierkegaard believed that the ethical must be *transcended* by the religious; Nietzsche believed the religious and the ethical should be *transvaluated*. As the title of one of his books indicates, modern man must go "Beyond Good and Evil." [20] God died and all theistic value died with Him. Modern man must find new values apart from these defunct traditional values.

1. *The Death of God and the Good* — In a famous passage in *Joyful Wisdom*, Nietzsche writes of modern man, " 'Where is God gone?' he called out. I mean to tell you! *We have killed him,* — you and I! We are all his murderers!. . . . Do we not hear the noise of the grave-

---

[19] Nietzsche, *Beyond Good and Evil*, Chicago: Henry Regnery Company, 1966.

[20] "One meaning is 'on the other side of good and evil,' indicating that good and evil together are on the same side of morality and that there exists another side. Another meaning of *jenseits* is 'aside from,' i.e., paying no attention to good and evil. When Nietzsche says that 'what is done of love always happens beyond good and evil,' he places the full meaning of 'beyond' at our disposal — the 'beyond' here is an 'above' and an 'aside from' and a 'without reference to.' " See Marianne Cowan's "Introduction" to *Beyond Good and Evil*, p. viii.

diggers who are burying God? Do we not smell the divine putrefaction? — for even Gods putrefy! God is dead! God remains dead! And we have killed Him!" [21] In his well-known work, *Thus Spoke Zarathustra*, Nietzsche exhorted, "I beseech you, my brothers, *remain faithful to the earth*, and do not believe those who speak to you of other worldly hopes! ... Once the sin against God was the greatest sin; but God died, and these sinners died with Him. To sin against the earth is now the most dreadful thing. ..." [22] Whether Nietzsche meant that a God who was once really alive has now *actually* died (as Thomas Altizer believes), [23] or whether he meant that God has died culturally in that modern men no longer believe in Him, [24] or whatever, the net ethical result is the same, viz., God and all traditional values have fallen.

Nietzsche called himself "the first immoralist" who desired to pass beyond all traditional morality the way chemistry passed beyond alchemy, and astronomy beyond astrology. [25] Even very general ethic principles, such as: "Injure no man, rather help all men so far as you are able," are questioned by Nietzsche. "In short, moralities too are but a *symbolic language of the passions*. ... " [26] The Christian morality of unselfish love is singled out for special attack by Nietzsche. "What? An act of love is supposed to be 'unegoistic'? Why, you idiots. ... 'How about praising the one who sacrifices himself?'" For "every unselfish morality which takes itself as an absolute and seeks to apply itself to Everyman sins not only against taste, but does worse: it is an incentive to sins of omission." [27] Indeed, Nietzsche reserves his most bitter words for Christian ethics. In *Ecce Homo* he wrote, "Christian morality is the most malignant form of all falsehood. ... It is really poisonous, decadent, weakening. It produces nincompoops not men." He adds elsewhere, "I condemn Christianity and confront it with the most terrible accusation that an accuser has ever had in his mouth. To my mind it is the greatest of all conceivable corruptions. ... I call it the one immortal blemish of mankind." [28]

2. *Revaluating Good and Evil* — Nietzsche's chief indictment against

[21] Nietzsche, *Joyful Wisdom*, translated by Thomas Common, Frederick Ungar Publishing Co., 1960, section 125 (pp. 167, 168).

[22] Nietzsche, *Thus Spoke Zarathustra*, translated by Walter Kaufmann, New York: Viking Press, 1966. Prologue, 3 (p. 125).

[23] See Altizer's *The Gospel of Christian Atheism*, Philadelphia: The Westminster Press, 1966, pp. 103, 68, 69, 92, and *passim*. See also *Radical Theology and the Death of God*, edited by T. Altizer and William Hamilton, The Bobbs-Merril Company, Inc., 1966, pp. 95, 125 - 126, and *passim*.

[24] See Walter Kaufmann, *Nietzsche*, New York: Meridian Books, Inc., 1960.

[25] *Beyond Good and Evil*, 32 Cowan trans. (p. 39).

[26] *Ibid.*, 186, 187 (pp. 92 - 94).

[27] *Ibid.*, 220 (pp. 144 - 145).

[28] Nietzsche, *Anti-Christ*, New York: Knopf, p. 230.

Christian ethic is that it is a morality of *weakness*. "From the very beginning, the Christian faith is a sacrifice, sacrifice of all freedom, all pride, all self-assurance of the mind; at the same time it is servitude, self-mockery and self-mutilation." According to Nietzsche, "'Become mediocre!' is now the sole morality that makes sense, that finds ears to hear." [29] And at the center of this morality of mediocrity is the Christian concept of love. "'Compassion for all' would amount to rigor and tyranny for *you* my dear neighbor!" he exclaims. Further, he says, "to love mankind *for God's* sake has up to now been the most distinguished and far-fetched feeling that mankind has reached."

This love ethic, as personified in the life of Christ, is "one of the most painful instances of the martyrdom that comes from knowing about love." It is the tragic end of a love ethic of weakness which stands in dire need of transvaluation. "Jesus said to his Jews," wrote Nietzsche, "Love God, as I do, love him as a son does. What do we sons of God care about morality?" God is dead, Jesus is dead, and Christian morality is dead. "Perhaps some day the solemn concepts about which we struggled and suffered most, the concepts 'God' and 'sin' will appear no more important to us than a child's toy or a child's grief appears to an old man." [30]

What is needed today, says Nietzsche, is a new morality, not of the weak but of the strong. The old morality is defunct; a new morality must be devised. Traditional morality is built on obedience of many to the few, and it produced "soft" virtues. It is a *flock* morality. What is needed today is a morality of the *individual* and of "hard" virtues, such as the warrior-like qualities of endurance, harshness, and suspicion. This morality of the "superman" will also include intelligence, honesty, and generosity that gives, not out of pity, but out of a superabundance of power. [31] But its goal is not uniformity of morality for all men but a variety of moralities. For "the demand of one morality for all means an encroachment upon precisely a superior type of man." There is an order of rank between men and there should be also between moralities. [32]

Whence comes this new morality? From creative geniuses, for "the real philosophers are commanders and legislators. They say, 'It *shall* be thus!' They determine the 'whither' and the 'to what end' of man-

[29] *Beyond Good and Evil*, 46 (p. 53), 262 (p. 211).

[30] *Ibid.*, 82 (p. 75), 60 (pp. 66 - 67), 269 (p. 220).

[31] Kaufmann contends that Nietzsche "means a war against accepted valuation, not the creation of new ones." *Nietzsche*, pp. 93, 94. He says, "The 'revaluation' is not a new value-legislation but a reversal of prevalent valuation — not from a new vantage point, nor arbitrary, but an internal criticism." But Kaufmann admits that there is a positive dialectic involved here, in that Nietzsche is negating a negative. In such a dialectic Nietzsche is not recreating the same old values but making new ones. This is what a dialectic does.

[32] *Beyond Good and Evil*, 164 (p. 87), 57 (p. 63), 228 (p. 155).

kind. . . . Their 'knowing' is *creating.*" It may be necessary for the genuine philosopher to have been a critic, dogmatist, skeptic, and historian. "But all of these are only prerequisites for his task. The task itself is something else: it demands that he *create values.*" Nietzsche is not concerned with the discovery of value but with its creation, and the supermen are the creators. The super individual's "will to power" replaces the saint's will to be overpowered by others. All group values are transformed into individual values, all absolutes into relatives, all morality into extramorality. Anything which increases the will to power is valuable. Moral good is found in affirmation of the will, and is strengthened by the ideal of the supermen. [33]

Just how should one approach ethics, then, if all value is relative to the individual will to power? The answer in one word is: experimentation. But this study of value-feelings and value-differences by experimentation is not to be directed toward establishing a *science* of morality but only to preparing a typology. "By the name with which I ventured to christen them, I expressly emphasized their experimentation and their delight in experimentation," wrote Nietzsche. And "in their passion for new insight, must they go farther in bold and painful experiments than the emasculate and morbid taste of a democratic century can approve?" [34]

But what is to keep this individualistic ethic of will to power from anarchy and chaos? Willing eternal recurrence is Nietzsche's answer. The superman accepts the final fact of a perpetual return of the same state of affairs. The eternal cycles will scare away insincerity from those who accept this new morality.

3. *The Rejection of All Absolute Value* — Not only did Nietzsche attempt to reject all *traditional* value and desire to re-evaluate it via recreation in the radical values of the rugged individualist, but he also emphatically rejected all *absolute* values altogether. "I shall repeat a hundred times," he wrote, "that 'immediate certainty' as well as 'absolute knowledge' and 'thing in itself' are all contradictions in terms." Both truth and value are on a sliding scale with no absolute standard. "Whatever forces us," Nietzsche asks, "to assume at all that there is an essential difference between 'true' and 'false'? It is not sufficient to assume levels of semblance, lighter and darker shadows and tones of semblance as it were, different 'values' in the painter's sense of the term?" The philosopher of absolute truth is prejudiced by the presupposition that there are opposites like true and false, good and evil. "The basic faith of all metaphysicians is *faith in the antithetical nature of values.*" It never occurs to them to doubt this presupposition," says Nietzsche. "But we may indeed doubt: first, whether

[33] See *Will to Power,* pp. 18, 19.
[34] *Beyond Good and Evil,* 211 (pp. 134 - 135), 186 (p. 91), 210 (p. 132).

antitheses exist at all, and second, whether those popular valuations and value-antitheses upon which the metaphysicians have placed their stamp of approval are not perhaps merely superficial valuations. . . . " [35] And the basic metaphysical belief that God is truth, that truth is divine is surely to be challenged. "But what if this itself becomes more untrustworthy," Nietzsche asks, "what if nothing any longer proves itself divine, except it be error, blindness, and falsehood; what if God Himself turns out to be our most persistent lie?" [36] Indeed, the whole of Nietzsche's *Anti-Christ* is devoted to the destruction of absolute truth. It was only the first part of a projected *magnum opus* (never completed) entitled by him, *A Revaluation of All Values.*

By way of summary, Nietzsche attempts to go beyond good and evil by transvaluating the very nature of good and evil. In his own words, he does this "in a *revaluation of all* values, in a liberation from all moral values, in saying Yes to and having confidence in all that has hitherto been forbidden, despised, and damned. . . . Morality is not attacked, it is merely no longer in the picture." [37] In brief, Nietzsche is without meaningful ethical norms in several ways: First, he is without any *absolute* norms. God is dead and all absolute values died with Him. Second, Nietzsche is without *objective* norms. Each individual creates his own variety of values. Third, he is without *Christian* norms. Nietzsche is deeply and irrevocably anti-Christian. Nietzsche himself, fearing that someone might one day canonize him (as Altizer did), [38] wrote, "I have a terrible fear that some day one will pronounce me *holy.*" [39] He was scarcely holy in the Christian sense, certainly not in his view of God and moral values built on God. He viewed "God as the declaration of war against life, against nature, against the will to live! God — the formula for every slander against 'this world,' for every lie about the 'beyond'! God — the deification of nothingness, the will to nothingness pronounced holy!" [40]

C. Sartre: Rejection of the Ethical

Kierkegaard began the modern existential move toward antinomianism, Nietzsche continued it, and it culminated in Sartre. Kierkegaard said that universal ethical norms can be *transcended* by the religious individual, Nietzsche said that objective ethical norms must be *transvaluated* into the irreligious individual's will to power, and Sartre said they must be *rejected* altogether. Kierkegaard posits a *supra-*

---

[35] *Ibid.,* 16 (p. 17), 34 (p. 41), 2 (p. 2).

[36] *Joyful Wisdom,* 344 (pp. 279 - 280). Cf. *Genealogy of Morals* III, 24.

[37] *Ecce Homo,* "Dawn" 1 (Kaufmann, *Basic Writings of Nietzsche,* pp. 746 - 747).

[38] Altizer, *The Gospel of Christian Atheism,* p. 25.

[39] *Ecce Homo* IV, 1.

[40] Nietzsche, *Anti-Christ,* p. 18.

moral realm for the religious man. Nietzsche designates an *extra-moral* domain for "supermen," and Sartre declares everything completely *amoral* for all men. The reason Sartre rejects any kind of objective ethics is that for him all of human life is absurd. This becomes evident upon examining Sartre's view of man.

1. *Man Is a Useless Passion* — Man is an empty bubble floating on the Sea of Nothingness. Men have an unquenchable but futile thirst for God. He writes, "The best way to conceive of the fundamental project of humanity is to say that man is the being whose project is to become God." For "to be man means to reach toward being God. Or if you prefer, man fundamentally is the desire to be God." [41]

The bitter irony, of course, is that the whole project is absurd and impossible. God is by definition a self-caused Being (*causa sui*) and to cause one's own existence is impossible for either God or man. [42] The "being-for-itself" (*être-pour-soi*) can never become the "being-in-itself" (*être-en-soi*); the contingent cannot become necessary; freedom cannot become determined; nothing cannot become something. In order to create oneself one would have to be able to stand outside oneself, he would have to be prior to himself, and that is impossible. In brief, man finds in himself a fundamental thirst for the transcendent with absolutely no ability to attain it.

2. *Man Is Condemned to Freedom* — At the heart of man's futility · is his freedom. Man is utterly free. He cannot be not free. Even when a man wants to escape his destiny he is freely fleeing it. "I am my freedom," he writes. "No sooner had you [to Zeus] created me than I ceased to be yours." So "I was like a man who's lost his shadow. And there was nothing left in heaven, no right or wrong, nor anyone to give me orders. . . . But I shall not return under your law; I am doomed to have no other law but mine. . . . For I, Zeus, am a man, and every man must find out his own way." [43]

Sartre accepts Dostoevsky's challenge that if there be no God then all is permitted. The best one can do is to be a heroic atheist, taking the *full* responsibility for his own acts. He creates his own life by his own free choices. In fact, he *is* his free acts. There is no God to assume ultimate responsibility for man's existence and choices. The most that one can do is sincerely to accept his own absurdity, i.e., to acknowledge that there is no explanation and no justification for his life outside of his own radical freedom.

There are no laws or norms in heaven or earth that can guide one in his choices. The study of Being will not help, for "ontology itself

---

[41] Sartre, *Being and Nothingness,* translated by Hazel Barnes, New York: Philosophical Library, Inc., 1956, p. 694.

[42] *Ibid.,* pp. 762, 766.

[43] *The Flies,* in *No Exit and Three Other Plays,* 121 - 123.

38 / ethics: alternatives and issues

cannot formulate ethical precepts. It is concerned solely with what is, and we cannot possibly derive imperatives from ontology's indicatives." [44] In David Hume's words, one cannot get "ought" from "is." Not only is man without ontological norms, he is also without any objectively meaningful utilitarian ends. Ethics is purely descriptive. "It indicates to us the necessity of abandoning the psychology of interest along with any utilitarian interpretation of human conduct. . . ." [45] In fact, there is nothing in the way of either ethical precept or project which a man ought to take seriously.

3. *Repudiating the Spirit of Seriousness* — According to Sartre, the principal result of an existential analysis "must be to make us repudiate the *spirit of seriousness*." The spirit of seriousness implies two things: "[1] It considers values as trancendent givers independent of human subjectivity, and [2] it transfers the quality of 'desirable' from the ontological structure of things to their simple material constitution. . . . Objects are mute demands, and he [man] is nothing in himself but the passive obedience to these demands." [46] All of this must be repudiated. For the extent to which men believe in transcendent values and objective demands they still believe they can accomplish their absurd project of finding a meaningful ground or justification for their life.

Actually, all that men discover is despair at their absurd thrust toward a transcendent meaning. "For they discover at the same time that all human activities are equivalent, since they all tend to sacrifice man in order that the self-cause may arise. . . . Thus it amounts to the same thing whether one gets drunk alone or is a leader of nations." There is no real difference because there are no real objective values to make a difference. Man must come to realize "that he is *the being by whom value* exists. It is then that his freedom will become conscious of itself and will reveal itself in anguish as the unique source of value and the nothingness by which the world exists." [47] There are no values outside of one's freedom which he should take seriously. All value is volitional, not ontological; subjective and not objective; amoral and not moral.

4. *Choosing for Others* — "What will become of freedom if it turns its back upon this value. . . . In particular is it possible for freedom to take itself for a value as the source of all value . . . ?" Sartre ends his famous *Being and Nothingness* with these questions. "We shall devote to them a future book," was a promise he never fulfilled. How then is one to relate his freedom to others? Does one have any re-

[44] *Being and Nothingness*, pp. 625, 626.
[45] *Ibid.*, p. 626.
[46] *Ibid.*, p. 626.
[47] *Ibid.*, p. 627.

sponsibility for other men? [48] Sartre's answer to these questions may be found in his concept of "authentic" freedom. That is, a man ought to choose for all men, and he ought to respect the freedom of others. However, Sartre contends that these "ought" statements are only logical and not valuational. [49] But if they are non-valuational, then they have no ethical force. And if they were valuational, then they would be normative, a position he has repudiated. In brief, Sartre's position is amoral in any ethical sense of that word.

Lacking external criteria for acting in authentic freedom for oneself and for others, how can one know what are the characteristics of an authentic act? Sartre gives two: lucidity and responsibility for others. But here again there are no standards by which these may be judged. In fact, there is no reason why one should be "responsible" for others, if each man is to be *fully* responsible for himself. Furthermore, as others have pointed out, there can be diabolical lucidity, and a ruthless use of power can have the supposed "good" of others in view. [50]

There are several other problems involved in assuming the responsibility of choosing for others. First, it is not really an ethical responsibility at all, if each man must be *completely* responsible for himself. One cannot really be responsible for another on Sartre's ground. Second, to choose for others means to order them as objects around oneself as a free subject. But this will not work; men will rebel against being used as objects since they, too, are free subjects. Society, then, is a form of mutual conflict. In Sartre's words, "Hell is other people." [51] Third, there is no ethical reason why a man ought to choose for others. Freedom is without reason to justify it and without norms to guide it.

5. *Attempting to Redeem Sartre's Ethics* — Sartre never wrote his promised work on ethics, but his wife did. In her book Simone de Beauvoir admits that the Sartrian ethic is individualistic but denies that it is solipsistic. That is, it is an ethic "which will refuse to deny *a priori* that separate existants can, at the same time, be bound to each other, that their individual freedoms can forge laws valid for all." [52] In this way it can be an ethic of the free without being anarchical. It begins in despair but need not end there. Absurdity is only the starting point; it is essentially an ethic of ambiguity. [53]

It is true that there is no absolute value outside man, no objective

48 *Ibid.*, pp. 627, 628.
49 See *Existentialism Is a Humanism.*
50 James Collins, *The Existentialists*, Chicago: Henry Regnery Co., 1952, pp. 52 - 55.
51 *No Exit*, p. 61.
52 Simone de Beauvoir, *The Ethics of Ambiguity*, New York: Philosophical Library, 1948, translated by Bernard Frechtman.
53 *Ibid.*, pp. 16 - 18, 156, 8 - 10.

or external justification for his existence, Beauvoir writes. Man *gives*, not *has*, reasons for his being. His attempt to be God is vain, but in the process he becomes man and this is not vain. Man cannot be right with God but he can be right with himself. So God's absence does not authorize license; it establishes man's responsibility. [54]

Even though man is free and cannot be not free in an ontological sense, nevertheless he must choose to be free in an ethical sense. That is, one cannot will himself unfree as a being, for this very act of will shows that he is free. Even in fleeing freedom in a positive sense one is exercising freedom in a negative sense. Every man is inescapably free in the ontological sense that he spontaneously casts himself into the world. But not everyone accepts this thrust in a positive way. It takes more than a stoic resignation; one must make a positive affirmation of one's being to be ethical. This positive affirmation is an ethical decision because the opposite (evil will) is possible. One can will not to accept his own project of giving objectively to his own subjectivity. That is, in man's very condition as man there is the possibility of not fulfilling it. [55]

Just what does man have to will to be free in an ethical sense? He must will in a positive sense the freedom which he cannot deny himself negatively. He must will his own freedom and the freedom of others. He must will to coincide with himself by surpassing himself. In brief, one must will his own ambiguity. But how can a man realize himself if he cannot do it in himself? Wherein can he find the grounds of his being? "Man can find a justification of his own existence only in the existence of other men." This is an irreducible truth: "The me-others relationship is as indissolvable as the subject-object relationship." So, "to will oneself free is also to will others free." This is another way, says Beauvoir, of affirming agreement with the Christian love principle or the Kantian principle of treating others always as ends, not as means. Or, in other words, "the precept will be to treat the other . . . as a freedom so that his end may be freedom." [56] We must use our freedom to help others realize their freedom.

This does not imply, of course, that every man should be given everything he wants. No man should use freedom to limit his freedom or that of others (as in drug addiction) nor to destroy his freedom (as in suicide) simply because he wants to do so. On the other hand, there are occasions when one may have to destroy freely the freedom of one man if not to do so runs the risk of letting ten innocent men die. The freedom of many men is better than that of one man. In any event, a man ought to affirm freedom(s) whenever and however

[54] *Ibid.*, pp. 11 - 16.
[55] *Ibid.*, pp. 24 - 35.
[56] *Ibid.*, pp. 72 - 73, 135.

he can. "For if it came to be that each man did what he must, existence would be saved in each one without there being any need of dreaming of a paradise where all would be reconciled in death." [57]

At first blush it may appear that Beauvoir has redeemed the Sartrian position from antinomianism. However, this would be a hasty conclusion for at least two reasons. First, her existential ethic is *volitionally* posited by the individual and is not an imperative imposed on the individual. All values are *chosen*, not essential. Second, she clearly repudiates any *objective* values. All values are subjectively selected and have no status independent of an individual's willing them. She would emphatically reject norms defined as prescriptive principles for human behavior, valid independently of individuals, i.e., with *objective* validity.

D. A. J. Ayer: The Elimination of the Ethical

A brief word should be said about the form of antinomian ethic known as emotivism. It grows out of a now defunct school of philosophy called Logical Positivism. The school of thought emanated from Vienna in the early 1930's and was represented by men like Rudolf Carnap, Moritz Schlick, A. J. Ayer, and others. The last named was perhaps the most forceful spokesman in English. Let us look at his now famous *Language, Truth, and Logic.* [58]

1. *Epistemological "Acognosticism"* — On the basis of a strict principle of empirical verifiability, Ayer allowed no statement to be meaningful unless it was purely analytic or tautological (as 7+3=10), *or* unless it could be verified some way through the experience of one or more of the five senses. In this way he thought not only to restrict metaphysical statements but to eliminate them altogether. For "surely from empirical premises nothing whatsoever concerning the properties, or even the existence, of anything super-empirical can legitimately be inferred." [59]

Leaning upon a similar distinction made earlier by David Hume between statements about relation of ideas (i.e., definitional) and statements about matters of fact (i.e., empirical), Ayer condemned all other statements as literally nonsensical. Such are all supposed metaphysical statements about substance, reality, being, God, etc. This is not to say that there *are* no such things as being, God, etc. It is only to say that if there are such realities no meaningful *statements* can be made about them. All God-talk is nonsensical.

In brief, Ayer's view is not an agnosticism which holds that it is at least meaningful to ask the question about God's existence. Rather,

[57] *Ibid.,* pp. 150, 159.
[58] A. J. Ayer, *Language, Truth, and Logic,* New York: Dover Publications, Inc., 1946.
[59] *Ibid.,* p. 33.

Ayer's position should be called an "acognosticism," because it denies that there is any cognitive meaning to the very word "God" in the question about His existence. There is simply no cognitive (i.e., verifiable) meaning for the word "God" in the question. Ayer did not categorically deny that there was a God or that the mystic could have intuitions of Him. He said, "We wait only to hear what are the propositions which embody his discoveries, in order to see whether they are verified or confuted by our empirical observations." [60] In other words, it may be possible to *experience* God but it is not possible to *express* this experience in cognitively meaningful statements — an epistemological "acognosticism."

2. *Ethical Emotivism* — The ethical consequence of "acognosticism" is emotivism. That is, no ethical statements are cognitively meaningful, since they are neither purely definitional statements nor mere statements about empirical fact. Ethical statements are simply emotive. Their significance is not that they state fact or commands but that they express the speaker's *feeling*. For example, the alleged command or "ought" statement, "You *ought not steal*," really means "I *dislike* stealing." Statements such as that are not imperative but they are merely *expressive* of the speaker's feelings and his desire to see others feel the same way. "You ought not lie" means "I don't like lying" and "I want you to dislike lying also." Ethical statements are not declarative of any factual state of affairs; they are *ejaculative* of one's feelings and attempts to influence the feelings of others. In view of this, "we can now see why it is impossible to find a criterion for determining the validity of ethical judgments," wrote Ayer. "It is not because they have an 'absolute' validity which is mysteriously independent of ordinary sense-experience, but because they have no objective validity whatsoever." [61]

Ayer admitted that his theory is "radically subjectivistic," but he distinguished it from traditional subjectivism on the grounds that his theory does not involve statements *about* how an individual feels (these would be true or false, depending on whether the individual really felt that way), but merely statements *of* one's feelings. For instance, one may express boredom (by gestures, e.g.) without making an assertion about his feeling of boredom such as, "I am bored." The assertion is verifiable, but the expression is not. Ethical statements are unverifiable expressions of feeling, not verifiable assertions about feelings. "They are pure expressions of feeling and as such do not come under the category of truth and falsehood." [62]

If ethical statements are not purely definitional or empirical, then

60 *Ibid.*, p. 118.
61 *Ibid.*, p. 108.
62 *Ibid.*

what kind of statements are they? They are of the same kind as aesthetic statements; they are statements of feeling. Both ethical and aesthetic statements express only one's subjective *taste* and not the objective *truth* about something. Both are value statements, and not factual assertions. "For we hold," says Ayer, "that one really never does dispute about questions of value." We argue only about matters of fact. Value is always presupposed, but it can neither be proven nor disputed. "Given that a man has certain moral principles, we argue that he must, in order to be consistent, react morally to certain things in a certain way." But "what we do not and cannot argue about is the validity of these moral principles." [63]

In brief, there are no ethical "oughts." No statements are normative or prescriptive for others. All alleged ethical norms are purely subjective and individualistic, expressive of one's feeling. They are emotive but not normative.

II. EVALUATION OF ANTINOMIANISM

Despite their dissimilarities, there is a basic agreement among the antinomian views discussed above. They are unanimous in their affirmation that ultimately what a man "ought" to do is individualistically and subjectively determined. There are no objective moral prescriptions universally binding on all men. The following evaluation will focus mainly on the central non-normative aspect which the above views have in common.

A. *Some Values in the Antinomian Ethic*

Not all is negative with the antinomian ethic. There are some positive values which are implied in or emerge from their approach. Some of the contributions of antinomianism include the following:

1. *It Stresses Personal Relationships* — One worthwhile factor implied in an existential kind of antinomian ethic is the emphasis on acting for other persons. This comes out in the concept of acting for other persons. Others, too, are persons and not mere things. In assuming responsibility for other persons, one is implying the value of persons. Persons, not things or even abstract rules, are the center of concern. Concrete human relations take precedence over abstract principles. Morality is person-centered. It is persons to whom commitments are made and for whom promises are kept, not mere precepts.

2. *It Stresses Individual Responsibility* — Ethics is ultimately a

---

[63] *Ibid.*, p. 110. If it were impossible to argue about values, then one could never change value systems nor "convert" someone else from one value system to another. Other emotivists have qualified Ayer's position in order to avoid this dilemma by suggesting that values are based at least in part upon facts and facts can be argued. Hence, one's values can be changed indirectly via education (viz., by new facts). See Charles L. Stevenson, *Ethics and Language*, New Haven, Conn.: Yale University Press, 1945.

matter of individual responsibility. Each man must choose for himself. There is a uniqueness about the individual situation. One's responsibility cannot be absolved by blending into a group. Groups are made up of individuals, and individuals are individually responsible for their choices. This often overlooked aspect of ethics is a welcomed reaction to an over-emphasis on the environmental and behavioristic determinants on human action.

3. *It Takes Cognizance of the Emotive* — Even if not *all* ethical statements are purely emotive, surely *many* are. It is to the credit of the positivist for focusing attention on this fact. That is, many of our statements are phrased in prescriptive language ("ought," "should," etc.), but there is no objective basis for these imperatives. In view of the emotivists' discovery it behooves every moralist to re-examine the repertoire of his "ought" statements to see whether or not there is more than a purely subjective basis for them. Perhaps much of what men take for objective moral imperatives are only subjective emotives.

B. *Some Problems With an Antinomian Ethic*

Even though antinomians are not necessarily irresponsible in their moral acts, nonetheless, there are some irredeemable difficulties with the position, even in its better forms. At least four problems will be pointed out here.

1. *It Is Too Subjective* — At the core of all the antinomian views reviewed above is a clear-cut subjectivism. A man's ultimate responsibility is without objective guides or norms. What antinomians fail to see is that an ethic need not be unprincipled in order to be personal. They fail to understand that an uncritical subjectivity is chaotic and self-destructive and that a critical subjectivity is *not* necessarily antinomian, since it may involve some standard or norm of criticism. A purely subjectivistic ethic is like a game without rules or a civilization without codes. Ultimately, it is really no ethic at all. It is a normless subjectivism in which each man feels and does his own "thing."

2. *It Is Too Individualistic* — Along with its subjectivism, the antinomian ethic is radically individualistic. The individual or the specific ethical moment is ultimate and radically different from all others. Every situation is atomically distinct. There is no community of values which transcends individuality. Each ethical decision is unique and autonomous. Such a radical dichotomy of men and moments does not provide any meaningful milieu for interpersonal relations. The best (yet inadequate) way antinomians can relate morally to others is through voluntaristically assumed projects. There are no laws transcending the individual and binding all men together in a moral community. There is really nothing which they *ought* to do.

3. *It Is Too Relativistic* — Concomitant with the inability of a norm-less ethic to provide a medium for moral interrelationships is its inability to resolve moral conflicts. If there is no ultimate standard, how can value *clashes* be resolved? Furthermore, on what basis should men choose their ultimate values? Without an ultimate normative basis there is neither objective grounds for beginning an ethical life nor is there any way to resolve tensions between conflicting life patterns. What happens when an ethic of egoism encounters an ethic of altruism, or when a morality of hate meets one of love? Which one is right, and how is the conflict to be resolved without a normative basis for deciding? Surely men are to do more than merely affirm their own individual freedom at the expense of others. Certainly they are to do more than merely emote their feelings at others without having an objective way of determining the value structures they pre-suppose. There must be an absolute to which all the conflicting relatives can be related and by which they may be resolved.

4. *It Is Irrationalistic* — In the final analysis, the antinomian ethic is irrational. That is, it attempts no rational resolution of ethical conflicts. Whether it is called an ethic of "paradox," "absurdity," "ambiguity," or "nonsense," it implies all of these by its unwillingness to make peace with the principle of non-contradiction. None of the forms of this view hold out for the rationality of one's ultimate responsibility. In the final analysis, what one *ought* to do is determined not by a rationally meaningful, non-contradictory principle but by a "leap" into the non-rational or non-cognitive. Whatever "resolution" there may be in these antinomianisms, it is not a rational but purely an existential or emotive one.

The problem with an ethic unwilling to subject itself to rational criteria is that it is a *meaningless* ethic. It does not provide any meaningful (i.e., thinkable, statable) basis for action. Indeed, such an ethic has two critical problems, a logical one and an ethical one. First, logically, there is no way to escape the principle of non-contradiction. There is no way to deny (even in thought) that it applies to ethical statements without affirming that it does apply in that very denial. Second, ethically opposite courses of action are equally acceptable if the law of non-contradiction is not applicable. "One ought to do *good*" would not preclude "One ought to do *evil*." If the opposite of "right" is not "wrong," then any meaningful ethic will be impossible.

46 / ethics: alternatives and issues

SELECT READINGS FOR CHAPTER TWO: ANTINOMIANISM

Ayer, A. J., *Language, Truth, and Logic*, New York: Dover Publications, Inc., 1946.

de Beauvoir, Simone, *The Ethics of Ambiguity*, New York: Philosophical Library, 1948, translated by Bernard Frechtman.

Greene, Norman N., *Jean-Paul Sartre: The Existentialist Ethic*, Ann Arbor: University of Michigan Press, 1960.

Kierkegaard, Sören, *Fear and Trembling*, New York: Doubleday and Company, Inc., 1954.

Nietzsche, *Beyond Good and Evil*, Chicago: Henry Regnery Company, 1966.

Sartre, Jean-Paul, *Being and Nothingness*, New York: Philosophical Library. Inc., 1956, translated by Hazel Barnes.

Stevenson, Charles L., *Ethics and Language*, New Haven, Conn.: Yale University Press, 1945.

3 / Generalism: There Are No Universal Norms

Most ethical positions reject the no-norm antinomian position in favor of some kind of meaningful guides for decision-making. One classical way of avoiding antinomianism on the one hand and the conflict of many absolute norms on the other hand is by holding to many ethical norms of general but not universal application. This position will be called generalism. Classical representations of this view may be found among utilitarians.

I. GENERALISM EXPLAINED

Utilitarians are not antinomians, since they believe in the value of ethical norms in helping the individual determine which action will probably bring the greatest good for the greatest number of people. On the other hand, utilitarians are generally not absolutists, since they usually repudiate universal norms representative of *intrinsic* value. It is true that the rule-utilitarians say that rules should not be broken because of the *extrinsic* value of the good results of rule-keeping. But the rule is kept not because it is really universally wrong to perform this forbidden act, but only because making exceptions to any ethic rule is a practice which leads to greater evil than good. In other words, the act is not judged by its intrinsic and universal value, i.e., by its form, but by its results. Even the rule-utilitarians, then, have no universal norms in the deontological and normative senses adopted in this study. [1]

[1] See chapter one for a further explanation of what is meant by a universal norm in the deontological sense.

47

This does not mean, of course, that utilitarians have no absolutes. They may have absolute *ends*, but they have no absolute *norms*. They may have an absolute or ultimate *result* by which they judge all actions, but they have no absolute *rules* enabling one to realize this ultimate end of the greatest good for the greatest number of people.

A. *Jeremy Bentham: Quantitative Utilitarianism*

Utilitarians are the heirs of hedonists who believe that pleasure is the greatest good *(summum bonum)* for man. Although the popular "Eat, drink, and be merry" is a perversion of what Epicurus taught, it was his ancient Epicurean followers who set forth the classic doctrine that seeking physical pleasure and avoiding physical pain is the chief aim in life. [2]

1. *The Pleasure Calculus* — Jeremy Bentham developed this ancient hedonistic pleasure calculus into a utilitarian position in his *Introduction to the Principles of Morals and Legislation* (1789). [3] According to Bentham, "Nature has placed mankind under the governance of two sovereign masters, *pain* and *pleasure*," [4] and "it is for them alone to point out what we ought to do, as well as what we shall do." These are summed up in the principle of utility which affirms the position "which states the greatest happiness of all those whose interest is in question, as being the right and proper, and only right and proper and universally desirable, end of human action." [5]

In view of this, "an action then may be said to be conformable to the principle of utility . . . when the tendency it has to augment the happiness of the community is greater than any it has to diminish it." [6] Furthermore, "when thus interpreted, the words *ought,* and *right* and *wrong*, and other of that stamp, have a meaning: when otherwise, they have none."[7] That is, no acts or words have any ethical meaning apart from their consequences. Everything is to be justified by its end, i.e., by whether it brings more pleasure than pain.

But how is the principle of utility itself to be justified? Bentham answers that it is not susceptible to any direct proof, "for that which is used to prove everything else, cannot itself be proved." Men everywhere naturally tend to embrace the principle of utility, although some have inconsistently rejected it. However,"when a man attempts

---

2 On Epicureanism see Epicurus' *On Nature*, fragments in Diogenes Laertius' *Lives and Opinions of Eminent Philosophers*, trans. R. D. Hick (Cambridge: Harvard University Press, 1950), IX, 51; or the Epicurean, Lucretius, *On the Nature of Things* in *Greek and Roman Philosophy After Aristotle*, ed. Jason L. Saunders (New York: Collier-Macmillan Limited, London), 1966.

3 New edition, Oxford, 1823.

4 *Ibid.*, Chapter I, i.

5 *Ibid.*, according to a note added by the author in July, 1822.

6 *Ibid.*, Chapter I, vi.

7 *Ibid.*, Chapter I, x.

to combat the principle of utility, it is with reasons drawn, without his being aware of it, from that very principle itself." [8] Further, if a man rejects the utilitarian principle in favor of his own feeling, "in the first case, let him ask himself whether his principle is not despotical, and hostile to all the rest of the human race," and "in the second case, whether it is not anarchical, and whether at this rate there are not as many different standards of right and wrong as there are men?" [9]

2. *Calculating Pleasure* — If pleasure and the avoidance of pain is the end of ethically good acts, then it is reasonable to ask how one is to measure relative amounts of these two elements. Bentham divides his answer into two parts: for individuals and for groups.

To an individual person the value of pleasure or pain in itself will be determined by four factors: intensity, duration, certainty or uncertainty, propinquity or remoteness. Two others may be added when considering the tendency of an act to produce other pleasures or pain, viz., fecundity (i.e., chances of producing others of its kind) and purity (i.e., chances of not producing the opposite kind of sensation). [10]

In applying the pleasure calculus to a group of people, seven factors must be considered in determining the value of pleasure or pain, viz., intensity, duration, certainty or uncertainty, propinquity or remoteness, fecundity, purity, and extent (i.e., the number of persons to whom it extends). So, to make a final calculation of the good of an act for a group one must first determine how much more pleasure than pain it will give to each individual and then add these all together. The total balance of pleasure over pain will give the general good tendency of the act. If there is more evil than good, then the general evil tendency will be revealed. [11]

Bentham admits that "it is not to be expected that this process should be strictly pursued previously to every moral judgment, or to every legislative or judicial operation." [12] Presumably this is because it is too psychologically and mathematically complex to be practical. It is at this point that the need for some kind of general norms is most obvious in Bentham's position. For if one cannot always calculate the balance of pleasure, then how is he to determine his course of action? The answer becomes more explicit in the utilitarian position of Bentham's successor, John Stuart Mill.

8 *Ibid.*, Chapter I, xiii.
9 *Ibid.*, Chapter I, xiv, 5 and 6.
10 *Ibid.*, Chapter IV, ii and iii.
11 *Ibid.*, Chapter IV, v, 5 and 6.
12 *Ibid.*, Chapter IV, vi.

B. *John Stuart Mill: Qualitative Utilitarianism*

There is at least one modification and one development of Bentham's position brought to light by Mill. The modification has to do with how pleasure (the end) is conceived, and the development has to do with how general norms can function in a utilitarian context.

1. *Pleasure Is Defined Qualitatively* — Bentham's hedonistic calculus (or pleasure principle) lends itself easily to a materialistic interpretation. He seems to be speaking of physical pleasure and pain, since they are measured by intensity and duration. Bentham tried in later years to soften the hedonistic implications of this by noting that "happiness" or "felicity" may be better words for describing what he meant by "pleasure." [13] However, he did not deny the materialistic way this "happiness" is to be measured nor the mathematical way it is to be calculated. John Stuart Mill, on the other hand, argued that pleasures differ in *kind,* and higher pleasures are to be preferred over lower ones. Pleasures do not differ merely in their amount or intensity. One is higher and more valuable than another simply because most people who experience both decidedly prefer one over the other.

The reason humans give marked preference to some pleasures as higher is that they have higher faculties than animals. "No intelligent human being would consent to be a fool . . . even though they should be persuaded that the fool, the dunce, or the rascal is better satisfied with his lot than they are with theirs." Indeed, says Mill, "It is better to be a human being dissatisfied than a pig satisfied; better to be Socrates dissatisfied than a fool satisfied." [14] And if the fool and the pig are of a different opinion, says Mill, it is because the pig knows only one side of the question; the fool knows both sides.

In brief, cultured pleasures are higher than uncultured pleasures. Intellectual pleasures are higher than sensual pleasures, and so on. There is a qualitative difference between them, and one is obligated to seek the highest kind of pleasure for the greatest number of people. But again it may be asked: How can one know what will bring about the highest good for the greatest number unless there are some guides or norms for his decisions? Surely the individual is seldom if ever in a position of being able to foresee the long-range results of his actions. Mill's answer to this question leads to the need for norms.

2. *Pleasure Is Determined Normatively* — The utilitarian position is not without norms. Mill refers to the great usefulness of the veracity norm. "Yet that even this rule, sacred as it is, admits of possible exceptions is acknowledged by all moralists." [15] That is, truth-telling is

---

[13] According to the author's note in July, 1822, *op. cit.*

[14] John Stuart Mill, *Utilitarianism*, Indianapolis: Bobbs-Merrill, 1957, Chapter II.

[15] *Ibid.*

a general rule, with some exceptions (e.g., lying is right to save a life), that can guide one in doing what will bring the greatest good to the greatest number of people.

Mill admits that one cannot always calculate the consequences of his actions. This is precisely why rules and norms are needed. Mankind has had ample time to formulate a "fund" of human experience on which one may draw to help him calculate the consequences of his actions. "During all that time, mankind have been learning by experience the tendency of actions," Mill writes. And unless we assume men to be complete idiots, "mankind must by this time have acquired positive beliefs as to the effects of some actions on their happiness." And "the beliefs which have thus come down are the rules of morality for the multitude, and for the philosopher until he has succeeded in finding better." [16]

In short, there are valid moral "rules," "beliefs," "codes," etc., to guide human decisions toward maximizing the good in society, but none of these are universal rules. None of these is exceptionless; all of them can and should be broken for the principle of utility, i.e., when the greater good is in jeopardy. For "the received code of ethics is by no means of divine right." It admits of indefinite improvement. "But to consider the rules of morality as improvable is one thing; to pass over the intermediate generalization [i.e., "rules," "codes," etc.] entirely and endeavor to test each individual action directly by the first principle [of utility] is another." [17]

Just because there is only *one* ultimate goal (viz., happiness) toward which all morality is directed, it does not mean there cannot be *many* moral norms directing us toward that one goal. It means only that these many norms are not absolute and when they conflict, the conflict must be resolved by the utilitarian principle. There is only one fundamental principle of morality and all others are subordinate to it.

3. *The Problem With Exceptions* — Mill admits that his position is open to the criticism that exceptions to moral rules will present a temptation to break moral rules indiscriminately for the supposed utility of it. His reply is twofold. First, this same criticism may be made of all moral systems. "It is not the fault of any creed, but of the complicated nature of human affairs, that the rules of conduct cannot be so framed as to require no exceptions. . . . " And "there is no ethical creed which does not temper the rigidity of its laws by giving a certain latitude . . . for accommodation to peculiarities of circumstances; and under every creed, at the opening thus made, self-deception and dishonest casuistry get in." [18] The utilitarian no more than other moralists

16 *Ibid.*
17 *Ibid.*
18 *Ibid.*

must overcome the misuse of exceptions by intellect and virtue. The utilitarian has a standard of morality, and though the application of it may be difficult, it is better than none at all. "While in other systems the moral laws all claim independent authority, there is no common umpire entitled to interfere between them." [19]

Secondly, Mill acknowledges that exceptions ought to be both recognized as exceptions and have their limits defined. The reasons for this, he says, are so that exceptions will not be multiplied beyond their need and so that they may not weaken one's confidence in the general rule. [20] Mill merely mentions but does not elaborate on these points. Other utilitarians have adopted an alternate approach to that of Mill, arguing for exceptionless moral rules or at least rules, though not exceptionless in themselves, that should never be broken for utilitarian reasons.

C. G. E. Moore: General Rules and Universal Obedience

Utilitarians handle the problem of "exceptions" in two basic ways. The act-utilitarians hold that each particular ethical act must be judged by its consequences. Hence, there may be exceptions to any ethical rule or norm which in a particular case would justify breaking it. Rule-utilitarians, on the other hand, argue that rules should never be broken (unless there is a conflict between them), since the consequences of rule-breaking are bad. G. E. Moore's position in some respects seems to combine a bit of each view.

1. *Rules Are Only Generally Valid* — According to Moore the assertion, "I am morally bound to perform this act," means: "*This* action will produce the greatest possible amount of good in the Universe." That is, the results of acts determine their morality. Furthermore, "with regard then to ethical judgments which assert that a certain kind of action is good as a means to a certain kind of effect, none will be *universally* true; and many, though *generally* true at one period, will be generally false at others. . . . Hence we can never be entitled to more than a *generalization* — to a proposition of the form 'This result *generally* follows this kind of action'; and even this generalization will only be true, if the circumstances under which the action occurs are generally the same." [21] Rules and norms are generally useful but are not really universal.

In fact, ethical rules are not really categorical but prove to be only hypothetical. They are saying that *if* we act this way under these circumstances then the greatest good will probably result. But since other circumstances may interfere, it is not possible to know this with

---

[19] *Ibid.*
[20] *Ibid.*
[21] G. E. Moore, *Principia Ethica* (Cambridge University Press, 1959), I, 16 (p. 22).

any more than probability. So then "an ethical law has the nature not of a scientific law but of a scientific *prediction:* and the latter is always merely probably, although the probability may be very great." Murder, for example, cannot be known to be universally wrong, since "we do, as a matter of fact, only observe its good effects under certain circumstances; and it may be easily seen that a sufficient change in these would render doubtful what seem the most universally certain of general rules." Thus, the general disutility of murder could be proved only if the majority of the human race persist in believing that life is worthwhile. "In order to prove that murder . . . would not be good as a means, we should have to disprove the main contention of pessimism — namely that the existence of human life is on the whole an evil." So "when . . . we say that murder is in general to be avoided, we only mean that it is so, so long as the majority of mankind will certainly not agree to it, but will persist in living." However, as long as most men continue to value life, the ethical consideration that "it is generally wrong for any single person to commit murder" seems capable of proof." The same holds true for other rules such as temperance and promise-keeping. [22]

Chastity, likewise, is only a general rule whose universal utility depends upon certain conditions which are considered necessary for the conservation of society. For instance, it is usually presupposed that chastity is necessary to avoid conjugal jealousy and to preserve paternal affection and that both of these are necessary conditions to preserve society. "But it is not difficult to imagine a civilized society existing without them." Hence, the rule of chastity is only a general and conditional rule that could be relinquished if society could survive without it. [23]

2. *Some General Rules Should Not Be Broken* — Notwithstanding the fact that moral norms are only general rules which have individual exceptions, Moore argues that the individual ought never disobey a rule which is held by most men to be true in general. He gives the following reasons. First, "if it is certain that in a large majority of cases the observance of a certain rule is useful, it follows that there is a large probability that it would be wrong to break the rule in any particular case." Further, "the uncertainty of our knowledge both of effects and of their value, in particular cases, is so great, that it seems doubtful whether the individual's judgment that the effect will probably be good in his case can ever be set against the general probability that that kind of action is wrong." Also, "added to this general ignorance is the fact that, if the question arises at all, our judgment will generally be biased by the fact that we strongly desire one of the

22 *Ibid.*, V, 94, 95 (pp. 154 - 156).
23 *Ibid.*, V, 96 (p. 158).

results which we hope to obtain by breaking the rule." In view of these factors, "it seems, then, that with regard to any rule which is *generally* useful, we may assert that it ought *always* to be observed," wrote Moore, "not on the ground that in every particular case it will be useful, but on the ground that in *any* particular case the probability of its being so is greater than that of our being likely to decide rightly that we have before us an instance of its disutility. . . . In short, though we may be sure that there are cases where the rule should be broken, we can never know which those cases are, and ought, therefore, never to break it." [24]

Even if one were to perceive clearly that in his case breaking the rule would be advantageous, yet insofar as such a rule-breaking action tends to encourage other unadvantageous breaches of the rule, it has a bad effect. For "in cases . . . where example has any influence at all, the effect of an exceptional right action will generally be to encourage wrong ones." According to Moore, the logic of this should be carried even one step further. For "it is undoubtedly well to punish a man, who has done an action, right in his case but generally wrong, even if his example would not be likely to have a dangerous effect. For sanctions [punishment] have, in general, much more influence upon conduct than example; so that the effect of relaxing them in an exceptional case will almost certainly be an encouragement of similar action in cases which are not exceptional." [25]

It should be noted that the above position that one ought *always* obey rules that are admittedly only *generally* applicable is limited only to those rules or norms which are known "certainly" to be of general usefulness. In cases where there is "doubt" of the general utility of a rule, Moore seems to agree with an act-utilitarian approach. "It seems," he says, "that, in cases of doubt, instead of following rules, of which he is unable to see the good effects in his particular case, the individual should rather guide his choice by a direct consideration of the intrinsic value of vileness of the effect which his action may produce." [26]

In either event, there are no actions or kinds of action which really are universally wrong; there are only some things *generally* wrong which one ought (for utilitarian reasons) to universally avoid. So there are at least two ways in which Moore's position does not provide any truly universal norms. First, the norms which one should *always* follow do not represent acts which are really universally right or wrong, but only acts which are generally wrong. In specific cases an exception may be justified. But since it brings more evil than good to claim that any given case qualifies as a legitimate exception, it

[24] *Ibid.*, I, 16 (p. 22); cf. V, 94 (pp. 154-155).
[25] *Ibid.*, V, 99 (pp. 163, 164).
[26] *Ibid.*, V, 100 (p. 166).

follows that the rule should never be broken. Secondly, Moore's general rules which should always be obeyed are not really normative universals in a categorical sense, since they are norms justified only by their results. They are not deontological. They do not represent kinds of actions with intrinsic value. [27] Moore is very clear in holding that no acts have intrinsic value; all acts are to be judged by their results. [28]

D. *John Austin: No General Rules Should Be Broken*

In the rule-utilitarianism of John Austin the question of "unbreakable" rules is carried one step further than in G. E. Moore. Moore argued only that some rules ought never to be broken, because of their general utility and because one could not be sure his case was a ligitimate exception, and even if it were, other offsetting bad consequences and influences would result from making an exception of it. Austin, on the other hand, argues that rules about a class of actions which if generally done would bring bad results should never be broken.

1. *Rules Are Justified by General Results* — Austin's position is decidedly utilitarian because the justification of keeping the rules is only the good results rule-keeping brings. He says, "Our rules would be fashioned on utility; our conduct on our rules. . . ." According to Austin's view, "our conduct would conform to rules inferred from the tendency of actions, but would not be determined by a direct resort to the principle of general utility." That is to say, "utility would be the test of our conduct, ultimately, but not immediately." [29] Rules are justified if keeping them brings greater good and/or if breaking them brings greater evil on society. However, rules are not about specific or individual acts but about classes or kinds of acts.

2. *Universal Rule-Keeping Is Justified by General Results* — Each individual act is not to be justified by its specific results as in act-utilitarianism. But the whole class of acts of that kind are judged by the results which those kinds of acts bring. As Austin stated it, "If we would try the tendency of a specific or individual act, we must not contemplate the act as if it were single and insulated, but must look at the class of acts to which it belongs." Further, "we must suppose that acts of the class were generally done or omitted, and consider the probable effect upon the general happiness or good. . . ." For "the *particular* conclusion which we draw, with regard to the single

---

[27] Furthermore, these general rules are always to be obeyed only *if* they are generally observed and generally useful. If either (or both) ceases to be a fact, then the rules lose their force and need not always be obeyed. Cf. *op. cit.*, V, 99 (p. 162).

[28] *Ibid.*, Cf. V, 92, 93, 104, 105.

[29] John Austin, *The Province of Jurisprudence Determined* (London: Weidenfeld and Nicolson, Ltd., 1954) p. 47; first published in 1832.

act, implies a general conclusion embracing all similar acts." [30] The only exception to this is when rules conflict or when a particular act falls under no rule.

Austin gives a number of examples of his position. A poor man should not steal from his rich neighbor on the grounds of the utility of this particular act (as an act-utilitarian would say), for if stealing were general, the effect would be disastrous on society. Nor should one evade the payment of a tax to devote the money to some good purpose, for "the regular payment of taxes is necessary to the existence of the government. And I, and the rest of the community, enjoy the security which it gives, because the payment of taxes is rarely evaded." [31]

In a similar way the punishment of an individual as a solitary event may do more harm than good. "But, considered as part of a system, a punishment is useful or beneficent. By a dozen or score of punishments, thousands of crimes are prevented." [32] That is, the individual punishment is justified by the good results of the general practices. Exceptions should not be made because the general results of disobeying general rules is generally bad.

II. Generalism Evaluated

There are some decided advantages to generalism as well as some serious drawbacks. Let us mention first the positive features of the generalistic approach to ethical norms.

A. Some Values of Generalism

The values of generalism vary with its various representations. But, taken as a whole, there are at least three of them which relate to the normative study undertaken here. First, it offers a possible solution to conflicting norms. Second, generalism reflects a need for norms. Finally, some generalists even argue for "unbreakable" norms.

1. *A Solution to Conflicting Norms* — A generalistic position does offer a solution to our paradigm problem (see chapter one) of what to do when there is a conflict of duty such as between truth-telling and life-saving. For to some generalists there are no universal rules which are really exceptionless. At best they are only general norms which may be broken if the occasion calls for it. In this way lying to save a life can be right, even though lying is generally wrong.

There is only one absolute end (the greatest good) and all the means (rules, norms, etc.) are relative to that end. In any given instance, when there is a conflict of means or norms, they may be resolved by a direct appeal to the utilitarian end. If lying in this situa-

<hr>

[30] *Ibid.*, pp. 47, 48.
[31] *Ibid.*, p. 39.
[32] *Ibid.*, p. 40.

tion would be more useful or helpful to most men, then one ought to lie.

As has been mentioned, the generalistic solution is neither antinomian nor situational. For antinomians admit of the value of no norms at all, not even general ones. And situationism (*a la* Fletcher) claims to have one absolute norm, whereas generalists claim no absolute norms at all. Of course, generalism has one absolute *end* which functions like a *norm* in helping to determine a given course of action when there is a conflict of general norms. But technically, the greatest good for the greatest number is not considered by generalists to be a norm by which the best end can be attained but it is the end itself in view of which the best norm should be chosen. So generalism is a mediating position, evading the no-norm position and offering a reconciliation when there is a conflict among accepted norms.

2. *The Need for Norms* — the generalist recognizes the need for norms. Even utilitarian ends need normative means for attaining them. There must be a road map for one's ultimate goal. Moral ends are not self-attaining. There is an evident need for criteria to guide one's conduct. It is to the credit of the utilitarians that they have recognized that without norms or other normative bases taken from the fund of human experience there is no way of determining the long range results of one's actions. That is, they are aware of the fact that in the absence of predictive powers men must draw upon principles which are known to produce good results when followed.

G. E. Moore argued that in view of the fact that one does not know the long-range future, he must gauge his action on the basis of the known short-range future, assuming they will be the same. But he frankly acknowledges that this is an unproven assumption. He adds, "It will be apparent that it has never yet been justified — that no sufficient reason has ever yet been found for considering one action more right or more wrong than another [via results]." [33] In view of this it is understandable that the utilitarian resorts to norms to save his position from collapsing.

3. *An "Unbreakable" Norm* — Other generalists offer a case for rules or norms which should never be broken. Even though they admit that there are exceptional cases which might in isolation justify breaking a general rule, they offer practical arguments for never breaking a rule such as life-saving, promise-keeping, etc. (unless, of course, there is a conflict of norms). The very desire to have meaningful and unbreakable norms for conduct is a commendable aspect of their ethic. It is a recognition of the many difficulties of an exceptionistic approach on the practical level.

Furthermore, generalists are not complete relativists. They have an

[33] Moore, *Principia Ethica*, V, 93 (p. 152).

absolute, even though it is not always considered an absolute *norm*. It is an absolute *end,* and it is used by them to discern among their relative means. In fact, without an absolute end it is difficult to see how generalists could either justify their choice among means or how they could argue that some rules should never be broken. For if there is no ultimate criterion for deciding on these issues, then how could one relative be chosen over another? Ranking separate actions by *intrinsic* value is not something generalists (of the utilitarian brand) are prone to do, for it is contrary to their premise of judging things by their *extrinsic* value (viz., usefulness).

B. *Some Inadequacies of Generalism*

Despite some positive things that may be said in favor of generalism, there are some serious problems with the position. First, it never really attains a universal norm. Second, it is not normative in an intrinsic sense. Finally, it evidences the need for an absolute norm (or norms).

1 *Generalism Has No Universal Norms* — There is a distinct difference between a *general* norm, which for practical reasons one ought always to obey, and a truly *universal* norm which is always intrinsically right to follow. The latter represents an intrinsically good act (which will be discussed in the next criticism), but the generalist offers only norms which have less than universal extension. There are always unspecifiable exceptions or else cases which are not covered by the rule. And even though generalists sometimes opt not to break these rules because of general utility, nevertheless, the rule itself is not essentially unbreakable.

In brief, if one is in search of meaningful norms for conduct which he ought always to follow because they will guide him in performing acts which are always the right thing to do, then he will be disappointed in generalism. The best a generalist can offer is a set of general norms which neither cover all cases nor are non-conflicting and for which, in order for them to be effective, one must have some other means of applying them in specific and often crucial cases.

2. *Utilitarian Acts Have No Intrinsic Value* — Another criticism may be directed toward the utilitarian generalists, viz., that the norms they do have do not represent any acts with intrinsic value. The attempt to save a life, e.g., is not an intrinsically valuable act. It has value only if the person is actually saved or if some other good comes from the futile attempt. According to the utilitarian premise, a gift of charity which never reaches the poor or an act of kindness to which there is no favorable response is not a good act. Indeed, no act in and of itself is good, unless good results from it. And no act is morally right unless it brings the greatest good to the greatest number of men. No benevolence, no sacrifice, no love has any value unless

it happens to have good results. And, conversely, if an act brings about good, it is a good act whether it was intended that way or not. Thus the utilitarian position reduces the ethical value of acts to the fates and fortunes of life. All is well that ends well. And what ends well is good. This would mean that the intentions of one's actions have no essential connection with the good of those actions. Presumably, one could will and perform an evil which by chance turned out for good and be credited with performing a good act. Surely fortuity and morality do not belong in such close proximity. [34]

3. *The Need for an Absolute Norm* — It is not possible consistently to maintain a group of general norms which may and do conflict without having an absolute norm by which the conflict can be resolved. This point seems to be evidenced by the need among utilitarian generalists to appeal to the end to resolve the conflict between norms. But when the end is so used, it serves a normative function. The end (viz., the greatest good) becomes the means of determining which means will be best for attaining the end. Not only is there a manifest circularity in so appealing to the end, but there is also an obvious need for an ultimate principle to resolve the tension among the less-than-ultimate principles or norms.

To state the point another way, relative norms do not stand alone. They must be relative to something which is not relative. So unless there is an assumed non-relative norm, the relative norms cannot properly function. In other words, general norms presuppose a universal norm or norms. Whether the number of absolute or universal norms is one or many will be discussed more fully in the next four chapters. It is sufficient for now to note that there must be *at least* one norm which is true under all conditions if the other norms are to be true under any conditions.

SELECT READINGS FOR CHAPTER THREE: GENERALISM

Austin, John, *The Province of Jurisprudence Determined*, London: Weidenfeld and Nicolson, Ltd., 1954.
Bentham, Jeremy, *Introduction to the Principles of Morals and Legislation.*
Mill, John Stuart, *Utilitarianism*, London: 1863. (New York: Meridian Books, 1962).
Moore, G. E., *Principia Ethica*, Cambridge University Press, 1959.
Singer, Marcus G., *Generalization in Ethics*, New York: Alfred A. Knopf, 1961.

[34] See also chapter one for further criticisms of the utilitarian or teleological position.

4 / Situationism: There Is
One Universal Norm

Contrary to what the word "situationism" might seem to imply, it is not taken here to represent a completely normless ethic. According to one of its most vigorous proponents, Joseph Fletcher, [1] situationism is located between the extremes of legalism and antinomianism. The antinomians have no laws, the legalists have laws for everything, and Fletcher's situationism has only one law.

I. SITUATIONISM EXPLAINED

Since Fletcher's situationism claims allegiance to one unbreakable norm, it will be treated here as a one-norm absolutism. For, according to Fletcher, his position is neither a lawless relativism nor a legalistic absolutism. It does not have laws for everything, and it does not say there is no law for anything. Rather, it contends that there is one law for everything, the law of love.

A. *Avoiding Two Extremes: Legalism and Antonomianism*

Fletcher fears both the radical right and the radical left in ethics. However, his position yields more readily to the criticism that it, too, is not distinguishable from antinomianism. [2] Between these two poles, he attempts to stake firmly one absolute norm which can be applied to every ethical situation.

[1] Joseph Fletcher, *Situation Ethics: The New Morality*, Philadelphia: The Westminster Press, 1966. There are other one-absolute situationists who might have been used for this study, but Fletcher is perhaps better known. See Emil Brunner, *The Divine Imperative*, Reinhold Niebuhr, *Moral Man and Immoral Society*, Bishop Robinson, *Honest to God*, and others.

[2] See the criticism of situationism at the end of this chapter.

60

1. *Legalism: Law Over Love* — The legalist is one who enters every decision-making situation encumbered with a bundle of predetermined rules and regulations. For him the letter of the Law, not the spirit of the law, prevails. The post-Maccabean Pharisees are singled out as a classic example of legalists. With their 613 (or 621) laws they were prearmed for any moral predicament. They had a preset and prescribed manual for morality. Along with Judaism, Fletcher classes both classical Catholicism and Protestantism as legalistic, though Judaism is less so than the latter two. The Jews stoned homosexuals and the Church burned them, says Fletcher. [3] Both were putting law over love. The legalist believes in the love of duty; the situationist holds to the duty of love.

2. *Antinomianism: No Law or Love* — At the other end of the ethical spectrum Fletcher locates the antinomians who are complete libertines with no norms whatsoever. Each of their moral decisions is spontaneous and unprincipled, based only on the there-and-then situation. Some antinomians claim to have a clairvoyant conscience, a kind of direct moral insight into right and wrong. As examples of the antinomian view, Fletcher lists the New Testament Libertines with their lawlessness, the early Gnostics with their "special knowledge," the modern Moral Re-armament movement with its "spiritual power," and Jean Paul Sartre's existentialism (discussed above in chapter two). Common to all these views, says Fletcher, is the rejection of all moral rules, even any generally valid ones. No norm is accepted, not even a love norm. From Fletcher's point of view, the antinomians throw out the whole ethical baby (of love) with the legalistic bathwater. [4]

3. *Situationism: Love Over Law* — Between these polar opposites of legalistic laws for everything and antinomian lack of laws for anything, Fletcher posits his situational absolutism of one law for everything. The situationist comes into every ethical battle armed with but one moral weapon — love. "Only the command to love is categorically good." Every other decision is hypothetical, viz., do this *if* it is loving. "We are 'obliged' to tell the truth, for example, only if the situation calls for it; if a would-be murderer asks his victim's whereabouts, our duty might be to lie." [5]

As far as other moral rules are concerned, they are helpful but not unbreakable. The only ethical imperative one has is this: "Act responsibly in love." Literally "everything else without exception, all laws and rules and principles and ideals and norms, are only contingent, only valid *if they happen* to serve love in any situation." [6]

---

[3] Fletcher, *Situation Ethics*, p. 20.
[4] *Ibid.*, p. 23.
[5] *Ibid.*, pp. 26, 27.
[6] *Ibid.*, pp. 28, 30.

The situationist has one law (*agapē love*), many general rules (*sophia*) which are more or less reliable, and the *kairos* or particular moment of decision "in which the *responsible self in the situation* decides whether the *sophia* can serve love there or not." The "legalists make an idol of the *sophia*, antinomians repudiate it, situationists use it," writes Fletcher. [7] The solidification of these generally valid rules into absolute norms is legalism, and the rejection of all value in them is antinomianism.

There are at least two basic reasons for accepting only one universal norm. First, universals cannot be derived by deduction from other universals like "middle axioms" — one cannot have a derived underived. Secondly, each situation is so different from every other situation that it raises a serious question as to whether a rule which applies to one situation can be applied to *all* situations like it (the others may not be really like it).[8] Only the single axiom or norm of love is broad enough to be applied to *all* circumstances and contexts.

B. *Setting Forth the Presuppositions*

According to Fletcher, there are four working principles of situationism. It is pragmatic, relativistic, positivistic, and personalistic. By claiming that his view is such, he does not intend that we should conclude that it is totally relativistic and non-normative. He means, rather, that within the framework of this absolute love norm everything else is pragmatic, relative, etc.

1. *Pragmatism* — By a pragmatic approach, which consciously inspired Fletcher's book, he means that "the right is only the expedient in our way of our behaving." [9] It is what "works" or "satisfies" for love's sake. He wants to put love to work in order to make it successful and to realize its "cash value." The pragmatic approach has nothing but disdain for abstract, verbal solutions to ethical problems; it seeks, rather, concrete and practical answers.

2. *Relativism* — There is only one absolute; everything else is *relative* to it. "As the strategy is pragmatic, the tactics are relativistic." The divine command of love is changeless in its *why* but contingent in its specific *what* and *how*. "The situationist," writes Fletcher, "avoids words like 'never' and 'perfect' and 'always' and 'complete' as he avoids the plague, as he avoids 'absolutely.'" Of course, it is impossible to be "absolutely relative." "There must be an absolute or norm of some kind if there is to be any true relativity. . . . In *Christian* situationism the ultimate criterion, as we shall see shortly, is 'agapic

---

[7] *Ibid.*, p. 33.
[8] *Ibid.*, pp. 32, 33.
[9] *Ibid.*, p. 41.

love.'"[10] But Christians should constantly remind themselves that *everything else* is relative to this one norm.

3. *Positivism* – A positivistic position, as opposed to a naturalistic view, holds that values are derived voluntaristically not rationalistically. A man *decides* on his values; he does not deduce them from nature. It is also called "emotivism" because moral values are thought to be expressions of one's feeling rather than prescriptions for one's life. [11] A positivistic or emotive ethic places art and morals in the same camp – both call for a decision or "leap" of faith. Ethical statements do not seek verification; they look for justification. [12] And only in the one norm of Christian love do all other moral expressions find their ultimate justification.

4. *Personalism* – Moral values are not only what persons express; persons are the ultimate moral values. There are no inherently good *things;* only *persons* are inherently valuable. Value only "happens" to things. Things are of value only to persons. "Things are to be *used;* people are to be *loved.*"[13] The reverse of this, which is loving things and using people, is the perversion of morality. According to Fletcher, considering only persons to have intrinsic value is what Kant meant by treating persons always as *ends* and never as *means.* So this is the meaning of love, viz., relating everything to the good of persons, who alone are good as such.

In brief, situationism is an ethic with a pragmatic strategy, a relativistic tactic, a positivistic attitude, and a personalistic value center. It is an ethic with one absolute to which everything else is relative and which is directed toward the pragmatic end of doing good to persons.

C. *Explaining the Propositions*

The situational position can be explained by six basic propositions. Each proposition is any elaboration of what it means to live situationally with only one absolute norm, love. The discussion here will follow the order in which they are given by Fletcher.

1. *"Only one 'thing' is intrinsically good; namely love: nothing else at all."*[14] – The realist argues that God wills something because it is good. Fletcher follows the nominalist (like Scotus, Ockham) who say that something is good because God wills it so. Nothing is good in and for itself. It is good only if it helps persons and bad if it hurts persons. The person who is "finding" the value may be divine or human, but only persons – God, self, neighbor – determine some-

---

[10] *Ibid.,* pp. 43, 44, 45.
[11] See chapter two for a discussion of emotivism.
[12] Fletcher, *op. cit.,* pp. 48, 49.
[13] *Ibid.,* p. 51.
[14] *Ibid.,* p. 57.

thing to be valuable. No act has intrinsic value. It gains its value only as it relates to persons. Apart from helping or hurting persons all ethical acts are meaningless.

All value, worth, goodness, and rightness are predicates, not properties. They may be predicated about persons, but they are not real things in themselves. God *is* goodness and love; all other persons merely *have* or *do* good. Love is an attitude, not an attribute. Love is something that persons give and something that only persons should receive, because only persons have intrinsic value. In fact, according to Fletcher, the image of God in man is not reason but love. Love and personhood constitute men's characteristic similarity to God. This is why the only human thing with intrinsic value is love — it makes man like God.

The other side of the proposition that only benevolence (love) is inherently good is that only malevolence is intrinsically evil. However, for Fletcher, the opposite of love is not hate (which is really a perverted form of love); the opposite of love is *indifference*. Hate at least treats the other as a *thou* or person. Indifference considers others an *it*. To totally ignore another and his needs is to depersonalize him. It is worse than attacking him, for an attack presupposes at least that the attacker considers the other person a person *worth* attacking.

Fletcher is opposed to calling some acts lesser and, therefore, excusable evils. A spy's lie, for example, is not wrong at all. "If a lie is told in love it is good, right." It is not an excusable evil; it is a positive good. "If love vetoes the truth, so be it." [15] Whatever one must do for love's sake is good, for only love is intrinsically good, nothing else whatsoever is good. Whatever is the loving thing to do in a given situation is the right thing to do, even if it involves sacrificial suicide under torture to avoid betraying one's comrades to the enemy.

2. *"The ruling norm of Christian decision is love: nothing else."* [16] — Love replaces the law. The spirit replaces the letter. "We follow law, *if at all*, for love's sake." One does not follow love for the law's sake; he follows the law only for love's sake. Traditionally, men believed that they kept love by obeying the law because the two were identical. But love and law sometimes conflict, and when they do, it is the Christian's obligation to put love over the law. It is not the love of the law but the law of love which one ought to follow. To repeat, it is not the love of duty but the duty of love.

According to Fletcher, Jesus summed up the Mosaic law and the Ten Commandments in one word, *love*. Indeed, there is no one of the commandments which may not be broken in some situation for

[15] *Ibid.,* p. 65.
[16] *Ibid.,* p. 69.

love's sake. "There are no 'universal laws' held by all men everywhere at all times, no consensus of all men." For "any precepts all men can agree to are platitudes such as 'do the good and avoid the evil' or 'to each according to his due.'"[17] That is, there are no universal laws except love. Every other law is breakable by love.

As Augustine put it, "Love with care and then what you will, do." He did not say, adds Fletcher, "Love with desire and do what you please."[18] Christian love is a *giving* love. Christian love is neither romantic love (erotic) nor friendship love (philic). Christian love is a sacrificial love (agapic). And it is also a responsible love which is no more subject to exploitation than the evasive motives of legalism. In fact, a legalistic refuge in the safety of universal laws can be a retreat from individual responsibility. One may be wishing the security of absolutes rather than the responsibility of relatives. The classical pacifist is, for Fletcher, escaping the responsibility of deciding which wars are just. It is an easier ethic if someone else decides what is right or wrong and simply tells us what to do.

3. *"Love and justice are the same, for justice is love distributed, nothing else."*[19] — Love and justice are identical. Love does more than take justice into account; love becomes justice. Justice means to give others their due, and love is their due. The apostle Paul said, "Owe no man anything except to love," quotes Fletcher. Even if love and justice differed (and they do not), the least love could do would be to give justice to every man.

In loving (i.e., in being just) one must be multi-directional, not just one-directional. The command is to love one's neighbors. Love is not merely a present activity to one's immediate neighbor. Love must have foresight. It must borrow the utilitarian principle and try to bring the greatest good (love) to the greatest number of men. For if love does not calculate the remote consequences, it becomes selfish. In short, justice is love using its head.[20]

Christian ethics welcomes law and order for love's sake. It even sees at times the need of a loving use of force to protect the innocent and it makes "rights" practical. Sometimes, one may have the moral (i.e., loving) responsibility to disobey unjust civil law. And on occasion love may demand a revolution against the state — if the state has gone beyond love's pale.[21]

4. *"Love wills the neighbor's good whether we like him or not."* — The fourth proposition stresses that love is an attitude and not a feeling. It stresses the distinctive characteristics of Christian love. "Where-

[17] *Ibid.*, pp. 74, 76.
[18] *Ibid.*, pp. 74, 79.
[19] *Ibid.*, p. 87.
[20] *Ibid.*, pp. 92, 95, 98.
[21] *Ibid.*, pp. 100, 101.

as in *eros* desire is the cause of love, in *agapē* love is the cause of desire." *Agapē* love is not reciprocal. A comparison of the three kinds of love reveals what Fletcher has in mind here.

Erotic love is egoistic. It says, "My first and last consideration is myself." Philic love is mutualistic. It says, "I will give as long as I receive." Agapic love, on the other hand, is altruistic, saying, "I will give, requiring nothing in return." It is this kind of love which is the ruling norm in situational ethics. The agapic kind of love is that by which one ought to love his neighbor as himself.

Fletcher outlines four interpretations of the command to love one's neighbor *as himself.* First, some say it means to love your neighbor just *as much as* you love yourself. Second, it may mean to love others *in addition to* loving yourself. Third, others (e.g., Sören Kierkegaard), hold that it means to love your neighbor *in the way you ought to* love yourself (e.g., rightly, honestly). Fourth, it is said that the command is to love your neighbor *instead of* loving yourself, i.e., as you have been doing but must now stop doing. Which is the true meaning of self-love?

Following the ladder of self-love suggested by Bernard of Clairvaux which climbs from (1) love of self for self's sake, to (2) love of God for self's sake, to (3) love of God for God's sake, to (4) love of self for God's sake, Fletcher outlines his own understanding of loving one's neighbor as oneself. We move, he says, from (1) love of ourselves for our own sake, to (2) love of our neighbor for our own sake, to (3) love of our neighbor for the neighbor's sake, to (4) love of ourselves for the neighbor's sake. The latter is the highest and the best. It is the right kind of self-love, viz., the love of oneself *for the sake of loving others.* [22]

When self-love and neighbor-love conflict, "the logic of love is that self-concern is obligated to cancel neighbor-good whenever *more* neighbor-good will be served through serving the self." A ship's captain or a plane's pilot, e.g., are to keep themselves alive, even at the expense of some passengers if need be, for the sake of the safety of the rest of the passengers.

In actuality, there is no real conflict between self-love and neighbor-love. One is to love himself only to the degree that it maximizes neighbor-love. All love is self-love, but it is the self loved *for the sake of* loving the most men possible. Love is one, but there are three objects: God, neighbor, and self. Self-love may be either right or wrong. "If we love ourselves for our own sakes, that is wrong. If we love ourselves for God's sake and the neighbor's, then it is right. For to love God and the neighbor is to love one's self in the right

22 *Ibid.,* p. 112.

way . . . ; to love one's self in the right way is to love God and one's neighbors." [23]

And in no case does loving one's neighbor imply that we must *like* him. In fact, love does not even necessarily involve *pleasing* our neighbor. Love demands that we will our neighbor's good, whether or not he pleases us and whether or not our love pleases him. Calculating the neighbor's good, even if it displeases him, is not cruel. A military nurse, e.g., may lovingly treat patients roughly so as to hasten their recovery and return to battle. Love, like a bride, needs a recipe and not mere feeling for the loved one. [24]

5. *"Only the end justifies the means; nothing else."* — If this were not true, no act would be justified. There are no intrinsically good acts except the act of love. Hence, the only thing that can justify an act is if it is done for loving ends or purposes. This is not to say that *any* end justifies any means but only that a *loving* end justifies any means. [25] For example, it might be the loving thing to steal a murderer's gun or to lie to a schizophrenic patient to keep him calm for treatment. What, asks Fletcher, justifies slicing into a human body with a knife? Surely not hatred of him as one's enemy. But would not the act of mutilating his body be justified if the end in view is to save his life from a diseased or cancerous organ? Does not the end justify the means in this situation?

In fact, what else besides the end could possibly justify the means, asks Fletcher? The means cannot justify themselves. Only ends justify means. Indeed, "no act apart from its foreseeable consequences has any ethical meaning whatsoever." [26] The meaning of the act comes from its purpose or end. And the only justifiable purpose for performing ethical acts is agapic love. Any means which is sought for its own sake is wrong. In fact, all ends are only means to higher ends, until one arrives at last at the ultimate end of love itself.

In response to those who charge, on the basis of the "wedge" principle, that it is dangerous to have exceptions to moral norms like truth-telling and life-saving, Fletcher argues that "abuse does not bar use." Just because some men will abuse the situationist position of responsible love by irresponsible actions does not disprove the value of the love norm itself. And the so-called "generalization" argument — "What if everyone did it?" — is no more than obscurantic, a delaying tactic of static morality. [27]

6. *"Love's decisions are made situationally, not prescriptively."* — The final expository postulate of situation ethics marks strongly the

23 *Ibid.*, pp. 113, 114.
24 *Ibid.*, pp. 116, 117.
25 *Ibid.*, pp. 120, 121.
26 *Ibid.*, p. 126.
27 *Ibid.*, p. 131.

difference between the basic ethical *principle* (i.e., the love norm) and the *application* of that principle in a given circumstance. The love principle is a universal but formal norm. It does not prescribe in advance what specific courses of action will be loving. For the precise prescription of love one will have to wait until he is in the situation. Love is free from specific predefinition. One cannot know in advance the "existential particularity" which love will take once it is in the situation. Love operates apart from a system of pretailored, prefabricated moral rules. Love functions circumstantially, neocasuistically. Love does not make up its mind before it has seen the facts, and the facts come from the situation. [28]

What the situationist does have in advance is a general (though not specific) knowledge of *what* he should do (viz., love), *why* he should do it (for God's sake), and to *whom* it should be done (his neighbors). He knows, of course, that love is altruistic and not egoistic. And he knows that it should be exercised toward as many neighbors as possible. He knows in advance how this love will probably operate in a general way by means of *sophia,* or wisdom. But he cannot say for sure what the loving thing to do will be in a particular case until all the particulars are known. For example, if Fletcher is asked, "Is adultery wrong?" he answers, "I don't know. Maybe. Give me a case." [29] In fact, Fletcher himself provides a case where adultery can be right if it is done in love (discussed below).

In brief, the situationist holds that the general *what* and *why* are absolute, but the *how* is relative. There is an absolute prescription, but it is only worked out in the relative situation. Love is ultimate, but just how one is to love is dependent on the immediate circumstances. By a closer examination of some difficult moral situations we will be able to understand even better just how Fletcher's one-norm absolutism functions in different contexts.

D. *Applying the Love Norm*

By the use of provocative illustrations throughout his book, Fletcher is able to explain more fully just why he holds to only one absolute norm and how it would probably be applied under differing conditions. Some of these marginal moral cases will now be examined.

1. *The Case of Altruistic Adultery* [30] — A German mother of two was captured by the Russians near the end of World War II. The rules of her Ukrainian prison camp allowed her release to Germany only by pregnancy, in which case she would be returned as a liability. The woman asked a friendly camp guard to impregnate her. She was sent back to Germany, welcomed by her family, gave birth to the baby,

[28] *Ibid.,* pp. 134, 136 cf. 27, 30, 55.
[29] *Ibid.,* p. 142.
[30] *Ibid.,* pp. 164, 165.

and made him a part of their reunited family. Was her adultery justified? Fletcher does not say explicitly that it was, but implies that it was by calling it "sacrificial adultery." Elsewhere, however, Fletcher speaks approvingly of wife-swapping for consenting adults, of a woman seducing a man who was pathologically attracted to a little girl, and of a young couple forcing parental approval of their marriage by engaging in intercourse. [31] The direct implication is that all of these things can be done lovingly and, therefore, can be morally right.

2. *The Case of Patriotic Prostitution* — A young woman working for a United States intelligence agency was asked to lure an enemy spy into blackmail by using her sex. In the guise of a secretary, she was to involve a married man who was working for a rival power. When she protested that she could not put her personal integrity on the block, as offering sex for hire, she was told, "It's like your brother risking his life or limb in Korea. We are sure this job can't be done any other way." [32] She was patriotic and wanted to serve her country. What was the loving thing to do? Here again Fletcher does not give his answer, but in view of the fact that he elsewhere approves of spies lying and men dying for their country out of love, there seems to be for him no reason why one might not be able to justify committing fornication for the Fatherland, too. [33]

3. *Cases of Sacrificial Suicide* — Is taking one's own life always morally wrong? According to situation ethics, it is not; suicide can be done in love. For example, if a man has only the choices of taking expensive medicine which will deplete family finances and cause his insurance to lapse just to live three more years or else refuse the medicine and die in six months but thereby leave ample financial provisions for his family, which is the loving thing to do? [34] It is not difficult to see how a situationist could approve of this rather indirect kind of sacrificial suicide. In fact, Fletcher speaks with approval both of Mother Maria's substitutionary death in the Nazi gas chambers for a young Jewess who was an ex-Communist, and of a captured soldier's taking his own life to avoid betraying his comrades to the enemy. [35] Suicide can be done for love's sake, in which case it is morally right, according to a situation ethic.

4. *The Case of the Acceptable Abortion* — Even though Fletcher favors birth control over abortion as a means of controlling the population, [36] nonetheless, there are circumstances when he comes out clearly in favor of abortion. He gives the example of an unmarried schizo-

[31] *Ibid.*, pp. 164, 165, cf. pp. 14, 80, 105.
[32] *Ibid.*, pp. 163, 164.
[33] *Ibid.*, pp. 65, 66.
[34] *Ibid.*, pp. 165, 166.
[35] *Ibid.*, pp. 74, 66.
[36] *Ibid.*, p. 122.

phrenic patient who became pregnant after being raped. Her father requested abortion but was refused by the hospital staff on the grounds that it was not a therapeutic abortion and was, therefore, illegal. Fletcher castigates this refusal as based on a legalistic ethic. "The situationist . . . would almost certainly, *in this case,* favor abortion and support the girl's father's request." [37]

In another case Fletcher gives tacit approval to a Rumanian Jewish doctor who aborted three thousand babies of Jewish mothers in concentration camps, because, if pregnant, the mothers were to be incinerated. That means that the doctor saved three thousand lives. And on the view that the embryos were human lives (which Fletcher rejects), the doctor, by "killing" three thousand lives, saved three thousand and prevented the murder of six thousand. [38] Surely this was the loving thing to do, according to situationism.

5. *The Case of Merciful Murder* — Should we actually turn our back on a man who is hopelessly caught in a burning airplane and begs to be shot? Would it have not been right to assassinate Hitler? Fletcher offers both illustrations and seems to indicate that either one could be a merciful and, therefore, justifiable murder. [39] He seems to favor the act of a mother smothering her crying baby in order to save their group from being detected and killed by hostile Indians. [40] The direct implication is that such an act might be performed in sacrificial love for the good of the whole group.

Fletcher clearly approves of throwing some men out of an overloaded rescue boat to save them all from sinking. The first mate of the ship *William Brown* out of Liverpool in 1841 was in charge of an overcrowded life boat. He ordered most of the males thrown into the sea to save the rest. Later, Holmes, the seaman who threw them into the sea, was convicted of murder, with mercy recommended. "Situation ethics says it was bravely sinful, it was a good thing." [41] According to Fletcher, Holmes actually acted in love for the greater number of lives.

There are many other marginal cases which Fletcher offers, such as refusing to respirate a monstrously deformed child, carrying a cancer-cure inventor out of a burning building rather than one's own father, the sterilization of someone marrying a syphilitic, and providing motherhood for single women by artificial insemination. [42] Time will not be taken here to discuss any more cases. The point, however, which arises from all of these situations and which needs emphasis

[37] *Ibid.,* p. 38.
[38] *Ibid.*
[39] *Ibid.,* p. 175.
[40] *Ibid.,* p. 125.
[41] *Ibid.,* p. 136.
[42] *Ibid.,* pp. 138, 115, 80, 126.

here is that in each situation there is a conflict of moral norms, which the situationist feels can be best resolved by appeal to a single higher norm. Often the norms which conflict are held by some men to be unbreakable, universal. But how can two or more norms be universal and unbreakable if they conflict? One cannot follow two opposing paths. He must choose. Surely he cannot be held responsible for obeying two conflicting norms when he can obey only one, can he? It is at this point that the situationist's solution shines. There is really only one universal and unbreakable norm, viz., love. All the other norms are at best general and can be broken for love's sake. The simplicity and logic of the solution has strong appeal, but there are also some grave difficulties. Let us turn our attention now to an evaluation of the one-absolute-norm position of situationism.

II. Situationism Evaluated

No comprehensive evaluation of the whole situational ethic will be attempted but only insofar as it bears on the question of norms. In this respect the evaluation will be both positive and negative. First, there are some clear merits to holding for only one absolute norm such as love.

A. *Some Advantages of the Situational Position.*

Critics from more traditional and absolutistic viewpoints tend to over-react to Fletcher's relativism, pragmatism, emotivism, and radical examples. But what is sometimes forgotten is that all of this is in the context of a clear claim of his ethic to be an absolutism — a one-norm absolutism. It is in this latter regard that many of the merits of the situational position emerge.

1. *It Is a Normative Position* [43] — First to be commended is Fletcher's attempt to lay down a *normative* approach to ethics. His second proposition reads, "The ruling norm of Christian decision is love: nothing else." In view of the fact that he gives a whole chapter to elaborating this, as well as repeatedly referring to this one absolute throughout the book, it seems quite unfair to summarily dismiss Fletcher as being totally normless and antinomian. Indeed, Fletcher spends much of the first chapter explaining that his view is not anti-

---

[43] In a later writing Fletcher denies that his approach has any universal norms ("What is a Rule?: A Situationist's View," *Norm and Context in Christian*, ed., Gene H. Outka and Paul Ramsey, New York: Charles Scribner's Sons, 1968). Fletcher distinguishes between (1) formal principles such as "Act as lovingly . . . as possible," (2) substantive principles such as "The good which should be sought or done is utility," and (3) normative principles such as "Loving concern for our neighbors calls for telling them the truth." Only formal principles, he says, are universal (pp. 337, 338). Possibly Fletcher means that there are no contentful universals and that the love principle which he calls "the ruling norm" of Christian ethics is only formally universal (Situational Ethics p. 69).

nomian. It is a one-norm absolutism, he claims.

The reasons for commending a normative approach to ethics have already been given, [44] so they will not be repeated here. It is sufficient to note in passing that norms are both inescapable and essential to a meaningful ethic. Without them one has no objective basis or guide for his ethical decisions.

2. *It Is an Absolutism* — Fletcher's view is not only normative, it is *absolute*. There is one unbreakable law, the law of love. And even though Fletcher deliberately avoids such words as "never" and "always" with regard to every other norm, yet he does not hesitate to emphasize that there are no exceptions to the love norm. "Only" love and "nothing else" justifies what one does, he argues. Furthermore, there is no such thing as total relativity. Relative norms must be relative to a norm which is not relative. *What, why,* and *who* are the Christian's three "universals," Fletcher says. That is, he knows that his neighbor should be loved for God's sake. These three "universals" are absolute; only the circumstances are relative. [45] He clearly holds that one ought *always* to love and should *never* hate or be indifferent to his neighbors. "*Christian* situation ethics has only one norm . . . that is binding and unexceptionable, always good and right regardless of the circumstances [viz., *agapē* love]." [46]

3. *It Resolves Conflict of Norms Issue* — Whatever one may think of the situationist's solution to the marginal cases where conflicting norms are involved, at least it presents a logical possibility. All other ethical norms are subordinate to the one absolute norm, in view of which it is ethically right to break any of them for the sake of this love norm. This solution is both logical and simple. It is simple, because it does not involve a complicated series of exceptions to norms, nor does it present a pyramid of norms but it posits a single norm which takes precedence over all others. It is logical in the sense that it is not internally contradictory. It never leaves any ethical dilemmas in conflict or tension; they are always resolvable (in theory at least) by appeal to the single love norm. In other words, situationism is never faced with the dilemma of having two absolute or universal norms in conflict — it does not have *two* absolute norms. [47] There is *one* absolute norm, no more and no less.

4. *It Gives Due Value to Differing Circumstances* — Another merit, of situationism, not to be undervalued, is its emphasis on the circumstance or the context of an ethical decision as bearing on its rightness or wrongness. However morally wrong falsifying may or may not be, surely it differs from context to context. Falsifying in fun to a friend

---

[44] See chapter one on the reasons in favor of a normative approach.
[45] Fletcher, *op. cit.*, p. 142.
[46] *Ibid.*, p. 31.
[47] See evaluations at ends of chapters five, six, and seven.

is probably amoral, whereas serious falsifying before a judge and jury is not. The circumstances do make a difference in the moral rightness or wrongness of the act. Likewise, taking another life accidentally, or in self-defense, or letting one die as an act of mercy are all markedly different situations from an intentional and malicious murder of another human being. The situation does condition the way one's norm (or norms) should be applied. Without due stress on the conditioning influence of the moral situation, one's ethics become legalistic and even inhuman. Indeed, as will be seen later, it is very difficult (if not impossble) to contend for a many-norm absolutism of any kind, unless contextual qualifications become part of the definition of the norm. Truth-telling and the duty to avoid or prevent life-taking (or at least letting one die) invariably come into conflict unless one has the prerogative to say that lying and life-taking *in certain contexts* is wrong. This will be discussed more fully later. For now it is sufficient to note that giving attention to the circumstances or context of ethical decisions is both unavoidable and desirable in elaborating a good ethical position.

5. *It Stresses Love and the Value of Persons* — From a Christian point of view (and even from many non-Christian perspectives), the stress on *agapē* love as the ruling norm is certainly commendable. Bertrand Russell wrote *Why I am not a Christian*, but he also said elsewhere, "What the world needs is Christian love or compassion." [48] Seldom do strong voices arise in defense of selfish love. [49] And from the Christian point of view love is the absolute moral character of God. "God is love" and "Love is of God," the New Testament says. [50] And when all else fades, love will abide forever. [51] Jesus summarized the whole of the Old Testament in the one word "love," as was stated in the Old Testament itself. [52] Indeed, according to Jesus, love was to be the characteristic earmark of His disciples. "By this all men will know that you are my disciples, if you have love one for another." [53] In view of this, it is very difficult to criticize from a Christian point of view the pre-eminence Fletcher gives to Christian *agapē* love.

Implied in this stress on loving others is the fact that they are to be treated as persons (in the image of God) and not as mere things. The neighbor is a *thou*, not an *it*. The other is a person to be *loved*, not a thing to be *used*. Others are *ends* in themselves and not merely *means* for our own ends. The intrinsic value of a person (because

[48] See *Human Society in Ethics and Politics*, p. viii.
[49] Ayn Rand is an apparent exception to this. Her concept of "enlightened self-interest" and the virtue of selfishness will be discussed in chapter eight.
[50] 1 John 4:7, 16.
[51] 1 Corinthians 13:1-13.
[52] Matthew 22:37-39; cf. Deuteronomy 6:5 and Leviticus 19:18.
[53] John 13:35.

he is a person like God) is, from a Christian point of view, a basic and significant emphasis for which Fletcher is to be praised.

B. *Some Inadequacies of One-Norm Situationism.*

Both from a general moralistic viewpoint and from a Christian perspective in particular, not everything in Fletcher's situationism is praise-worthy. Time will not be taken here to elaborate on his critical and inconsistent view of the gospel records of the New Testament,[54] nor the implications of holding that God can be loved *only* through one's neighbor. [55] Rather, attention will be centered on the inadequacy of having only one norm for an ethic.

1. *One Norm Is Too General* — A one-norm ethic, especially a norm as broad and general as Fletcher's love norm, is *in most cases* (though not necessarily in all cases) little better than having no norm at all. A single universal norm by its very nature must be broad and adaptable, or else it could not apply to *all* circumstances. But its versatility is also a liabilty, for it necessitates an ambiguity about what the norm means, as far as concrete relationships are concerned. And if the absolute love norm is without concrete content apart from the relative situation, then the specific meaning of love is relative and not absolute. Indeed, Fletcher admits that the content of love varies from situation to situation. [56] Therefore, the command, "*Love* in all cases," means little more than "Do X in all cases." For unless there is advanced cognitive content to the term "love," then one does not really know what he is being commanded to do. Fletcher flatly announces that the love principle is factually contentless. "This is why I say it is a 'formal' principle, which rules us and yet does so without content." [57]

In actual practice, Fletcher does seem to imply that there is in advance of the situation *some* understanding of what love means. But the question is *how much?* Is there enough content in the universal love norm to raise it above a mere platitude? "Do the *loving* thing" is scarcely more specific than "Do the *good* thing." The question in both instances is: What *kinds* of acts are good or loving? So his

[54] On one occasion Fletcher sides with Judas' view against Jesus about whether the costly perfume should have been sold and the money given to the poor *(Ibid.,* p. 97). He also rejects Jesus' view on divorce (p. 133). At the same time, Fletcher (inconsistently) accepts from the same gospel records Jesus' teaching on love.

[55] *Ibid.,* pp. 55, 158. According to part of the gospel record which Fletcher apparently does accept, Jesus said that *one* way to love God is through loving others (cf. Matthew 25:45), but Jesus did not say it was the only way. In fact, Jesus made a clear distinction between loving others *as* one's self and loving God *with* one's self.

[56] *Ibid.,* p. 27.

[57] See "What is a Rule?" *op. cit.,* p. 337.

one-term ethic of love is no more helpful than an ethic of natural law which says, "Follow Nature" or "Live according to Reason." Instead of "What does 'love' mean?" the question becomes: "What is meant by 'Nature' and 'Reason'? But the result is the same, viz., one is left without any specific ethical direction. An appeal to the situation to provide content or meaning for love will not suffice — Fletcher admits that the situations are relative and even radically different. If the meaning of love is dependent on the circumstances, then the significance of love is really relative to the situation and therefore not absolute. This leads to a second criticism.

2. *The Situation Does Not Determine the Meaning of Love* — The meaning of the love norm is not completely determined by the conditions of the situation but is merely *conditioned* by it. Circumstances do not effect norms which judge them, they only *affect* them. That is, the context in which a norm is applicable does not dictate how the norm will be applied but only *influences* its application. If the complete determination of meaning came from the situation, then the alleged ethical norm would not really be normative at all. The situation would be determining the norm rather than the norm being determinative for the situation. [58]

Here again, Fletcher does not claim that the situation *completely* determines what the norm means. He says only that what love will mean in advance of the situation cannot be known with any "existential particularity," it can be known only *in general*. However, what is known in advance "in general" may turn out to be the wrong meaning of love in a particular circumstance. No general wisdom *(sophia)* or norms are universal and unbreakable. There is no rule apart from the general (and ambiguous) rule of love which ought never be broken. But this is precisely the problem. The meaningful norms are breakable, and the only unbreakable norm is not meaningful in any specific or practical sense of the word. Perhaps Fletcher should not have dismissed so summarily the possibility that there are *many* universal and unbreakable norms.

3. *The Possibility of Many Universal Norms* — There seems to be several reasons why situationism dismisses the possibility of having many universal norms, none of which reasons is definitive. First, Fletcher argues that the many-norm position would be legalistic. [59] This does not follow. A many-norm ethic *may* be legalistic but there is no reason why it *must* be legalistic. It all depends on *what* the norms are, *how* they are related to each other, and how they are applied to life whether or not the view is legalistic. As a matter of fact, one could be legalistic with one norm. Second, it is implied that there is

[58] Fletcher, *op. cit.*, pp. 76, 46.
[59] *Ibid.*, cf. p. 37.

no other way to resolve the conflict of norms unless there is one absolute norm to which all other norms are only relative. But this is not so. There are at least three other ways to relate many universal norms, viz., (1) show how they really do not conflict, or (2) show why it is wrong to break either when they do conflict, or (3) show how one of the norms is of a higher order and takes priority over those of a lower order. [60] Third, Fletcher sees no way to derive universal norms from a universal norm. He thinks that "middle axioms" is a contradiction in terms; they are derived underiveds. [61] But there is no reason a deduction cannot be as certain as its premises.

But apart from whether there really *are* many universal norms, Fletcher certainly does not eliminate the *possibility* that there are such. He does not disprove that they can be arrived at by *deduction* the way postulates are derived from axioms in geometry. He does not disprove that they could come from *revelation* such as many Christians find inscripturated in the Bible. [62] Nor does Fletcher definitely dismiss the possibility that many universal norms could be known *intuitively* to have a separate status of their own. In brief, the *possibility* of there being many universal norms should not be given up either (1) until it is shown to be logically impossible, or (2) unless no universal norm besides love is ever found. In view of the fact that candidates for universal norms will be introduced and evaluated in subsequent chapters, we will withhold judgment until then as to whether or not there really are many universal norms. It will be enough at this point to observe that Fletcher does not prove that there is *only* one universal norm, since he does not prove that it is impossible that there may be many universal norms.

4. *A Different Universal Norm Is Possible* — Not only is it possible that there are *many* universal norms (as opposed to Fletcher's *single* norm), but it is also possible to opt for a *different* single norm (as opposed to the love norm Fletcher uses). In other words, why not a one-norm ethic built on hate instead of love? Why not Buddhistic *compassion* instead of Christian love? Why not the *negative Golden Rule* rather than the positive one, i.e., "*Do not* do to others what you do not want them to do to you," as opposed to "*Do* unto others what you would have them do unto you"? Surely, Fletcher has not demonstrated that *all* ethical principles mean exactly the same thing (at any rate, not those as different as love and hate). Then, on what basis is one to choose the single norm on which he is to build his whole

---

[60] For a discussion of the three ways to relate many-norm ethics see chapters five, six, and seven.

[61] Fletcher, *op. cit.*, pp. 31, 32.

[62] See Carl Henry, *The Christian Personal Ethic*, chapter seven.

ethic? There must be some way to justify one's basic ethical presupposition if it is not to be entirely arbitrary. [63]

In brief, the problem of a one-norm ethic is this: *which* norm? Prima facie, there are many ethical norms which claim obedience. Which one should be given the special position of being absolute and unbreakable? Could not a case be made for using truthfulness at any cost as the single absolute? Could not such a position be worked out with internal consistency in the same way as Fletcher's love norm can be? And if one absolute norm can be just as internally *consistent* as another, then on what basis is one norm to be preferred over another? By evaluating the *consequences* of each? If the one absolute norm is chosen on the ground that it brings the best consequences for most people in the long run, then there are several problems. First, we do not know the long run, and some things that are not really best in the long run work very well for very many people in the short run (e.g., dishonesty and dictatorships). In fact, many things which are distinctly wrong (on almost any ethical basis) obviously work too well for too many people for too long a time (e.g., cheating, hating, warring). Second, to choose the norm on the basis of its consequences (if this were possible) would be to depart from a normative basis for ethics in favor of a utilitarian basis, with all the problems that view entails. [64] As a matter of fact, utilitarianism depends on norms for its own operation, which brings the argument full cycle. That is, this would be saying that ends are needed to justify norms and these ends in turn depend on norms to establish them. But this really demonstrates that norms are at the basis of ethics, in either event. Norms are necessary; the question remains: *which* norms and *how many* are there? We turn next to an examination of the many-norms views to seek an answer to these questions.

---

[63] For an answer to this problem from a Christian point of view see chapter seven.

[64] See chapter one for further criticism of judging ethic norms by their consequences. And in view of the fact that Fletcher frankly, but reluctantly, admits his view is utilitarian, perhaps this criticism should be stressed more. See Fletcher, "What Is a Rule?," *op. cit.*, p. 332.

SELECT READINGS FOR CHAPTER FOUR: SITUATIONISM

Bonhoeffer, Dietrich, *Ethics*, New York: The Macmillan Company, 1955.

Brunner, Emil, *The Divine Imperative*, Philadelphia, Penn.: The Westminster Press, 1947.

Fletcher, Joseph, *Situation Ethics: The New Morality*, Philadelphia, Penn.: The Westminster Press, 1966.

Niebuhr, H. R., *The Responsible Self*, New York: Harper & Row, Publishers, Inc., 1963.

Robinson, John A. T., *Christian Morals Today*, Philadelphia, Penn.: The Westminster Press, 1964.

Sittler, Joseph, *The Structure of Christian Ethics*, Louisiana University Press, 1958.

Tillich, Paul, *Morality and Beyond,* New York: Harper & Row, Publishers, Inc., 1963.

5 / Non-Conflicting Absolutism: There Are Many Non-Conflicting Universal Norms

Probably the most common position among traditional absolutists is to hold or imply that there are many absolute norms which never really conflict. Each norm covers its own area of human experience and it never really conflicts with another absolute norm. Often this view is only assumed, but sometimes it is given explicit defense.

I. Non-Conflicting Absolutism Explained

Among traditional absolutists there is no unanimity as to the number of universal norms, but all agree that there is a plurality of norms. The problem, of course, is how these universal norms relate to each other, particularly when there is an apparent conflict between them. There have been many absolutistic positions, especially within religious circles, but only a few of the more notable ones will be discussed here.

A. Plato: Universal Ideas of Morality

Probably the most notable source of a pluralistic absolutism is the writings of Plato. According to his earlier writings especially, Plato espoused the doctrine that there are independent universal Forms for each of the cardinal virtues. The problem which he faced, of course, was just how these separate universal Ideas relate to each other.

1. *Universal Forms* — In the famous cave analogy Plato argues that the present state of men is like that of prisoners living from birth in an underground cavern, facing the back wall and chained so that their heads cannot move. [1] All they can perceive are the shadows of sensi-

79

ble objects cast on the wall by a fire behind them. If one of the prisoners were released his eyes would be dazzled by the unexpected brightness of the light. It would be necessary for him to habituate himself first to the light of the fire and then, outside the cave, to reflected light, then the light of the moon and the stars. Finally, he would be able to look on the sun itself, the source of all light. Only in the light of the sun would he truly understand all things in their true perspective.

In this illustration the sun represents the Idea of the Good which gives birth to all lesser forms of good. Below the Good and participating in its goodness (and light) is the realm of Forms or Ideas which all other things (e.g., empirical things) imitate for their likeness. There is, for example, in the moral realm the Idea of Justice and those of coordinate virtues. These Ideas or Forms are all fixed, unchangeable and eternal. They are the intelligible patterns emulated by all virtuous acts. As the immovable Ideals of all right conduct, they are not subject to either death or decay. Anyone who acts wisely or correctly in public or private is doing so by virtue of the changeless virtues derived from these absolute Forms of goodness. True education, then, consists in knowing the eternal Ideals which participate in this goodness, for those who know what is virtuous will perform it, says Plato. Since "to make for what one believes to be evil, instead of making for the good, is not, it seems, in human nature, and when faced with a choice of two evils no one will choose the greater [evil] when he might choose the less." [2]

2. *Some Absolute Virtues* — Much of the thrust of Plato's teaching is directed to combat the relativism of certain sophists of his day. It established the absolute nature of virtue against the Protagorean relativism that "man is the measure of all things" [3] or Cratylus' flux doctrine that "everything is in a state of transition and there is nothing abiding." [4] Plato argued firmly for fixed Forms or universal Ideas of basic virtues. The basic forms of virtue set forth by Plato are courage, temperance, wisdom, and justice.

Courage, Plato says, means "the power in all circumstances, a conviction about the sort of things that it is right to be afraid of — the conviction implanted by education which the law-giver has established." That is, courage is "the conviction, inculcated by lawfully established education, about the sort of things which may be rightly feared." It is a conviction "never to be washed out by pleasure and

[1] Plato, *Republic,* Book VII. Unless otherwise noted the Plato quotations come from *Plato: The Collected Dialogues,* edited by Edith Hamilton and Huntington *Cairns* (New York: Pantheon Books) 1964.

[2] *Protagoras,* p. 358 d.

[3] *Republic,* Book IV, pp. 428 - 429.

[4] *Ibid.,* p. 441.

pain, desire and fear, solvents more terribly effective than all the soap and fuller's earth in the world." [3] And, Plato adds, "we shall call an individual brave in virtue of this spirited part of his nature, when, in spite of pain or pleasure, it holds fast to the injunctions of reason about what he ought or ought not be be afraid of." [4]

"*Temperance* surely means a kind of orderliness, a control of certain pleasures and appetites." It "means that within the man himself, in his soul, there is a better part and a worse; and that he is his own master when the part which is better by nature has the worse under control." [5] That is to say, one is "temperate by reason of the unanimity and concord of all three [parts of the soul, viz., reason, spirit, and appetite], when there is no internal conflict between the ruling element and its two subjects, but all agreed that reason should be ruler. [6] In brief, a man is temperate when his reason rules his spirit and appetites.

Wisdom is a form of knowledge which will enable one "to take thought, not for some particular interest, but for the best possible conduct of the state as a whole in its internal and external relations." [7] In the individual the virtue of wisdom is manifest when it is "the business of reason to rule with wisdom and forethought on behalf of the entire soul; while the spirited element ought to act as its subordinate and ally." So, the wise man is the one whose reason rules well for the other two parts of him, viz., his spirit and his appetites. [8]

Justice is the principle "that everyone ought to perform the one function in the community for which his nature best suited him." It means minding one's own business. It is the "quality which makes it possible for the three we have already considered, wisdom, courage, and temperance, to take their place in the commonwealth. . . . " Wisdom is "the principle that each one should do his own proper work without interfering with others." For a disordered or unjust arrangement is the worst evil in a society. [9]

As to justice in the individual, "we shall conclude that a man is just in the same way that a state was just. And we have surely not forgotten that justice in the state meant that each of the three orders in it [viz., rulers, administrators, and citizens] was doing its own proper work." So, Plato continues, "We may henceforth bear in mind that each one of us likewise will be a just person, fulfilling his proper

3 *Republic*, Book IV, pp. 428 - 429.
4 *Ibid.*, p. 441.
5 *Ibid.*, p. 430.
6 *Ibid.*, pp. 441 - 442.
7 *Ibid.*, p. 427.
8 *Ibid.*, p. 441.
9 *Ibid.*, p. 434.
10 *Ibid.*, p. 442.

function, only if the several parts of our nature fulfill theirs." That is, justice occurs when each "part of his nature is exercising its proper function, of ruling or of being ruled." In this way "justice is produced in the soul, like health in the body, by establishing the elements concerned in their natural relations of control and subordination, whereas injustice is like a disease and means that this natural order is inverted." [11]

Plato was not unaware of the fact that whenever there are many forms of virtue, there are possible conflicts among them. In his earlier writings he attempted to resolve this by showing that all the basic virtues are one — like the many parts of a face are one. [12] All of the virtues find their unity in knowledge of the Good. [13] That is, the many forms of good find their unity in the super Form, the Good, which is the source of all goodness. [14] Despite this alleged unity of virtues in the Good, Plato struggled to show — and with debatable success — that the separate forms of virtue on earth did not really overlap or contradict each other. In a later work Plato acknowledged the conflict between the different parts of virtue as moderation and courage, saying, "Is there not . . . something inherent in them which keeps alive a family quarrel among them?" [15]

The problem, then, will be how to resolve the conflict between ethical norms. If they are all absolute, what does one do when they conflict? Indeed, if there is between any two a conflict or overlap, it would seem to be difficult to maintain that both are really absolute.

3. *Resolving the Conflict of Forms* — In his later dialogues Plato seemed to recognize the problem of relating separate but absolute Forms. In his earlier works he taught that Forms were simple, indivisible unities which differed from one another fundamentally. "We are saying," he wrote, "that the opposite *itself* can never become opposite to *itself* — neither the opposite which is in us nor that which is in the real world. . . . We maintain that the opposites themselves would absolutely refuse to tolerate coming into being from one another." [16]

Not only were the Forms individually distinct but they were absolutely indivisible. "It seems to me," he wrote, "not only that the form of tallness itself absolutely declines to be short as well as tall, but also that the tallness which is in us never admits smallness and de-

---

[11] *Ibid.*, p. 444.
[12] *Protagoras*, p. 329b; cf. *Meno*, p. 73c - 74a.
[13] See A. E. Taylor. *Plato: The Man and His Works*, New York: Meridian Books, Inc., 1960, pp. 28, 57, 257.
[14] *Republic*, Book VII, p. 517.
[15] *Statesman*, 306 b-c.
[16] *Phaedo*, 103 b-c.

clines to be surpassed." [17] In the famous cave analogy Plato describes the indivisibility of the Forms in terms of numbers. In the Forms "each unity [is] equal to every other without the slightest difference and admitting no division into parts." This is why, he says we "are speaking of units which can only be conceived by thought, and which it is not possible to deal with in any other way." [18]

A possible re-examination of this earlier view of absolutely separate and indivisible Forms is signaled in Plato's *Parmenides*. [19] In this dialogue Plato asks, "Do you not recognize that there exists, just by itself, a form of likeness and again another contrary form, unlikeness itself, and that of these two forms you and I and all the things we speak of as 'many' come to partake . . . ?" And "even if all things come to partake of both, contrary as they are, and by having a share in both are at once like and unlike one another, what is there surprising in that . . . ?" [20] In other words, the problem regarding the doctrine of indivisible and independent Forms is how there can be any relationship between them. For if they remain *only* indivisible unities, then there is no way for them to relate to each other. This dilemma leads to the so-called "third man" argument against Plato which states that when two particular things owe their similarity to an idea that there must be something to which we may ascribe the similarity between the idea and the two particulars, and so on ad infinitum. [21]

Plato's answer to this problem is stated in the *Sophist* where he writes, "We shall find it necessary in self defense to put to the question that pronouncement of father Parmenides, and establish by main force that what is not, in some respect has being, and conversely that what is, in a way is not." [22] That is, between and among the existing Forms there is a principle of interrelatedness called non-being. Being or reality is one complex whole, a dynamic of identity and diversity, of the changeless and the changing. "Like a child begging for 'both,' he must declare that reality or the sum of things is both at once — all that is unchangeable and all that is in change." [23] Plato seems to recognize that a complete isolation of each absolute Form from the others would destroy any relationship, even the possibility of discourse itself. [24] In view of this he suggests that each Form is related to the

---

[17] *Phaedo,* 102 d.

[18] *Republic,* Book VII, 526 a-b.

[19] John Burnet says, "This dialogue contains a direct criticism of the doctrine of the forms as that stated in the *Phaedo* and the *Republic*." *Greek Philosophy* (London, 1964), p. 192.

[20] *Parmenides,* 129 a-b.

[21] See Leonard J. Eslick's criticism of Plato's view in "The Platonic Dialectic of Non-being," *The New Scholasticism,* XXIX, No. 1 (January, 1955), p. 49.

[22] *Sophist,* 241 d.

[23] *Ibid.,* 249 d.

[24] Plato recognizes this in *Sophist* 259 e.

others by way of "Non-being" or the principle of "Otherness." In the *Philebus* he calls this the "unlimited," in the *Timaeus* it is the "receptacle," and it is the indefinite "Dyad" of Plato's oral teaching. But in each case it is the principle of differentiation by negation; it is relation by negation.

Even granting that Plato's answer is adequate (which we do not), [25] the problem then is how the Forms can be absolute and changeless when they are subject to changing interrelationships. For, as Plato seems to admit, the Forms themselves appear to change when they are related in broader unities. "Perhaps," he wrote, "we ought to have assumed that the syllable was not the letter but a single entity that arises out of them with a unitary character of its own and different from the letters." [26] So if broader unities made up of smaller unities or Forms are actually different from the smaller ones, then how can the smaller parts be absolute if they change in the whole?

Plato does not say just how he would resolve a conflict between two or more of his absolute and independent Forms of virtue. In his earlier view of separate and individual Ideas the assumption would seem to be that various Forms of virtue do not overlap, but each is a distinct kind of its own, drawing its value from the absolute Good. But in his later attempt to interrelate Forms he seems to find it difficult to maintain the changeless and absolute nature of interrelating and/or overlapping Forms.

B. *Immanuel Kant: The Categorical Imperative*

Plato's is not the only absolutistic position which must face the problem of apparently conflicting norms of morality. Immanuel Kant argued for a plurality of moral principles drawn from one's sense of absolute duty. He believed that there were unconditional duties which men ought to perform and which were always wrong to disobey.

1. *The Basis of the Categorical Imperative* — For Kant, ethics has neither an empirical nor a hypothetical basis. It is not empirically based, because experience reveals only what *is* but not what *ought* to be. Empirical facts provide only data but not duties, conditions of life but not commands for life. All that experience can tell us is what men do, not what they should do. If there is to be a norm for life, then it must be an imperative outside of the merely declarative state of affairs in which men find themselves. "Empirical grounds of determination are not fit for any universal external legislation, and they are just as little suited to an internal," writes Kant, "for each

[25] For a critique of Plato's doctrine of non-being see Eslick's article, *op. cit.*, and James T. Regan, "Being and Non-Being in Plato's *Sophist*," *Modern Schoolman*, XLII (March, 1965), 305-314.

[26] *Theaetetus*, 203 e.

man makes his own subject the foundation of his inclination and in each person it is now one and now another which has preponderance." And "to discover a law which would govern them all by bringing them into unison is absolutely impossible." [27] Neither can ethics be based on hypothetical or conditional grounds, such as: Do this and good life (i.e., happiness) will result. For happiness cannot be the determinate of our actions since it is purely subjective. "When one's own happiness is made the determining ground of the will, the result is the direct opposite of the principle of morality," Kant says. [28] If we suppose all rational creatures to be unanimous in what feelings brought them pleasure or pain, "even then they could not set up the principle of self-love as a practical law," says Kant. "For the unanimity itself would be merely contingent. The determining ground would not have the necessity which is conceived in every law, an objective necessity arising from a priori grounds. . . ." [29] Furthermore, if ethical duties were only conditional upon resultant happiness, then one might justify torture or cruelty because of the pleasure it brings to sadists.

For Kant, the only valid basis for ethics is a categorical one — duty for duty's sake, not duty for the sake of happiness. There is an unconditional command to do what is right whether it pleases us or not. This is called the categorical imperative. It is categorical because it is an unconditional duty — there are no "ifs, ands, or buts" about it. It is an "imperative" because it does not merely describe what men do but, rather, it prescribes what they ought to do. [30]

2. *Statements of the Categorical Imperative* — Kant states his categorical imperative in several different ways. The first statement of it is found in his *Foundation of the Metaphysic of Morals* (1785). [31] It reads, "Act only according to that maxim by which you can at the same time will that it should become a universal law." The second statement says, "Act as though the maxim of your action were by your will to become a universal law of nature." The third says, "Act so that you treat humanity, whether in your person or in that of another, always as an end and never as a means only." In his *Critique*

[27] *Critique of Practical Reason,* translated by Lewis W. Beck (New York: Bobbs-Merrill Company, Inc., 1956), p. 28.
[28] *Ibid.,* p. 36.
[29] *Ibid.,* pp. 24-25.
[30] *Ibid.,* pp. 24-31.
[31] Cf. *The Philosophy of Kant as Contained in Extracts From His Own Writings,* selected and translated by John Watson (Glasgow, 1888, 1891) as abridged in Chapter 19 of Melvin Rader's *The Enduring Questions* (New York: Holt, Rinehart and Winston, 1969) second edition, pp. 582-604. A more complete edition of Kant's ethical works may be found in Thomas K. Abbott's *Kant's Critique of Practical Reason and Other Works* (London: Longmans, Green and Co. Ltd., 1909), pp. 1-84.

of Practical Reason (1788) Kant offers still another formulation of his ethical imperative: "So act that the maxim of your will could always hold at the same time as a principle establishing universal law." [32]

In amplification of what is meant by his categorical imperative Kant offers these further comments. "Nothing in the whole world, or even outside of the world, can possibly be regarded as good without limitation except a *good will.*" "The true object of reason then, insofar as it is practical, or capable of influencing the will, must be to produce a will which is *good* in itself, and not merely good *as a means* to something else." What is meant by good will, says Kant, can be clarified by a sense of duty. Acts of good will are those done *from* a sense of duty, not merely those done *in accordance with* a sense of duty. For example, one might desire to preserve his life not in accordance with a sense of duty but primarily from a natural inclination to self-preservation. Such a desire is not a moral one. But if adversity and hopeless sorrow tempt one to suicide, then to prolong one's life from a sense of duty would be a moral act. It follows that "*duty is the obligation to act from reverence for law*" and not merely a natural inclination for an object. [33] In brief, Kant is defending duty for duty's sake. He is arguing for doing what is intrinsically right, however the chips may fall.

Kant's explanation of the third statement of the categorical imperative casts further light on what is meant by acting according to intrinsic values. Treat men as ends and not means, for non-rational beings are "called *things.* Rational beings, on the other hand, are called *persons,* because their very nature shows them to be ends in themselves. . . ." Persons are intrinsically valuable and should be treated as such. Things should be *used,* and persons should be *loved.* One should never *use* persons as a means to other ends nor *love* things as an end in themselves. For "persons are not purely subjective ends, whose existence has a value *for us* as the effect of our actions, but they are *objective ends,* or beings whose existence is an end in itself, for which no other end can be substituted." [34]

So one ought to treat others as persons who are ends in themselves. And, furthermore, what one *ought* to do, one *can* do. That is, duty implies ability; responsibility presupposes the ability to respond. For in Kant's view, "ought" implies "can." [35]

3. *In Defense of the Categorical Imperative* — In defense of the categorical imperative, Kant argues that to will otherwise would be self-destructive. For instance, one must will truth-telling as a universal law in accordance with the categorical imperative. For if one were

[32] *Critique of Practical Reason,* p. 30.
[33] *The Philosophy of Kant,* etc., pp. 592-594.
[34] *Ibid.,* p. 602.
[35] *Critique of Practical Reason,* pp. 126f.

to will the opposite of truth-telling, viz., lying, as a universal law, then there would be no truth about which one could lie. In this case, then, even lying would become impossible (for if one were to lie about a lie, he would be telling the truth). In Kant's words, "If lying were universal, there would, properly speaking, be no promises whatever. I might say that I intended to do a certain thing at some future time, but nobody would believe me, or," he continues, "if he did at the moment trust to my promise, he would afterward pay me back in my own coin. My maxim thus proves itself to be self-destructive, so soon as it is taken as a universal law." [36] Likewise, murder is always wrong, for to will it as a universal law would be to will the possibility that there could be no more people to murder. That would be both self-destructive and irrational.

Kant is not primarily concerned, however, with the fact that lying, murder, etc., are self-destructive, but with the fact that they are impossible and unreasonable laws. "I only ask myself: Canst thou also will that thy maxim should be a universal law?" writes Kant. "If not, then it must be rejected, and that not because of a disadvantage accruing from it my myself or even to others, but because it cannot enter as a principle into a possible universal legislation, and reason extorts from me immediate respect for such legislation." [37] In other words, Kant does not wish to give a utilitarian justification for his non-utilitarian (deontological) principle. He does not intend to base the validity of categorical imperative on the fact that if one disobeys it bad results ensue. He desires, rather, to note that one could have neither rational nor moral respect for its contrary because its contrary is neither rationally possible nor morally respectable as a law.

Furthermore, according to Kant, "although common men do not conceive it in such an abstract and universal form, yet they always have it really before their eyes, and use it as the standard of their decision." In fact, "it would be easy to show how, with this compass in hand, men are well able to distinguish, in every case that occurs, what is good, what bad. . . ." And "we only, like Socrates, direct their attention to the principle they themselves employ; and that, therefore, we do not need science and philosophy to know what we should do to be honest and good, yea, even wise and virtuous." [38] Indeed, the categorical imperative is only another way of stating the Golden Rule. "'Love God above all and thy neighbor as thyself,' agrees very well with this," Kant writes, "for as a command, it requires respect for a law which orders love and does not leave it to

[36] See Rader, *The Enduring Questions,* pp. 595-596.
[37] *Foundation of the Metaphysical of Morals,* translated by Thomas Abbot, pp. 19-20. (From *Kant's Critique of Practical Reason and Other Works*).
[38] *Ibid.,* p. 20.

arbitrary choice to make love the principle."[39] In other words, the Golden Rule, like the categorical imperative, commands duty, the duty of loving others or treating them like persons with intrinsic value.

4. *Conflicts in the Categorical Imperative* — In accordance with the categorical imperative, Kant concluded that there are many absolute and inviolable norms for human conduct. Among these, the prohibition of murder and the duty of truth-telling are specific examples. One ought never to take an innocent life, and one ought never to tell a lie. From this, of course, emerges the problem of the conflict of norms. What if one is in a situation where he could save a life by telling a lie? Would this not be a legitimate lie? And if it would be justifiable to lie, then how can lying be universally wrong? It would seem that Kant would either have to give up truth-telling as a universal moral principle or else concede that murder is right.

In actual fact, Kant accepts neither of these two alternatives. Rather, he retains the absolute nature of both norms. He argues, first, that one should never tell a lie, not even to save a life. Second, that when one gives an occasion for someone else to murder because of the truth one tells, it does not follow that one is morally guilty. In other words, he holds that there is no real conflict between two absolute moral principles. And if this position is carried through consistently it is a non-overlapping absolutism. Each moral absolute has its domain and it never really clashes with another moral principle; thus it never forces the individual to break an absolute.

First, let us see why Kant argues that one should never lie even to save a life. According to Kant the question is this: ". . . whether a man — in cases where he cannot avoid answering Yes or No — has the right to be untruthful." The answer is: "Truth in utterance that cannot be avoided is the formal duty of a man to everyone, however great the disadvantage that may arise from it to him or any other." For "although by making a false statement I do no wrong to him who unjustly compels me to speak, yet I do wrong to men in general in the most essential point of duty, so that it may be called a lie . . . and hence that all rights founded on contract should lose their force; and this is a wrong which is done to mankind." Furthermore, when a lie is defined as an intentional falsehood toward another, it need not be added that it must injure him (as jurists add). "For it always injures another; if not another individual, yet mankind in general, since it vitiates the source of justice."[40] Lying, then, is essentially wrong and it never really helps but always harms men by undermining the truth which holds mankind together. Truthfulness is the cohesive that makes

[39] *Critique of Practical Reason*, pp. 85-86.
[40] Kant, "On the Supposed Right to Tell Lies from Benevolent Motives," ed. Abbott, *Kant's Critique of Practical Reason and Other Works*, p. 362.

society possible and, therefore, it is a sacred and inviolable duty to perform it.

But what about cases where to tell the truth will obviously harm innocent men such as being truthful to a would-be murderer concerning his victim's whereabouts? First of all, Kant is not so sure that truth-telling, even in this case, would necessarily bring harm. "It is possible that whilst you have honestly answered Yes to the murderer's question, whether his intended victim is in the house, the latter may have gone out unobserved, and so not come in the way of the murderer, and the deed therefore have not been done." On the other hand, "if you lied and said he was not in the house, and he had really gone out (though unknown to you), so that the murderer met him as he went, and executed his purpose on him, then you might with justice be accused as the cause of his death." Furthermore, "if you had spoken the truth as well as you knew it, perhaps the murderer while seeking for his enemy in the house might have been caught by neighbors coming up and the deed been prevented." In brief, "whoever then *tells a lie*, however good his intentions may be, must answer for the consequences of it . . . however unforeseen they may have been." For "to be *truthful* (honest) in all declarations is therefore a sacred unconditional command of reason, and not to be limited by any expediency." [41]

As for the possibility that the truth might lead to the murder of the victim (and a lie would have saved him), Kant is prepared to say, "It was merely an *accident (casus)* that the truth of the statement did harm to the inhabitant of the house; it was not a free *deed* (in the juridical sense)." In other words, there is no moral blame since the truth-teller did not *intend* the murder, nor did he *do* the harm. In brief, "every man has not only a right, but the strictest duty to truthfulness in statements which he cannot avoid, whether they do harm to himself or others." [42] And even if a given lie might help a given individual, yet it does harm to all men by violating the general principle of justice. Hence, the alleged conflict of norms is not a real conflict. One's duty is only to do what is truthful.

C. *Other Pluralistic Absolutists: Some Implied Premises*

The view of pluralistic absolutism is not uncommon among traditional Jewish, Catholic, and Protestant thinkers. Many of them contend for two or more principles which ought never to be broken. And what is often implied is that these norms never really conflict. Like Kant, these thinkers often imply that God (or Providence) will not permit universal moral norms to conflict, and that when they do conflict, one course is not really evil. Further, it is sometimes implied

[41] *Ibid.*, p. 268.
[42] *Ibid.*, pp. 267-270.

that God will not permit an evil to result from doing one's absolute duty.

1. *Evil Does Not Result From Doing One's Duty* — Kant clearly contended that it is a greater evil to lie to save a life than to let the man be killed. Lying affects the relationship of men in general and erodes the whole basis of society, whereas permitting a murder involves only individual men. He also hinted that God might intervene through circumstances and save the victim by means of escape (or help from the neighbors). It is this suggestion, along with some concrete examples, which has led some to contend that God will not allow a greater evil to occur as a result of our doing what is intrinsically right. Illustrations may be provided of men who told the truth about potential victims and whose lives God miraculously spared, thus apparently rewarding their truthfulness. Other illustrations may be given as to how God spared men from the dilemma of having to lie by not allowing them to be forced into a situation where they cannot be silent and fear to tell the truth. Indeed, it might be contended that silence, even to the point of sacrificing one's own life for the truth, would be better than lying — and it would avoid allowing the murderer to kill someone else.

In any event, whether or not an immediate evil is occasioned by obeying a universal norm, two things are clearly involved in this absolutistic position. First, that ultimately (if not immediately) the consequences for good will be greater by doing what is intrinsically and universally right. Second, that when there is a conflict of moral principles, the one which is best to do is not really the lesser of two *evils*. Rather, it is the decidedly *right* thing to do. It may be the occasion for someone else to do evil or for evil to happen accidentally, but it is not an intentional evil in itself.

2. *Falsifying Is Not Always Evil* — In order to justify the contention that there is really no conflict between truth-telling and falsifying to a would-be murderer, some absolutists take a narrower definition of what a lie is. In this way they may hold the position that intentionally giving false information to a murderer is not wrong. In other words, working from the same general premise as Kant, that lying is always wrong, they come to an opposite conclusion (viz., it is right to falsify to save a life). The reason for the different conclusions is the different way they define a lie.

For Kant, any intentional falsehood is a lie. For other absolutists, however, an enunciated falsehood need not be a lie. They contend that "it is not every *enunciatio falsi* which is a falsehood. This enunciation may be made through ignorance or mistake, and therefore be perfectly innocent." Furthermore, "it may even be deliberate and intentional. This we see in the case of fables and parables, and in works of fiction." One does not regard the *Iliad* or *Paradise Lost* a repertoire of lies. Nor would one want to conclude that Jesus' parables were untrue because they were intended to represent things in a way which is not literally so. [43]

It is sometimes argued that there are numerous cases within the Bible where intentional falsehoods are not condemned. That is, sometimes the Scriptures even command or commend intentional falsehood. The Hebrew midwives were commended for deceiving Pharaoh with regard to his order to kill all of the male babies (Exodus 1:19, 20). In 1 Samuel 16:1, 2 God ordered the prophet to deceive Saul as to the real purpose of his journey. In 2 Kings 6:14-20 Elisha the prophet intentionally deceived the Syrian soldiers about his own identity. Even Jesus is said to have fooled the two disciples into thinking He would continue the journey on alone, whereas He knew that He would eat with them (Luke 24:28). "On these grounds it is generally admitted that in criminal falsehood there must be not only (1) the enunciation or signification of what is false, and (2) an intention to deceive, but (3) also a violation of some obligation." [44] That is, not all falsehoods or intentional deceptions are lies. A lie is an intentional deception *which violates someone's right to know the truth.*

There may be circumstances in which one has no right to tell or to expect the truth. For example, "a general is under no obligation to reveal his intended movements to his adversary; and his adversary has no right to suppose that his apparent intention is his real purpose." Surely no one would hold a householder morally culpable for leaving the house lighted while on vacation so as to deceive robbers into thinking someone is home. And, what is more, "if a mother sees a murderer in pursuit of her child, she has a perfect right to mislead him by any means in her power. . . . " In other words, it is not really a lie to falsify for the sake of saving an innocent life. For that is a situation in which there is no obligation to give the correct information. One ought always to tell the truth, but it is not a lie to intentionally deceive a robber, murderer, or military enemy. The question, then, is not whether it is ever right to lie (it is *not*); the question is what constitutes a lie. The answer to this question is this: a lie must have three elements: "(1) The enunciation of what is false. (2) The intention to deceive. (3) The violation of a promise; that is, the violation of the obligation to speak the truth. . . . " [45] Without this third element it is merely a justifiable falsehood and not a lie, i.e., it is not communication for which one is morally culpable. So by a more careful definition of a lie the alleged moral conflict can be avoided.

[43] Charles Hodge, *Systematic Theology* (Grand Rapids, Michigan: Wm. B. Eerdmans Publishing Company, 1952), p. 440; first published by Scribner, Armstrong, and Company, 1872.

[44] *Ibid.,* p. 441.

[45] *Ibid.,* pp. 441-443, 445.

II. Non-Conflicting Absolutism Evaluated

Whatever liabilities the position of non-conflicting pluralistic absolutism may have, it must be granted that it is not only a possible position but that it may be defended with a certain degree of plausibility. There *may* be many moral absolutes, and it just *may* be that they never really conflict, once they are each understood in their proper context.

A. Some Positive Features of Pluralistic Absolutism

There are several appealing features to the position of pluralistic absolutism. First, its attempt to save moral absolutes is commendable. Second, its desire to reconcile the conflict of moral principles is good. Third, its recognition of the need to define moral principles more carefully is needed.

1. *The Attempt to Preserve Moral Absolutes* — From Plato to the present, great thinkers have seen the need for moral absolutes. Some of them have contended for many moral absolutes governing respectively the various dimensions of life. They have seen that without permanent principles of morality society would be like a ship without a rudder or a traveler without a map. The way each absolutist determines the number of such principles and how he justifies their unbreakable character is debatable. But their contention that everything cannot be totally relative and that there must be a foundation for morality is unshakable. Without the recognition that right is right no matter how few people practice it and wrong is wrong no matter how many men do it, the future of society is uncertain, if indeed it is possible at all. [46]

2. *The Desire to Reconcile Conflicting Moral Principles* — It is one thing to affirm many absolutes and another thing to reconcile the apparent conflict between them. It is to the credit of Plato that he spent his mature years in grappling with this problem. And although Plato's solution seems less than satisfactory, nevertheless the fact that he saw the problem and made an attempt to solve it is commendable. For if there are to be many absolute forms or norms for virtue then one must show both the basis for their absoluteness and how they relate when they do overlap. Apart from the success or failure of Plato's attempt to show how the Forms interrelate by "otherness," there still remains the question of how they maintain their absolute status when they enter into changing relationships. These are critical questions; Plato must be given some credit for facing them.

Kant's answer to conflicting norms may appear disappointing to some, but it is not without some plausibility. He does show how many unbreakable norms can be derived from one categorical com-

[46] Compare also the criticism of total relativism at the end of chapter two.

mand. And he does face the issue of what to do when there is an apparent conflict. Furthermore, when Kant implies that part of the solution may be a providential intervention, he interjects new light on the basic difference between utilitarians and deontologists. The latter assume God, providence, or a pre-established harmony which guarantees that if one does what is intrinsically right then ultimately it will bring the greatest good. The utilitarians, who feel they have no such normative basis for denoting intrinsically good acts, must resort to "guessing" results or "funding" experience to help them do what is right. Kant shows that if a man trusts God (or providence) to work 'out the greatest good, then he can do what is right and let the chips fall where they may, without worrying about the consequences of his action.

3. *The Recognition of the Need to Define Norms More Precisely* — Plato was constantly grappling with the problem of definition. But special recognition should be given to those who, facing the full force of conflicting norms, attempt to reconcile the problem by a more precise definition of terms. It is a commendable effort to point out that a lie, e.g., is more than an intentional falsification. Surely there are numerous justifiable kinds of falsification that occur in daily living, from practical jokes to faking in athletic contests and on to the more serious deceptions like military maneuvers and spying.

Other areas of redefinition might be profitably explored as well. For instance, murder is surely more than intentional life-taking. There are no doubt some justifiable cases of killing in self-defense, some legitimate cases of capital punishment, and/or some justifiable wars. Furthermore, more attention might be focused on the meaning of "human." Perhaps the proper intent of the command not to take a human life does not extend to human "vegetables" whose miserable and hopeless existence is being perpetuated only by machines. In brief, a redefinition of the traditional "Thou shalt not kill" may have the minimal meaning of "One ought not to intentionally take the life of an innocent *human* being, etc." By defining more carefully in this way, it may be possible to avoid many apparent conflicts in the more loosely defined traditional norms. [47]

B. *Some Problems With Pluralistic Absolutism*

Despite the commendable effort to preserve absolutes and even to reconcile them by redefinition, the position of non-conflicting pluralistic absolutism suffers from serious problems. First, in its more popular versions it tends to be naively authoritarian. Second, even in its philosophical form it does not show how many absolutes can interrelate, nor, third, does it resolve all the conflicts between its redefined norms.

---

[47] The question of legitimate life-taking will be discussed more fully in chapters ten and thirteen.

1. *The Naive Acceptance of Absolutes* — There is the tendency among pluralistic absolutists, at least on the popular level, to yield uncritically to norms as absolutes simply because they appear to be absolute. That is, there is the temptation to cling to norms as absolute without thoroughly examining the basis for this view. Absolutes are a necessary weapon in the arsenal of authoritarians and legalists. Consequently, the critical thinker must constantly be on guard against the naive acceptance of a multitude of universal norms for which there is provided no adequate justification. In a socratic fashion, the thinking moralist should conclude that the unexamined "absolutes" are not worth following as such. Anything which claims utter and absolute obedience ought to present some worthy credentials or reasons for its demands. Especially should one be defensive about the naive acceptance of so-called absolutes which conflict with each other or which, at least, do not interrelate.

2. *The Need to Show the Interrelation of Absolutes* — Even in a more sophisticated form of pluralistic absolutism, there is often lacking any explicit information on how these many "absolutes" can interrelate. Indeed, the first problem would be to demonstrate that there can be more than one norm which is really absolute. The answer that there can be many norms, each absolute in its own sphere, can make sense only if one assumes spheres which are entirely separate and non-overlapping. This assumption, however, is very difficult to reconcile with a wholistic view of human experience. That is, it seems to assume (contrary to fact) that the various relationships and spheres of human activity are entirely isolated from each other. This compartmentalization of the several areas of human responsibility makes a neat theory, but it does not accord well with the brute realities of life. Like many other idealistic positions, non-conflicting pluralistic absolutism is a beautiful theory which is destroyed by a brutal gang of facts.

3. *The Unresolved Conflicts of Norms* — What are the realities in the face of which non-conflicting absolutism becomes inadequate as a total solution? Numerous incidents of conflict of universal norms can be given, [48] but only a single case need to be demonstrated to show the inadequacy of the view of non-conflicting absolutism. Let us speak here of the conflict between truth-telling and life-saving mentioned above. It seems that in the form of the argument given by Kant his answer is sufficient. That is, if the moral choice is *only* one between truth-telling and not *taking* a life, then one has no real dilemma. For by telling the truth about the victim's whereabouts he is not thereby performing the act of taking his life. The problem,

[48] See chapter four for many more illustrations of conflicting norms.

however, does not have such an easy ethical solution. The real dilemma is this: If I tell the truth then I am not doing what I could do (viz., giving false information) to save a life. Surely, this is a case where one is morally obligated to do what is best, and it is surely better to *save* an innocent life that not to do so. And a simple deception might very well save the life. In fact, in Commander Bucher's case, some very sophisticated falsification was able to save a whole crew.

Of course, if one is willing to redefine a lie (as Kant was not) to include the overriding authority of another moral principle, then the dilemma can be solved. However, once it is admitted that one principle or norm overrides another, then one has taken a hierarchical position which has new problems of its own. [49] That is, if the conflict is resolved by saying one obligation is higher than the other, then the basic problems are to establish the hierarchy of values and to show how a duty (such as truth-telling) can be universal if it is sometimes to be broken. Insofar as the view of non-conflicting absolutism is concerned, there is no way, on its ground alone, to separate the various domains of responsibility to the point of no conflict without appealing to some norms as higher than others. But this is no longer non-conflicting absolutism but hierarchicalism.

There is at least one more way to face the dilemma of conflicting absolute norms which has not yet been discussed. One could hold that the universal norms are all (equally?) binding, and that when they conflict both are wrong to do. In other words, the individual trapped in this dilemma will be guilty either way. The "out" of this dilemma is by pardon or forgiveness. This position will be taken up in the next chapter.

[49] This is the problem discussed in chapter seven.

96 / ethics: alternatives and issues

SELECT READINGS FOR CHAPTER FIVE: NON-CONFLICTING ABSOLUTISM

Curran, Charles E. (ed.), *Absolutes in Moral Theology?*, Washington, D. C.: Corpus Books, 1968.

Frankena, William K., *Ethics*, Englewood Cliffs, N.J.: Prentice Hall, Inc., 1963.

Gustafson, James M., "Contest Versus Principles: A Misplaced Debate in Christian Ethics," in *Harvard Theological Review*, Vol. 58, No. 2 (April, 1965), pp. 171-202.

Kant, Immanuel, *Critique of Practical Reason*, translated by Lewis W. Beck, Indianapolis: The Bobbs-Merrill Company, Inc., 1956.

————————, "On the Supposed Right to Tell Lies From Benevolent Motives," in T. K. Abbott's *Kant's Critique of Practical Reason and Other Works*, London: Longmans, Green and Co. Ltd., 1909.

Plato, *Republic*.

Ramsey, Paul, *Deeds and Rules in Christian Ethics*, New York: Charles Scribner's Sons, 1967.

————————, (ed.), *Norm and Context in Christian Ethics*, New York: Charles Scribner's Sons, 1968.

6 / Ideal Absolutism: There Are Many Conflicting Universal Norms

There are three positions which contend for many absolute norms: non-conflicting absolutism (discussed in chapter five) which holds that these many norms never really conflict or overlap, hierarchicalism (to be discussed in chapter seven) which says that some norms are higher than others, and ideal absolutism which contends that these norms do sometimes conflict. According to the first view, all conflicts of norms are only *apparent,* whereas the other two views admit that there are real conflicts. In the first view the tensions among norms is resolved by pointing out third alternatives or redefining the norms so that they do not overlap. Hierarchicalism resolves the conflict by affirming that it is always right to follow the norm which imposes the higher obligation. Ideal absolutism, on the other hand, is not willing to admit that it is ever right to disobey any absolute norm. For those who hold this view, it is not a question of doing the higher of two *goods* (for when norms conflict it is wrong to disobey either) but rather a case of doing the lesser of two *evils.* The evil may be excusable or pardonable because of the tragic dilemma one finds himself in, but it is an evil nonetheless. Ideally, neither norms should have been broken. But because of the realistically evil conditions of life, what ideally ought not happen (viz., a conflict of norms) does in fact happen. And when it happens the best one can do is the least evil possible.

I. IDEAL ABSOLUTISM EXPLAINED

It is difficult to find clear-cut examples of this position. Apparently the position is more often spoken and implied than clearly written.

However, because it is both a possible position and one with some specific implications and consequences, especially in Christian ethics, it deserves attention.

A. Some Basic Tenets of Ideal Absolutism

Since specific examples of this ethical position are rare, the reader is not to imply that all of the men quoted in connection with this view are really proponents of it. References will be used on the basis of their similarity with one or more of the basic or associated tenets of ideal absolutism as it is explained here. In the actual elaboration of this view conclusions will be drawn which are thought to be consistent with the basic premises, even if no specific example is provided of someone who has stated it that way.

1. *There Are Many Absolute Norms* — The most basic assumption of ideal absolutism is that there are many absolute norms, many ethical principles which ought never to be broken. The basis of this assumption may be either philosophical or theological. The absolute nature of these many norms could be defended philosophically like platonic Forms or like Kant's categorical imperative. Theologically, many absolute norms could be presupposed as part of a divine revelation with or without any kind of verification. These and other positions have been held with regard to pluralistic absolutisms. The point, however, is not so much the basis for holding that there are many absolutes but in showing how they relate. As has already been noted, there are three pluralistic positions. The primary difference between them is not the basis for holding to absolutes (though the basis varies); the real difference is how an attempt is made to relate these absolutes. For most absolutists would be willing to grant that there are many absolutes (as opposed to only one), if there were a satisfactory way of showing how they all harmonize. So far as ideal absolutism is concerned, then, it is most basic to note that, for whatever reason, it holds fast to *many* absolute norms.

2. *It Is Wrong to Break Any Absolute Norms* — It is necessary also to point out that from the viewpoint of ideal absolutism it is always *wrong* to break an absolute norm. Unlike the hierarchical position, which is willing to approve ethically of superceding lower norms to keep higher ones, ideal absolutism disapproves of breaking any absolute norm. There are several possible reasons for taking this position. Perhaps the most basic reason is that it seems to the ideal absolutists to be contradictory to hold that a norm is both an ethical absolute and one which can sometimes be justifiably broken. How can it be universally valid if there are some legitimate exceptions to it? Another possible reason for holding that it is always wrong to break a universal norm is that the consequences of doing so are bad. This, however, is a rule-utilitarian kind of justification of norms by norm-

breaking acts which turn out not to be intrinsically wrong acts but acts which, if practiced widely, would bring generally bad results. [1] And it does seem a bit inconsistent to justify an intrinsically valid (i.e., deontological) norm with a utilitarian (i.e., teleological) argument. It would be a much stronger argument simply to stress the first point, viz., that it seems meaningless to speak of norms as "absolute" or "universal" if they can be disregarded without incurring ethical guilt. What could be the difference between a "universal" norm which can sometimes be legitimately set aside and a "general" norm? In other words, the ideal absolutist contends that hierarchicalism is not really an absolutism at all. For in the event of a conflict of norms the hierarchicalist reneges on his moral obligation to the lower principle.

Of course, to contend that it is always morally wrong to break universal norms, which admittedly conflict on occasion, is to lay oneself open to another problem. If both of the only two alternative courses are wrong in a situation where one must act, then how can the individual be blamed for doing what he could not avoid? What about freedom and intention? Is it really wrong to do what one did not want or intend to do? In Kantian words, does not the fact that one *ought* to do something imply that he *can* do it? This problem may be answered from the ideal absolutist's point of view by any of the following associated tenets.

B. *Some Associated Tenets of Ideal Absolutism*

This moral dilemma does not mean that all is hopeless for ideal absolutism. There are several factors implied or stated by those who defend positions which are associated with ideal absolutism which help to explain, if not resolve, the ethical predicament of this view. Basically, the answer is two-directional: first, *ideally,* there is no conflict between norms and, second, there is a way out of the conflict without making excusable exceptions to the universal norms.

1. *Ideally the Absolute Norms Do Not Conflict* — The many norms are designed not to conflict. Each has its own separate sphere of human activity which *ought not* overlap with that of another. Ideally speaking, the intent of having many norms is that each should cover a given area of human relations without infringing on another area. For example, lying has to do with the truth relationship, stealing with the property relationship, adultery with the marital relationship, and so on. These are distinctly different relationships which humans have with each other and *as such* they do not overlap. Of course, if it is admitted (as indeed it must be) that life is so complex that these

---

[1] See chapters one and three for further explanation and criticism of the rule-utilitarian kind of "universal" norms.

relations will inevitably overlap, then it would follow that there is at least the *possibility* of conflict among norms inherent in the very nature of things.

However, the possibility of moral dilemmas does not mean that there ought to be any conflicts. And the ideal absolutist can content himself with the fact that no conflicts are either intended or necessitated by the nature of things. That is to say, it is not the fault of the moral structure of the universe that there are moral dilemmas. It is good to have absolutes covering every area of human relationships, and it is good that they are designed not to overlap. If for some other reason they do conflict, then one cannot blame the nature or intent of absolute norms for the result. Or, in theistic terms, one cannot blame the Moral Law-Giver for the actual conflicts among moral laws which He designed not to conflict. [2]

2. *Real Conflict of Norms Results From Sin* — If conflict of norms is neither intended nor necessitated by the nature of things, then just how does it come about? The Christian answer to this is called depravity. Man is sinful and he lives among sinful men. Such a world was not the moral intent of God and it is not ideal. In a depraved world men find themselves in moral dilemmas which are neither the fault of the moral law nor of the Moral Law-Giver. This doctrine was stated most emphatically by the great Protestant Reformers. Martin Luther may be taken as a classical source.

According to Luther, "In Adam's fall we sinned all." That is, "by one sin Adam makes all those who are born of him guilty of this same sin. . . . " Luther bases his doctrine of hereditary sin on verses like Psalm 51:5: "Behold, I was brought forth in iniquity, and in sin did my mother conceive me," and Ephesians 2:3: "And so we were by nature children of wrath, like the rest of mankind." This inborn depravity of human nature is both original and basic. It is the root of all other sins. Even pious parents beget children who are totally corrupt. "We are utterly lost; from head to foot there is nothing good in us; we must absolutely become new and different people," Luther wrote. And "even if no actual sin is present, the tinder of original sin hinders the entrance into the kingdom of heaven." Luther admits that the doctrine of original sin is difficult to justify before human reason. This is so, he says, because "it is hidden to all the world, and

---

[2] Of course, one could "blame" God for creating the *possibility* of moral conflict, even though the actual conflict comes about against His moral intent. Theists, however, could answer that God's intending the very possibility of moral conflict was a good intent in that it made freedom and moral perfection possible. See C. S. Lewis, *The Problem of Pain* (New York: The Macmillan Company, 1962), chapters six and seven.

our powers, our reasoning and thinking, do not reveal it, but rather obscure, defend, and excuse it." [3]

Despite Luther's refusal to defend depravity philosophically, one might argue for the ideal absolutist's position on the ground that there would be no moral dilemmas if men always obeyed the moral law. as they ought to do. This might be argued as follows. First, if no one anywhere ever disobeyed any moral precept, there would probably not be a moral dilemma, since conflict of norms usually arises because some antecedent evil has been committed. For example, no mother would ever be forced into the dilemma of either lying or letting her baby be killed unless there were sinful men who force on others this kind of dilemma. Likewise, no man would be forced into the lesser evil of killing others in war if there were no sinful and unjust aggressors in the world. Nor, perhaps, would a doctor be forced to choose between the duty of perpetuating the life of a human "vegetable" and the responsibility of turning off the machine which is keeping him alive, if someone else somewhere had performed his duty to prevent the kinds of disease which cause such a condition. That is, it is just *possible* that all sickness and human calamities are the result of previous neglect and antecedent sin.

Indeed, this is how many Christians have interpreted verses like the following: "Therefore as sin came into the world through one man [Adam] and death through sin, and so death spread to all men because all men sinned [in Adam]," and "the creation was subjected to futility, not of its own will but by the will of him who subjected it in hope." [4] In brief, it is logically possible, and in many cases quite probable, that there would be no conflict of moral norms if there were not the breaking of some antecedent norm which forced the dilemma. And if this is so, then one would not be forced either to give up his many absolutes or to deny that moral blame is involved when there is a conflict.

3. *Ought Does Not Imply Can* — Even granting the above defense against the charge that ideal absolutism does not explain how there can be moral guilt for performing either of two unavoidable alternatives, there is still a residual difficulty. Why should the blame or guilt be placed on the one who could not do otherwise? Why not place the guilt on those who committed the antecedent evils? Why not follow the Biblical pronouncement that "the soul that sins shall die. The son shall not suffer for the iniquity of the father . . . the righteousness of the righteous shall be upon himself, and the wickedness of the wicked shall be upon himself"? [5] That is, why should the individual

[3] Taken from *What Luther Says*, St. Louis, Missouri: Concordia Publishing House, 1959, compiled by Ewald M. Plass, pp. 4149 - 4157, 4170, 4178.

[4] Romans 5:12; 8:20.

[5] Ezekiel 18:20.

in the moral dilemma be held responsible for doing the best he could do in a bad situation which was created by someone else's evil acts? The answer sometimes given to this is frank and to the point. "Ought" does not necessarily imply "can." Kant was wrong. There can be moral responsibility even where it is not possible to perform what one ought to do. Carl F. H. Henry, e.g., writes, "Modern dialectical moralists, faced by the writings of Barth, Brunner, and Niebuhr, have revolted against the optimistic Kantian formula 'I ought, therefore I can.'" [6] In place of it "they have reverted to the Pauline-Augustinian alternative, 'I ought, but I cannot,' even though their conception is based on a profoundly non-biblical theory of the fall of man. . . ." Nonetheless, Henry agrees with them against Kant, saying, "Classical theology had a series of Latin phrases by which it emphasized these facts. Before the fall Adam was *posse non peccare* — able not to sin, and not merely *posse peccare* — able to sin." However, "after the fall he was *non posse non peccare* — not able not to sin." Furthermore, writes Henry, "the formula, 'I ought, but I cannot,' summarizes the predicament of fallen and unregenerated man. It fixes attention on the inability of the sinner to meet the demands of the moral law because of the corruption of his nature." [7] Of course, Henry is not speaking here of moral dilemmas but the principle he lays down is the same one used by the ideal absolutists to justify imputing guilt to one who disobeys either one of two conflicting norms. But how, we may still persist in asking, does this "justify" imputing guilt to one who did his *best* in a bad situation which was not of his own making? An answer to this question may be found in another associated implication of this ethical position.

4. *Doing the Lesser of Two Evils Is Excusable* — Granted that all of the possible alternatives are evil, the best that can be expected under the circumstances (and even the best is an evil) is to perform the lesser of the available evils. However, assuming the individual did not cause his own dilemma by antecedent evil acts of his own, his lesser-of-two-evils option may be considered *excusable*. He is not really guilt-free, but his response is understandable and even pardonable. That is, somehow the penalty for such a sin may be softened and even suspended in view of the tragic circumstance. For instance, in the case of the seaman who threw some men out of an overcrowded

<hr>

[6] Some of these existential theologians take the position that there are moral dilemmas wherein either alternative is wrong when mere relative (non-absolute) norms conflict. But as Paul Ramsey notes, "On their view, a policy may be inept or erroneous, but it is difficult to see how decisions could be wrong." *War and the Christian Conscience*, Durham, N. C.: Duke University Press, 1961, p. 13. That is, if the norms aren't absolute or universal, then why should one consider it wrong to break one in order to bring about the best results possible?

[7] Carl F. H. Henry, *Christian Personal Ethics*, pp. 168, 393.

life boat, the court found him guilty of murder but recommended mercy. [8]

A similar position is taken by the late Edward J. Carnell with regard to Rahab's lie told to save the children of Israel. "Christians are sometimes troubled by the fact that God justified Rahab the harlot, even though she told a lie (Hebrews 11:31). They would not be troubled if they were not already confused about the reality of tragic moral choices." For "what, may I ask, *should* Rahab have done?. . . . God, who reads the heart, saw that she would have told the truth if she had been morally free to do so. She was a good woman because she hated the very thing she did." According to Carnell, "a choice is tragic when one consciously chooses evil in order that a greater good may come." [9] What Rahab did was evil and she hated to have to do it, but it was, nonetheless, the best thing for her to do. Hence, she could find "justification" in God's sight.

Paul Ramsey alludes to this position in a recent writing. Speaking about the woman who committed adultery to escape from a prison camp and return to her family, Ramsey admits, "There is something to be said in behalf of holding that in the order of ethical justification Mrs. Bergmeier's *act* was *wrong*, that the *blame* for this rested elsewhere or upon others or the evil system of regulations, and that *she* was excusable." [10] That is, it was an evil act but a lesser evil than the other alternative.

Now there are at least three ways in which an ideal absolutist may respond to a moral dilemma. First, he may consider all sins to be equally bad or of equal consequences, in which event it does not really matter which alternative he chooses. From a Christian point of view it seems clear that sins are not all equal. Jesus said there were "weightier" matters of the law, that there were/are "greater" sins, and Paul taught that there is even a "greatest" virtue. [11] However, men as far back as Cicero *(Paradoxes,* III, 1) have stated the view that all sins are equal, and unorthodox Christians have restated it from time to time. [12] Most ideal absolutists, on the contrary, have not held that all sins are equal, as is obvious from the popular "choose the lesser of two evils" principle.

[8] Recorded in Joseph Fletcher, *Situation Ethics: The New Morality,* Westminster Press, pp. 136, 196.

[9] Edward J. Carnell, *Christian Commitment,* New York: The Macmillan Company, 1957, pp. 229, 223.

[10] Paul Ramsey, "The Case of the Curious Exception," in *Norm and Context in Christian Ethics,* ed. by Gene H. Outka and Paul Ramsey, New York: Charles Scribner's Sons, 1968.

[11] Compare Matthew 23:23; John 19:11; 1 Corinthians 13:13.

[12] Thomas Aquinas charged Jovinian with holding falsely that all sins are equal. See *Summa Theologica* I - II, 73, 2.

A second way to respond to a conflict of moral absolutes is to assume that one norm commands an intrinsically higher act than another, in view of which one is to break the lesser norm in order to keep the higher norm. This position is more common and seems to be more defensible. Examples of this view are not difficult to find. The problem is that they often so closely resemble the position of hierarchicalism that they are difficult to differentiate. Both positions hold that one ought to obey the higher principle. The basic difference is that ideal absolutism contends that in obeying the higher principle the individual is morally guilty for breaking the lower principle. Hierarchicalism, on the other hand, holds that it is *not wrong* to disobey a lower principle in order to keep a higher one. But whether one is guilty or not guilty for breaking the lower norm is not the point here, and whether or not a hierarchy of norms is a good way to resolve the conflict between norms will be discussed in the next chapter. Here we may merely note that it is a possible solution for the ideal absolutist as to what he should do when there is a conflict of norms and that it has the value of maintaining the intrinsic value of actions over against a utilitarian justification of norms.

A third and, perhaps, more common way of deciding which of two conflicting norms one should follow is to judge which will bring the least evil consequences. This is clearly utilitarian and pragmatic, and as such comes under the criticisms already stated against this position. [13] But to clarify at least what the position is contending it should be noted that implied in the "excusability" of the evil choice is the fact that one did pursue the best alternative available. If he had chosen the greater of the two evils there would be no excuse. His sin can be "overlooked" or "pardoned" only if he does that which will bring the least evil to the least number of people.

5. *Doing the Lesser of Two Evils Is Forgivable* — It may be asked on precisely what grounds such a choice of lesser evil may be "pardoned," since it is an evil for which one is held guilty. In a general moralistic way the answer is that pardon is offered on the basis of understanding mercy; in a specifically Christian way the answer is divine grace or forgiveness. Since the latter position is more explicit it will be discussed in more detail. But first a word about mercy.

On a kind of humanitarian ground one could expect amnesty for the individual who did his best in choosing the lesser evil. After all, if he had taken the other alternative he would have brought more pain and suffering on mankind. The least that can be expected is that he be rewarded for saving men from a greater evil. Surely if he is not praised for his deed, he should not be punished for it either, at least not as much as one who did the same thing when there was no con-

---

[13] See chapters one and three.

flict of norms involved. In other words, if the verdict must be guilty at least the sentence should involve leniency or clemency.

On a Christian view of atonement the reason is more explicit as to why the guilty individual should be forgiven. Working on the assumption that man is sinful and cannot atone for his own sin, the doctrine of the atonement declares that God in grace has provided a way of escape from guilt. Christ died, the just for the unjust, that He might bring man to God. The divine holiness is offended by man's sin but appeased by Christ's sacrifice. Jesus paid the penalty for man's sin and provides forgiveness as a free gift to all who will receive it. The rationale is this: God is just and must punish sin, but God is loving and wishes to forgive the sinner; therefore God devised the atonement as a way to satisfy His justice so that He could free His love. That is, the only way God could be just and yet justify unjust men is to have Christ die, the just for the unjust. In this way, despite man's moral dilemma of being faced with what he ought to do but cannot do, he is offered a way of escape by way of what Christ has done for him. [14] Sin and guilt are inevitable for man, but salvation is possible. An individual may be held guilty even where he could not do otherwise, but there is always the possibility of forgiveness offered to him which he *can* receive.

Of course, the doctrine of the atonement is directed primarily to man's inability not to sin in general, but it applies equally well as a solution to the problem of conflicting moral norms. It says, in essence, that even though one is guilty for doing evil in a moral dilemma where he cannot do otherwise, nonetheless, the evil is forgivable through the atonement.

6. *Confessing One's Guilt* — However, evil is not forgiven automatically. It must be confessed. One must hate the very evil he does. He must really desire forgiveness. There must be a willingness to come to God as one unable to help himself and who is completely dependent on God's grace. This is true of all sin but particularly true of those tragic moral choices arising out of a conflict of absolute norms. One must break the moral law only under the command of God only with "fear and trembling," as Sören Kierkegaard painfully observed. For no one can rightly go beyond a moral law who does not deeply desire to live in accord with it. There must be anguish over one's sinful dilemma. [15] But granting that one is in a moral dilemma and really desires to do what the situation does not permit him to do, it follows that he will want to do the very best he can which is the lesser of the alternate evils. And on the basis of this desire, or of his confession and desire for forgiveness, his sin is excusable or pardon-

[14] Compare 1 Peter 2:24; 3:18; Romans 3:21-28.
[15] See chapter two where Kierkegaard's position is discussed.

able. There is a way out of the dilemma. Even if there is no way to avoid it, there is a way to remove the guilt which cannot be avoided.

B. *Some Examples Examined*

Perhaps the position of ideal absolutism will come to focus better through some specific examples. Numerous situations are available from both inside and outside of the Christian Scriptures. Let us select a few illustrative cases and reason as to what one should do who believes that there are many absolute norms which do conflict and one is guilty for disobeying any of them. The first examples are those offered by Joseph Fletcher. [16]

1. *Maternal vs. Marital Love* — What should the German mother have done who could not return to her family unless she became pregnant in her Russian prison camp? There is a clear conflict between her duty to care for her family and her sexual faithfulness to her husband. If she believed that neither of these moral principles should ever be broken, then she should painfully submit to the lesser of two evils and ask God to forgive her breach of marital fidelity (i.e., assuming that duty to her family was the greater good). Such a decision, of course, could not be made easily or lightly. One would have to examine his motives to make sure that there is not merely a conflict between duty and desire in which desire is winning out. The conflict must be between duty and duty, and the decision must be to violate the duty which would be (or bring) the greater evil.

2. *Fornication for the Fatherland* — If prostitution is the only way one can obtain vital espionage information which may save the lives of many soldiers or even save one's country, then what should one do? Assuming that among the individual's unbreakable norms are both the duty to save the lives of her countrymen and the duty to be faithful to the sanctity and purity of her own body, then she is faced with a moral dilemma. It is conceivable that in such a circumstance a morally upright person might reluctantly and remorsefully commit the sin of fornication in the conviction that it was the lesser of the two evils. If this were the case, then sacrificing her personal integrity for her country, undesirable and painful as it might be, could be "justified" by the greater good it accomplishes or at least be forgiven by the God to whom she confessed this lesser evil.

3. *Murder vs. Mercy* — Certainly no moral man relishes taking the life of another human whatever the circumstances may be. However, when it is a case of being humane and merciful to this person vs. the desire and duty not to take another's life, then one is faced with a moral dilemma. For example, the request of a man hopelessly caught

[16] Taken from Fletcher's *Situation Ethics.* See our discussion of these above in chapter two.

in a burning airplane who pleads to be put out of his misery ought not to fall on deaf ears, at least not if they are moral ones. What should one do, be merciless or commit murder? On the grounds that it is always wrong to take another human life and, also, that it is never right to be merciless, one is faced with a painful dilemma. He should choose the lesser sin, which might be showing the mercy, and then ask God for mercy on himself for the sin of taking another human life.

4. *Duty to Man vs. Duty to God* — Within the Scriptures there are a number of cases where two of the Ten Commandments conflict, often one from the first table (duty to God) conflicting with one from the second table (duty to man). The life of Christ provides several such illustrations. On one occasion Jesus counseled a disciple to violate the law of filial piety, saying, "Follow me, and leave the dead to bury their own dead." On another occasion Jesus said, "He who loves father or mother more than me is not worthy of me." [17] Presumably, then, if one's parents commanded him not to love God, one would have to break the fifth commandment to keep the first commandment. A classic example of moral conflict is where God commanded Abraham to kill his son Isaac. What does one do when his duty to God and his love for his only son come into such irresolvable tension? Abraham chose to sacrifice his duty to Isaac in order to secure his duty to God. The Bible contains other illustrations as to when it is necessary to break one of the laws of the Old Testament. Examples of such are the Scriptures that affirm that one should show mercy rather than keep the letter of the law. [18] In which cases breaking the law is the lesser evil.

5. *Duties to God vs. Duties to Government* — Another form of moral conflict is that between responsibilities to the civil law and those of the moral law. Socrates argued that one should never disobey even unjust civil laws. [19] As a matter of fact he died by this conviction. Christians were exhorted by the apostles to obey Roman rulers, some of whom martyred them, on the ground that government was ordained of God. "Let every person be subject to the governing authorities," wrote Paul. "For there is no authority except from God, and those that exist have been instituted by God. Therefore he who resists the authorities resists what God has appointed. . . ." [20] This would mean, then, that a conflict between a civil law and a moral law would be a conflict between two laws which God has ordained, since God or-

[17] Matthew 8:21; 10:37.
[18] Genesis 22:1ff. See also Sören Kierkegaard's treatment of this above in chapter two. Cf. Matthew 12:1ff; 23:23.
[19] Plato, *Crito*, 51, c-e.
[20] Romans 13:1-2; cf. Titus 3:1; 1 Peter 2:13.

dained both. If they come into conflict, as they obviously do when a government issues the comand to take innocent lives, then one must choose the lesser of two evils. A clear example of this is found in Exodus 1:15-22. The king of Egypt commanded the midwives to kill every Hebrew male child born. The midwives disobeyed the civil law and let the innocent children live. They chose the lesser of the two evils.

Examples of this kind can be multiplied. Not every ideal absolutist would agree that all of these instances represent legitimate cases of irresolvable conflict of unbreakable moral rules. What they would agree on, however, is that when there is a clash of absolutes it is wrong to violate any of them. The only excusable or pardonable choice is to do the lesser evil and plead mercy for one's action.

II. Ideal Absolutism Evaluated

Because of its many forms and few identifiable proponents, the ideal absolutistic position is difficult to evaluate. Therefore, most of our evaluation will have to center on some of the essential elements and implications of the view. First, some positive features will be noted.

A. Some Positive Contributions of Ideal Absolutism

Ideal absolutism may be commended for several things. It is an attempt to preserve an unshakable basis for human conduct. It does attempt to handle the problems of conflicting norms. Furthermore, in so doing, important light is cast on the nature of guilt, responsibility, and forgiveness, especially from a Christian standpoint. Finally, it provides a solution without making exceptions to norms.

1. *The Desire to Preserve Many Absolutes* — The very fact that there are a number of attempts to preserve absolutes is indicative of at least the need felt by many moralists to have a firm basis for founding human interrelationships. The ideal absolutist should be commended for his efforts, vain or not, to find a fixed basis for morality. Since no specific examples were given of just what is the basis for these many absolutes, there is no need here to evaluate these arguments. It is sufficient to note that whether the basis is revelational, presuppositional, intuitional, or whatever, the ideal absolutist rightly sees the need for maintaining an unshakable basis for morality. The problem is to demonstrate that the ethical norms one uses, whatever their origin may be, are indeed worthy of unwavering allegiance. This problem becomes especially acute in view of the admission that these norms sometimes clash with one another.

2. *Some Light shed on the Nature of Responsibility and Grace* — It must be admitted that the solution of ideal absolutism to moral dilemmas becomes more plausible in view of a Christian concept of

enabling grace — more so than on purely naturalistic grounds. For, rationally speaking, why should there be any responsibility when there was no ability to respond? Why should one be condemned for not doing what he could not do? Rationalistically, the fact of responsibility would seem to imply the ability to respond. However, the picture changes somewhat when a supernatural dimension is introduced. For it does make more sense to say that one is not able to do what he should do, *if* there is someone who can enable him to do it. So what does not make good sense on a purely moralistic ground, viz., a command to do what is humanly impossible, does make sense when there is some way to make it divinely possible. That is, it is meaningful to affirm that *ought* does not necessarily imply *can* on a purely human level, if there is some superhuman help available which *can* accomplish what ought to be done. In brief, one can be held morally responsible for not being able to do by sheer human effort what he ought to do, if God makes available to him supernatural power by which he can do it. In other words, a man can be held morally responsible for not being willing to avail himself of the grace which could enable him to do what he ought to do.

3. *A Solution Without Exceptions* — In comparison with some of the other solutions to the problem of conflicting norms, ideal absolutism has an unadulterated simplicity about it. No complex calculations are needed to determine guilt. No elaborate ordering of moral principles is necessary to pinpoint responsibility. A universal norm should never be broken, and that is that! If it is broken, conflict or no conflict, then one is guilty and he must recognize it. If finality and simplicity are the only criteria, then ideal absolutism would be virtually impeccable.

Even in a less eulogistic sense ideal absolutism should be commended for maneuvering to an exceptionless position. Unlike situationism and generalism, once a norm is established for ideal absolutism there are absolutely no exceptions to undermine its validity. It has the decided advantage of laying down norms for living without any conditions. There are simply no conditions or circumstances under which one can transgress these absolute norms without incurring guilt. In view of the complexity and subtlety of other ethical positions which involve a rather detailed overlay of values or a tortuous procedure of casuistry, ideal absolutism must come as a pleasant breeze to those desiring simple solutions.

B. *Some Serious Difficulties With Ideal Absolutism*

Despite its appeal to those seeking finality and simplicity, ideal absolutism has some grave difficulties. Not all ethical norms possess finality or universality, and ethical decisions are not always simple. Among the problems entailed in the ideal absolutist's position may be named its tendency to legalism, a misapplication of the doctrine of depravity, a misunderstanding of individual moral responsibility, and a futile attempt to hide behind incomprehensibility.

1. *The Tendency to Legalism* — Contrary to Fletcher's contention, [21] we would argue that a position may hold to many norms without being legalistic. It is not essential to a many-norm ethic that it over-extend or abuse its norms, which is what the legalist's does. The use of many norms, even absolute ones, does not automatically make an ethic legalistic. However, when the position shows no willingness to arrange and apply these norms so that ethically responsible acts can be performed without guilt, then the position does tend to be legalistic. This is precisely the case with ideal absolutism. It shows no willingness to acknowledge the ethical rightness of performing over-riding obligations. Why should a man who chooses the *best* of his available alternatives be held guilty for performing an *evil*, even if it is considered a lesser and forgivable evil? It seems unnecessarily and inflexibly legalistic to hold a man to the letter of one law when he obeyed the demands of a higher one. Why should he be held guilty at all when he did the good, i.e., the best alternative?

Indeed, in some of the very illustrations used from Scripture it is clearly stated that it was right or *good* (not a lesser evil) to perform the higher obligation. In the conflict of mercy and Sabbath-keeping Jesus said pointedly, "So it is lawful to do *good* on the Sabbath." In the case of the Hebrew midwives it is written, "So God dealt *well* with the midwives; and the people multiplied and grew very strong. And because the midwives feared God he gave them families." Likewise, Abraham was justified before God for his willingness to offer Isaac and was not condemned for committing a lesser evil. [22] In each case the act performed was not a lesser evil but *the greatest good.* Surely no one should be held personally and morally guilty for the act of doing the greatest good possible, whatever the circumstances. [23]

2. *Misapplication of the Doctrine of Depravity* — Whatever else may be intended by the biblical doctrine of depravity, it certainly does not mean that personal moral responsibility is eliminated by the atonement. But that is precisely what would happen if ideal absolutism were carried to its logical conclusion. For it inconsistently holds that one is held responsible for not doing good when only evils are possible. This would mean that one is not free not to sin (even by

[21] Fletcher, *op. cit.*, chapter one.

[22] Compare Matthew 12:12; Exodus 1:20, 21; Hebrews 11:17-19.

[23] If an individuals's moral dilemma is caused by antecedent choices of his own, he may be held guilty for doing what he could not avoid. For then his personal freedom was antecedent. That is, he could have freely chosen previously not to permit himself to get into a position where he would lose control of his freedom. For example, one who drinks heavily, knowing he must drive, is guilty for whatever injuries he inflicts as a drunken driver.

God's enabling grace). It would mean that God asks men to do what He knows they cannot do (and what He will not help them do) and holds them responsible for not doing it, so that He can forgive them for doing it. If this were so, it would not be a moral tragedy; it would be a kind of divine comedy. God would be forcing men to sin just so He could forgive them. Perish the thought! Indeed, if sin is inescapable, then Christ could not be impeccable.

Even if men are *not able* not to sin on their own power, certainly they are *able* not to sin by God's enabling power. And surely this power is available to all men who are *willing* to have it. For if men are to be justly condemned for not doing their duty, then there must be some possible way of doing it. Sin in general may be unavoidable, but each sin in particular could have been averted. That is, men inevitably will sin, but there is no individual sin which could not have been resisted by God's enabling grace. But on the ideal absolutist's solution to a conflict of absolute norms, God provides no way to avoid guilt. A man is personally responsible for a moral evil which he could not avoid. It is true that where guilt like this is inevitable the grace of forgiveness is available. But the question is not whether unavoidable sins are forgivable; the question is why the greatest good a man can do should render him guilty. In other words, on the ideal absolutist's position there is no way to maintain the justice of God in view of human responsibility.

3. *A Misunderstanding of Moral Responsibility* — It is not clear whether depravity is misunderstood because moral responsibility is not understood or vice versa. In either event, the two are closely connected. And if moral responsibility were clearly conceived there would be no need at all to misapply depravity to relieve the dilemma. For as was noted earlier, it does make sense to say that grace is the answer to guilt, that forgiveness is the answer to sin, etc. But it does *not* follow from this that grace or forgiveness can be used to save an inadequately conceived ethical system from collapse. That is, one should not hold an individual personally and morally responsible for not doing what he had no way of doing. For even if the individual does not possess the power to do it "on his own," he must at least be able to get the enabling grace from God. Otherwise, the divine commands would be unreasonable, for God would be commanding the impossible. It must be assumed that there is some way for the individual to fulfill his moral duty or else a reasonable and moral God would not prescribe it for him. And whether the moral agent fulfills his duty by using human or divine resources is not the point. In either case, the command implies the possibility of performing it. Responsibility does imply the ability to respond; ought does imply can in an overall sense.

Not only is moral responsibility meaningless without the available moral ability to respond, but moral accountability makes no sense if each sin is inevitable. Why should a man be punished for doing his *best?* He should be rewarded for doing the so-called "lesser of two evils" for it is really the "greater of (two) goods." Or, if one alternative is evil, then at least one alternative must be good. So it would be better to say that the one ought to do the greater good and not the lesser evil. These positions are not identical. Both positions may choose the same alternative in a given case. But for the ideal absolutist it is morally *wrong* to do it because it is an evil, lesser or not. On the other view it is not morally wrong to break a lower norm in order to keep a higher one. There is always at least one right thing to do. For, as the apostle Paul said, "God is faithful, and will not let you be tempted beyond your strength, but with the temptation will also provide the way of escape, that you may be able to endure it." [24]

4. *A Serious Christological Problem* — Perhaps the most telling objection against ideal absolutism from a Christian point of view is that it would render the sinlessness of Christ either impossible or meaningless as a paradigm of Christian morality. If there are moral situations where sin is really inevitable, then Christ surely faced them and is sinful Himself. But if He sinned, then He is not the sinless Savior which the New Testament claims He is. [25] This would render the doctrine of the substitutionary atonement ineffective. For Christ would not be the sinless sacrifice for sin.

But if Christ were Himself sinful, then how can He be the example of Christian perfection? And, on the other hand, if Christ did not encounter such moral dilemmas, then He was not really tempted in all points as we are (Heb. 4:15). That is, if Jesus never really faced any of the tragic moral choices we have, then how can He be the meaningful moral exemplar for our lives? So, on the thesis of ideal absolutism, either Jesus was sinful or else He did not face the realistic kinds of moral conflicts which His disciples do.

It seems obvious enough that neither of these alternatives is the case. The Scriptures clearly indicate that Christ was without sin and yet He faced victoriously all of the kinds of temptation to sin. From this it follows that sin is not necessary. There are no situations where the only alternatives are sinful. Jesus never faced any and neither do His disciples.

[24] 1 Corinthians 10:13.
[25] This point was suggested to me by a colleague, Dr. Arthur Klem.

SELECT READINGS FOR CHAPTER SIX: IDEAL ABSOLUTISM

Baier, Kurt, *Moral Point of View: A Rational Basis of Ethics,* Ithica, N.Y.: Cornell University Press, 1958.

————, *Values and the Future,* New York: Free Press, 1968.

Elert, Werner, *Christian Ethos,* trans. by Carl J. Schindler, Philadelphia, Penn.: Muhlenbard Press, 1957.

Forell, George W., *Faith Active in Love,* Minneapolis, Minn.: Augsburg Publishing House, 1960.

Koeberle, Adolf, *Quest for Holiness,* trans., by J. C. Mattes, Minneapolis, Minn.: Augsburg Publishing House, 1936.

Montgomery, John W., "The Moral Point of View," in *The Bible — the Living Word of Revelation,* Grand Rapids, Mich., Zondervan Publishing House, 1965.

Ramsey, Paul, "The Case of the Curious Exception," in *Norm and Context in Christian Ethics,* ed. by Gene H. Outka and Paul Ramsey, New York: Charles Scribner's Sons, 1968.

7 / Hierarchicalism: There Are Hierarchically Ordered Universal Norms

There are at least three positions possible on universal norms. First, there is non-conflicting absolutism which holds that the many universal norms never really conflict. The problem with this view is that no matter how carefully one defines the various norms, there are still real conflicts between them. Second, there is ideal absolutism which holds that ideally the norms would not conflict and when they do conflict one ought to do the lesser of the two evils. The difficulty with this position is that it holds the individual guilty for doing his best in an unavoidably bad situation. A third possibility is called hierarchicalism which maintains that whenever norms conflict one is morally right in breaking the lower norm in order to keep the higher one.

I. Ethical Hierarchicalism Explained

Ethical hierarchicalism is so named because it maintains a hierarchical arrangement or ordering of ethical norms based on the relative scale of values they represent. It implies a pyramid of normative values which *in and of themselves* are objectively binding on men. But when any two or more of these values happen to conflict, a person is exempted from his otherwise binding obligation to a lower norm in view of the pre-emptory obligation of the higher norm.

The precise nature of hierarchicalism can be seen by way of comparison. The antinomian *excludes* all objective ethical norms. The situationist holds out for one *exclusive* norm of an absolute nature. The generalist views all norms as being subject to *exceptions*. In non-conflicting absolutism it is contended that norms never really conflict but there is always a way of *escape* from the apparent dilemmas. According to ideal absolutism, when there is a conflict of norms, evil is inevitable but *excusable* or forgivable. But in hierarchicalism, one is not guilty for breaking a lower norm but has an *exemption* from it in view of the overriding duty to the higher norm. [1]

A. *The Basic Thesis of Hierarchicalism*

Historically, there have been many examples of hierarchically ordered values, most of them springing from the neo-plotinian fountainhead, Plotinus. [2] The premise common to all hierarchicalism is basically the same, namely, things are ordered on a scale of good, ranging from least to most good. Ethically speaking, some things are better than others. Values must be weighed, and one must act accordingly. Lesser goods must give way to greater goods. As might be expected, not all ethical value scales are identical. Some acts or deeds weigh more heavily in one view than in another. There is, however, a large area of agreement on some basic values. And in order to simplify the analysis and facilitate evaluation, the author assumes responsibility for the position of hierarchical absolutism outlined here.

The first question to face is: when norms representing different values conflict, which value is intrinsically higher? Since on the hierarchical position one ought always to do the highest good possible (even if it means doing a lower evil), then one must have some way of knowing which values are intrinsically higher. The following principles are offered as a guide for decision-making in view of possible conflicts of value.

1. *Persons Are More Valuable Than Things* — The first basic principle of hierarchicalism on which one can expect wide agreement is that *persons* are more valuable than *things*. This is why persons are to be *loved* and things are to be *used*. And, conversely, things should not be loved, and persons should not be used. In Kant's words, persons are to be treated as *ends* but never as *means*. Or, in Martin Buber's words, one should maintain an I-thou relation with persons and an I-it relation with things. That is, no other subject should be treated like a mere object but as another subject with its own subjectivity and freedom.

Several implications of this principle may be noted. First, persons are intrinsically higher than things because subjects are more valuable than mere objects. A subject can view other things as objects (even itself), but an object cannot know either itself or another object. Subjectivity involves self-awareness such as men possess but animals do not. Man is not only conscious (as are the higher animals), but he is

[1] See chapter one for a comparison and contrast of these six views.
[2] See Plotinus, *Enneads*, trans. Stephen MacKenna, London: Faber and Faber Ltd., 1956.

self-conscious. Man has a subjectivity which transcends his objectivity. For when man views himself as an object, there is the viewer (i.e., the subject) over and above what is viewed (i.e., the object). There is the "I" which views and makes the affirmations about the "me" or "it." So the subject's ability to transcend mere objectivity manifests his intrinsically higher value than a mere object.

Second, a personal subject is intrinsically higher than an object as is manifested by the subject's ability of self-determination. Objects can be determined, but only subjects can determine. And only personal subjects like men can self-determine. In other words, a person is an intrinsically higher being than a thing because persons are free. Persons, unlike things, are completely subject neither to the fortunes of indeterminacy nor to the sheer mechanics of determination; persons have the power of self-determination. In this way persons may be said to be more valuable than things in the way that autonomy is more valuable than complete dependence. For the self-sustaining are more valuable than the dependent; men are more valuable than puppets.

Third, persons are intrinsically of more value than things, for persons can relate personally to other persons; things cannot. Persons are subjects and subjects can relate to other subjects via a web of inter-subjectivity; objects cannot. Only persons can have I-thou relations with other persons. An object is an "it" and as such does not enter into personal relationships. In fact, objects or things cannot *relate* to others; they can only *be related*. For only subjects have the power to relate things. A subject is active but an object is passive. Hence, personal subjects are more valuable as such than are objects.

2. *Infinite Person Is More Valuable Than Finite Person(s)* — Assuming a theistic framework, it must be held that the infinite source of all finite persons is of more value than they are. In fact, infinite person is the most valuable thing of all. For it would be a strange logic to hold that the source of all value is itself not valuable. [3] On the contrary, God is of infinite value. He is not only the basis of all good but He is the essence of good itself. Furthermore, He is not only the Creator of all personality but He is essentially personal Himself. He is the infinite Subject by which all subjects can be related. God is the infinite "I" who is the nexus of relationship for all finite "I's."

The implication of this is obvious. Whenever there is a conflict between the value of finite persons and the infinitely personal Being, one must choose in favor of the latter over the former. All personhood and personal relationships are valuable. But the personhood of the in-

---

[3] On the surface, Plotinus seems to hold that the source of all does not possess the good which the things which emanate from it possess (Cf. VI, 7, 15). But on closer examination it is clear that he believes the source of all good to be good in a superior way (Cf. V, 2, 1).

finite and personal relationships with the infinitely personal Being are of unlimited value. In the language of Scripture, whenever there is a conflict between divine and human values, "we must obey God rather than men." [4]

3. *A Complete Person Is More Valuable Than an Incomplete Person* — Another principle involved in ethical hierarchicalism is that the complete is of more value than the incomplete. A whole person is of more value than a partial person. Maturity of personhood is of more value than immaturity of personhood, whether the immaturity is in the direction of childishness or in the direction of senility. The mature person is to be preferred to either the childish or senile, and the childish has some advantage over the senile in that it yet has the chance to mature. [5]

There are several ways a person can be incomplete. He may be incomplete mentally. In this case the sane is of *more* intrinsic value than the insane. This is not to say that insane persons have *no* value. They have great value as persons, only they are incomplete persons. The mentally ill are human but their value as humans is lessened because of their incapacitation. They cannot engage in the full function of interpersonal relations nor bear the full responsibility of personhood. They need the help of other persons. In fact, their recovery is dependent on being treated as persons by persons. Nonetheless, the incompleteness of their personhood makes their personhood of less value as such than a person who is not so limited in the free expression of his distinctively human powers.

A person may also be incomplete by way of physical handicaps. The blind and the maimed have definite limitations on their personal activities. It is true that these limits are often the occasion of a greater development of their other powers, but they are limits nonetheless. It is intrinsically better not to be crippled or physically incapacitated. A person who is physically complete has a better manifestation of humanity than one who is not. This is not to imply that the mentally retarded or physically handicapped are not *equally* human with those who are not. What they possess of human nature is just as human as that of the healthy; they simply do not possess all there is to be possessed. Their personhood would be more valuable if it were complete.

4. *An Actual Person Is of More Value Than a Potential Person* — Another point in the hierarchy of values is that an actual person is more valuable than a potential person. An actual person is one that *is;* a potential person is one that *may be.* The actuality of something is more important than its mere potentiality. An actual oak tree is

[4] Acts 5:29.
[5] Matthew 18:3.

better than a mere acorn. An actual person is of more value than a potential person because the former has full reality while the latter has it only potentially. *Being* fully human is better than the mere possibility of *becoming* fully human.

And just as the actual plant is more valuable than the seed (potential plant), so a mother is more intrinsically valuable as a person than the fertilized ovum within her womb. For the mother is an actual person, whereas the embryo is only a potential person. She *is* a mature, free, autonomous subject; the unborn has only the potential to *become* such. Hence, it would follow that when there are *irresolvable conflicts* between the values involving potential humans and actual humans, the actual should take precedence over the potential. More about this later.

In view of the principle that actual persons have more value than potential persons, one should not draw the hasty conclusion that potential persons have *no* value. On the contrary, as the next principle illustrates, potential persons are highly valuable.

5. *Potential Persons Are More Valuable Than Actual Things* — So valuable is personhood that even potential personhood is better than mere thinghood. This is why one must highly respect human life even at the embryonic state. An unborn embryo is a potential human being; an appendix is not. The human embryo *can* and (conditions being favorable) *does* become another free and autonomous human person; a human appendix does not. Therefore, it is a serious and sacred thing to tamper with potential personhood. This is the flaw in the appendage theory. Further, genetic manipulations which may affect one's future personhood have definite and grave moral implications.

A potential person is of such great value that it should not be sacrificed for any *thing* in the world. The most highly trained dog as such is not to be compared to the value of an unborn child of a poor and unknown woman. As John Stuart Mill's unhappy man is better than a happy pig, so a potential man is better than any actual animal in the world. For the sheer potential to become human is incomparably superior to the actual value of a famous race horse. The most sophisticated computer and the most educated animal cannot enter into personal relationships. They cannot love, and even if they can in some way help men, yet they cannot know that they are being helpful. A human person can do both of these and much more.

Of course, a *potential* person cannot love any more than a machine or an animal can. So it might be contended that, therefore, a potential person (i.e., an embryo) has no more value than a mere thing. This would be both a hasty and an unwarranted conclusion, for several reasons. First, because potentialities are really different in *kind*. For example, jello has the potentiality to be molded into small forms for the table, and steel has the potentiality to be structured into large buildings. But jello does not have the potentiality to be made into skyscrapers, whereas steel does. There is a *real* difference in their respective potentials. Or, to use another illustration, an acorn has the potential to become an oak tree but a pebble does not. This means that there is a difference in the kind of reality each possesses. One thing can become an oak tree and the other cannot. Even so, there is a reality (not yet matured, to be sure) within a human embryo that makes it more valuable, even as a potential person, than any fully developed non-personal beings in the universe.

There is a second reason for preferring a potential personal being to an actual non-personal being. It is better to have the potential to be a person, even if this potential is never actualized, than not to have this potential at all. It is better because the object having such potential *might* become a person, whereas a stone, which has no potential to become a person, *cannot* become a person. It is better to have the opportunity to be or do something good which never actualizes than not to have that opportunity at all. In fact, a potential person is better than a mere object or thing even if the potential person develops personhood and then ruins or rejects it. For "it is better to have loved and lost than never to have loved at all." It is better to be free even if one brings bondage on himself through his freedom than not to be free at all. That is, the potential for the greater good of personhood is to be preferred to the actuality of the lesser good of mere thinghood. [6]

6. *Many Persons Are More Valuable Than Few Persons* — If one person has intrinsic value, then two persons have more value, and the most persons possible have most value. This would mean that if one were faced with a decision which involved the possibility of saving either five lives or one life, then he should save the most lives possible. For many persons have more value than one person. And the greater value is not based on the mere quantity of persons but on the potential for interpersonal relationships and the enhancing of the personhood of all the persons involved. That is, there is something qualitatively higher about many persons over a few persons. If personhood and

[6] This does not necessarily mean that the mere potentiality of every higher good is better than the actuality of *every* lower good. There may be instances where the actual good "in the hand" is worth two higher potential goods "in the bush," especially if the chances for actualizing the potential for the higher are not good. But this is not so with the value of persons. For a potential person is worth risking any *thing* one can, provided that it does not involve the sacrifice of other persons. That is, one should not use up the resources needed to preserve actual persons in attempting to save a potential person.

interpersonal relationships are intrinsically good, then reduplicating and enriching this good is certainly a greater good.

Overcrowded cities and the threat of an overpopulated world may appear to be exceptions to the principle that many persons are better than few persons. Indeed, at face value, the principle might appear to be saying that the largest family possible would be the greatest good possible for all parents. These conclusions should not be drawn, for they reflect a basic misunderstanding on several levels. First, the word "possible" places some limitations on the principle. If a family, nation, or even a race reaches the point where it stretches to exceed its own possibilities, then there are inbuilt ways of leveling off the populations such as starvation, plagues, and war. Further, the number of persons in a given space ought not to be multiplied beyond the possibility of all of them having a complete "personhood." That is to say, it is conceivable that in a time-space world like ours there could be too many people for each individual to fully develop his personhood. If this were so, it would be an evil. For the principle that many persons are better than few extends only as far as the word "person" permits. When individuals can no longer be persons, then one is under no obligation to further increase the number of individuals.

7. *Personal Acts Which Promote Personhood Are Better Than Those Which Do Not* — There are many acts performed by persons with respect to other persons, but they are not all of equal value. Some acts of persons are impersonal, e.g., indifference to other persons in need. Some acts of persons are anti-personal, e.g., hatred toward men of another race. And of the remaining personal acts, some promote interpersonal relations better than others. In each case, the higher are to be preferred to the lower. That is, personal acts are more valuable than impersonal acts, and more highly personal acts are better than less personal acts.

In the event of a conflict, then, between levels of value among possible human acts, one should always yield to those courses of action which make for better personal relationships. For if persons have intrinsic value, then personal acts which best promote personhood are the best kind of acts. And since personhood is developed only in interpersonal relationship with other persons, then the personal acts which best promote this interpersonal relationship are superior to those which do not. In view of this principle, if one is caught in a moral dilemma where he must choose between an equal number of persons living while the others die, then the decision should be based on which person (or persons) will probably promote the best truly interpersonal relationships if he lives. On this basis, a general might be saved and a soldier sacrificed or a minister kept alive while a murderer dies. This, of course, is to be applied only in cases where there is an *unavoidable conflict* of ethical norms. It is in this sense that one person (say, the apostle Paul) is more valuable than another (say, Hitler), not intrinsically more valuable, but because of their relative value to other persons.

B. Some Illustrations of Hierarchicalism

To show precisely how hierarchicalism is worked out in experience may be helpful to further illustrate its basic tenets. By taking some of the classical moral dilemmas and resolving the conflict by discovering which norms represent intrinsically higher values, it may be more fully appreciated what ethical hierarchicalism means. Some illustrations will be taken from the Scriptures and others from human experience in general.

1. *Abraham and Isaac* — The classical example of a conflict of moral principles is found in the command of God to Abraham to sacrifice his son Isaac. Sören Kierkegaard understood this as an instance when one's religious duty of direct obedience to God transcends his ethical responsibility to men. It is a case in which one's subjective religious obligation suspends his objective moral duty. Abraham's obedience to God's command to kill his own son was a teleological suspension of the ethical. This does not mean, said Kierkegaard, that it was a destruction of the ethical but only a temporary dethroning of it in view of his overriding religious obligation.

What Kierkegaard did *not* hold, but ethical hierarchicalism does hold, is that the moral law forbidding murder was suspended for a higher *moral* law. For Kierkegaard, the moral law can be transcended only for religious ends but not for higher moral purposes. Morally, Abraham was a murderer. But his religious leap of faith was able to reverse this and transform a moral tragedy into a religious triumph. According to Kierkegaard, Abraham was not a tragic hero on moral grounds but a knight of faith on religious grounds. There was absolutely no ethical justification for what Abraham was willing to do.

Ethical hierarchicalism, on the contrary, takes issue with Kierkegaard's analysis, claiming that there was a higher ethical purpose or principle in view of which Abraham was ethically justified in his decision. The higher principle was his duty to obey God which always transcends one's duty to another man. For the person of God and one's personal relation to God are of higher value than the person of man or personal relations with a man. In the scale of ethical values the duty to infinite Person always transcends that of the duty to finite persons.

Furthermore, according to Kierkegaard, this higher duty to God (which he calls religious and we call moral) is subjective, personal, and paradoxical. For hierarchicalism, on the contrary, one's duty to

God is statable in rational and propositional form. Perhaps it was Kierkegaard's inability to appreciate how a personal relationship can be stated in meaningful propositional form which forced him to dub it as completely subjective and beyond stating in a cognitively meaningful way. But whatever the reason for Kierkegaard's retreat to the "irrational," it is plain that he did not consider the higher duty to be an *ethical* duty. Hierarchicalism, on the other hand, views Abraham's dilemma as one where he had to choose between two universally valid ethical norms. And in view of the fact that one norm represents an intrinsically higher value, hierarchicalism concludes that Abraham was *morally* justified in obeying the higher norm. It was not the lesser of two evils; it was the greatest good that a man could do, viz., fulfilling his duty to the infinitely valuable Person.

2. *Bucher's Lie to Save His Crew* — In the first chapter the case of Commander Lloyd Bucher was examined. Under the threat by his captors that they would kill his crew unless he signed false confessions, he lied to save their lives. His conflict was between faithfulness to the lives of his crew and faithfulness to the truth. Which ethical norm should he have followed? According to ethical hierarchicalism, it was right for him to lie (i.e., to intentionally falsify) in order to perform the greater good of saving these many lives. The norm against lying was not destroyed but it was dethroned by a higher obligation. Truth-telling was temporarily suspended but not revoked. No exception was made to truth-telling but an *exemption* was made in view of a higher obligation to human lives. Bucher's duty to the lives of his crew was higher than his obligation to tell the truth to his enemies.

Since Bucher's was a choice between relating truthfully to persons who were threatening to do an antipersonal act with his telling the truth (viz., the killing of his crew) and being a faithful person in a personal and loving way to other persons (viz., his crew) with whom he wanted to perpetuate personal relations, the act of lying was more beneficial to promoting true interpersonal relationships than telling the truth would have been. In other words, Bucher did that which promoted the highest personal value. He treated his crew as persons; the Koreans wished to treat them as things. In fact, one could even argue that by lying to his captors he saved them from performing the decidedly antipersonal act of murder. It is true that the act of lying to them was not itself a personal act. In and of itself, lying is impersonal and unloving. But when one can gain an overriding personal value by suspending truth-telling, then it is morally justifiable and personal to do so.

3. *Some Other Biblical Examples* — There are numerous examples in the Scripture where a lower norm is broken in order to keep a

higher one. Jesus urged His followers to love God more than their parents. [7] The apostles sometimes found themselves in contention with the very human laws which they reminded their followers were ordained of God. [8] Jesus said that God desired mercy more than animal sacrifices and justice more than tithing. He said there were weightier matters of the law and there were greater sins. [9]

In the Old Testament the Hebrew midwives both disobeyed the king and lied to save innocent lives and God blessed them for it. Rahab told a lie to save the spies and the nation of Israel. Daniel and his friends disobeyed the law of the land and were preserved and blessed of God. [10] And even though not all of these are conflicts between two absolute moral laws (some of them being civil laws), nevertheless some of them are, and the rest illustrate the general hypothesis that lower principles (of whatever kind) ought to be "broken" when it is necessary to keep higher ones.

4. *Some Other Non-Biblical Illustrations* — The general thesis of ethical hierarchicalism can be illustrated by some ethical dilemmas from human experience in general. Most of these cases have been stated before but are repeated here to illustrate the hierarchical position in practice.

Therapeutic abortion can be justified on the grounds that saving an actual person (the mother) is more valuable than saving a potential person (the baby). The mother has both personhood and interpersonal relationships, the unborn baby has neither. And since the mother has the higher finite values which the baby does not, then the act of saving her life is intrinsically higher than that of saving the baby's.

We reject any such reasoning that would contend that if the mother were a bad person (morally, physically, etc.), then the baby should be saved, since it is a potentially good person. This position is utilitarian. It neglects the intrinsic value of personhood and judges according to whether or not the person happens to *do* good or bad things. Furthermore, there is no guarantee that the mother could not become a better person nor that the baby might not grow up to be a worse person than the mother. In order to justify saving the baby and sacrificing the mother on such a ground one would have to be omniscient. And playing God is a dangerous role! Finite man should content himself with doing what is intrinsically right and leave the consequences to God.

In the case of the overcrowded life-boat it is surely intrinsically

7 Matthew 10:37. In Matthew 12:5 Jesus said, "Or have you not read in the law how on the sabbath the priests profane the sabbath, *and are guiltless?*" [Emphasis added.]

8 Cf. Acts 4:19; 5:29; 1 Peter 2:13.

9 Matthew 12:7; 23:23; John 19:11.

10 Exodus 1:15-22; Joshua 2:5; Judges 11:31; Daniel 3 and 6.

right to save the most lives possible. Of course, one should always seek third alternatives. But if no one volunteers to leave and if after a vote is taken the losers still refuse to jump off, then it becomes the responsibility of the leader to do whatever is necessary to save as many lives as possible. And what must be done to save the maximum amount of lives is not wrong; it is morally *right*.

In the cases of lying and of having sexual relations outside of marriage for one's country, at least part of the problem cannot be answered until it is determined whether or not war is ever justifiable. This will be discussed in a later chapter. At this point it can be said that *if* a given war is justifiable on the grounds that it will save more persons and promote better interpersonal relations, then it is conceivable that lying and spying which are *necessary* to winning that war can be justified. But the problem is too complicated for any generalization here.

Mercy "killing" is another example of the conflict of moral principles. In the case where human "vegetables" are being kept alive by machines, the higher norm would seem to dictate turning off the switch. For in their case one is not perpetuating personhood in any meaningful sense of the word. It is an incomplete and destroyed person whose physical body is being forcibly kept in existence. If the possibility of personal relations with others has passed and if the persons related to the victim will relate better as persons because of it, then it would be better to withdraw the medicine or machine for the incurable patient and let him die. Of course, this is not really a killing (i.e., a *taking* of someone's life) which is being discussed, but rather allowing a merciful death to happen naturally (i.e., *letting* one die).

It goes without saying that letting a real person (or even a potential person) die without resisting would be morally wrong. The determining factor as to whether or not one is a "person" is whether or not they can function with some measure of self-consciousness and freedom. If they are subjects who can love and understand that they are being loved, then they are persons and ought to be kept alive as such at all cost. (This would certainly include retarded individuals.) Any deliberate interjection into their life system which would knowingly lead to their death would be morally wrong.

In the case of the man hopelessly caught in a burning airplane, one should *not* shoot him even if he requests it. There are other alternatives. First, the human body has a natural threshold of pain which takes one into unconsciousness when he is faced with more pain than he can bear. In the event of death by fire the fumes usually induce unconsciousness before the body suffers prolonged pain. Whatever outside help is available should be exerted in the direction of saving the man's life, or, if this is impossible, in making his death as painless as possible. Shooting a tranquilizer into his body would be an act of mercy. *Taking* his life in any way would be morally wrong; *letting* him die as mercifully as possible would not be morally wrong.

II. HIERARCHICALISM CRITICIZED

Illustrations of ethical hierarchicalism could be multiplied, but by now the reader can anticipate the conclusions. What is perhaps not yet perfectly clear is how it can be maintained that (1) a norm can be universal and unbreakable when it is sometimes right to break it, and (2) on what basis one is to determine which norms are higher and which are lower. These two points comprise the main criticisms against the hierarchical position.

A. What Is the Basis for Determining the Hierarchy of Values?

Many different value scales are possible. Why should one follow the arrangement of values suggested above? What is the basis for determining which norms are higher and which are lower? Do not different ethical hierachicalists hold to different orders of ethical priorities? The simplest way to reply is to acknowledge that many different value arrangements are possible but that not all of them are logically and morally consistent. It seems to this writer that the only consistent ethical positions are variations of a love ethic built on the intrinsic value of persons. And of the love ethics, the Christian love ethic is superior to other kinds of love ethics.

This may be defended on two grounds: intuitive and revelational.

1. *The Intuitive Basis of Ethical Hierarchicalism* — Rational and moral creatures know intuitively that love is to be preferred to hate and that some forms of love are higher than other forms. That love is intuitively understood as the basis for human relationships is strongly evidenced by its presence in all of the great ethical creeds from ancient to modern times. [11] As C. S. Lewis observed, no culture ever taught that it was right to rape or to be cruel to children. No ethical pronouncements ever held it to be right for a man to take *any* woman he wanted or to take any man's life he wished to take. No moral norms have been discovered anywhere which commend men for double-crossing their benefactors or breaking a promise any time they want to do so. [12] Rather than being vastly or totally different, most ethical creeds are quite similar. And at the core of their similarity is some kind of love norm. It is true that this is sometimes stated negatively as in the Confucian "Silver Rule," which says, "Do not do unto others what you would not have them do unto you." Sometimes it is stated positively as in the Christian Golden Rule, "Do unto others what you

[11] C. S. Lewis, *The Abolition of Man*, New York: The MacMillan Company, 1947.
[12] C. S. Lewis, *Mere Christianity*, New York: The MacMillan Company.

would have others do unto you." But in either case there is an implied respect for the other person.

So, too, are Kant's categorical imperatives and Buber's I-thou relation really love principles. [13] Both men clearly affirm that this rule means that others are to be treated as persons or ends and not as means or things. And this is precisely what love implies. Whether it be Buddhist compassion or Christian concern or general benevolence, there is an essential similarity of intent based on an intuitive recognition that others should be treated consistently with one's own basic desires. Of course, not everyone acts toward others in a way which is consistent with his own desires, and that leads to the next point.

Even *if* some men or some creeds would not recognize some form of the love principle, nevertheless they *ought* to do so. That is to say, they are morally inconsistent for not believing that they ought to love others. They want to be loved or treated as persons, and hence they *ought* to treat others this way. In other words, what a man *would* practice if he were consistent and what he *does* inconsistently believe may be different. But if men are consistent with their own basic desires and needs, they will believe in some form of the love norm. For all persons who recognize their personhood surely want to be treated as persons. And if they are convinced that personhood should be valued and respected in them, then they should value and respect it in others wherever it is found. What men *do* toward others or even what they *say* ought to be done toward others does not necessarily prove that this is what they *ought* to do or say. What is said and done can be a cover-up for negligence for one's basic duty to love others. In the final analysis, the intuitive proof for the love norm rests on the insistence of all men that *they* ought to be loved by others. From there it is a simple matter of consistency that everyone like *them* should also be loved. Hence, to deny the validity of extending the love norm to someone is tantamount to denying their personhood. (What implications for racial prejudice!)

Granting that the love norm is held (or *ought* to be) at least negatively and implicitly by all rational and moral beings, does it follow that the hierarchy of love's relationships is also known intuitively? Do men know intuitively that it is better to love God than man and better to save many lives than one, etc.? It may sound bold to venture a positive answer to these questions, especially in view of the fact that some men claim not even to believe in God, but this is precisely what is being suggested here. Perhaps this will be better understood if it is cast in hypothetical terms. That is, yes, everyone who believes God to be the ultimate source of all value also holds that it is better

[13] See chapter five above on Kant's categorical imperative.

to affirm His ultimate value than some lesser value when the two conflict. In other words, *if* there is an ultimate value (God or whatever), then men see intuitively that it is of more value than things which are less ultimate. Of course, if one has no ultimate value (and this is probably not possible),[14] then he has no conflict of the ultimate and the less than ultimate. But whenever men have ultimate values in view, then they see (or *ought* to see) that the ultimately valuable is more valuable than what is less than ultimately valuable. Furthermore, when there is an ultimately valuable or *best*, then there is immediately the grounds for rating everything else as better or proper in comparison to it. What is ultimately good makes it possible to grade everything else as more or less good by comparison, i.e., hierarchically.

Surely there are differences in value structures, even if these basic intuitively known distinctions be granted. But other than those culturally relative differences (which do not affect the basic norm involved), the significant differences are no doubt due to the fact that one position is worked out more consistently than another. The ethical hierarchicalism which is worked out most consistently with what men really intuit as right for themselves (and which, therefore, they *ought* to apply to other persons) is the one which best exemplifies the true hierarchy of values. It is the inconsistency of men which causes the confusion, not their basic intuitions or inclinations.

2. *The Revelational Basis for Ethical Hierarchicalism* — For those who, as this writer does, accept the Christian Scriptures as an authoritative revelation of God, there is yet another source for ethical hierarchicalism.[15] There are some decided advantages in a revelational approach to ethics. First, it is much more definitive than human intuition. For there are propositionally revealed rules of conduct such as the moral principles contained within the Ten Commandments. The Bible contains divinely inscripturated ethical norms. Furthermore, the Scriptures provide a hierarchical arrangement of norms. They reveal which norms are the higher principles and which, therefore, represent the greater values in life.

The first point to establish is that the Scriptures do present a hierarchy of moral values. This seems to be very clear from a number of passages as well as some direct implications. First, Jesus referred to some sins as *greater* than others. He said to Pilate, "Therefore he who delivered me to you has the greater sin." On another occasion

---

[14] Tillich argues convincingly that every man has something which he values ultimately. This object of one's ultimate concern may not really be of ultimate value in itself (it may be something finite), but it is at least held to have ultimate value by the individual. See Tillich's, *Dynamics of Faith*, New York, Harper & Row, Publishers, 1957, p. 106.

[15] See *General Introduction to the Bible*, Chicago: Moody Press, 1968, chs. 1 - 9 by Norman L. Geisler and William E. Nix.

Jesus compared tithing with justice and mercy, declaring the latter to be *"weightier* matters of the law." When asked which was the *greatest* commandment, Jesus unhesitatingly answered, "You shall love the Lord your God with all your heart, and with all your soul, and with all your mind. This is the great and first commandment." He did not say that it was the *only* commandment, but that it was the *first* commandment in importance. For Jesus added, "And a *second* is like it, You shall love your neighbor as yourself." In his famous Sermon on the Mount Jesus distinguished at least three degrees of ill will, saying, "Every one who is *angry* with his brother shall be liable to judgment; whoever *insults* his brother shall be liable to the council, and whoever says, 'You *fool!'* shall be liable to the hell of fire." Jesus even pronounced one sin as the very *worst:* the blasphemy of the Holy Spirit which will never be forgiven. [16]

The rest of the Bible, too, speaks of virtues and vices as better or worse. The apostle Paul, e.g., speaks of love as the *"greatest"* virtue. Elsewhere Paul refers to himself as the *"foremost* of sinners." And the entire legal system of the Old Testament is built on the fact that there are differing kinds of sins for which there are to be commensurate punishments. "An eye for an eye, a tooth for a tooth, and a life for a life," clearly indicates that sins were not all considered to be equal. Indeed, the whole concept of degrees of punishment for evildoing and degrees of rewards for doing good implies that there are different kinds of vices and virtues. "For he [God] will render to every man according to his works." [17]

In view of the clear teaching of Scripture that sins are not all equal, it is strange to hear Christians so often saying that all sins are alike to God. Sin is sin, they say. Little ones and big ones are all alike to God. Sometimes James 2:10 is cited in support of their position: "For whoever keeps the whole law but fails in one point has become guilty of all of it." But on closer examination this verse does not teach the *equality* of all sins but the *interrelatedness* of all sins. It says that the law is a unity and, therefore, it cannot be *partially* broken. When someone breaks even one tiny point, he is a law breaker. All sin is sin, no matter how small a sin it might be. But not all sins are equally sinful. Some sins are worse than others.

Sometimes one hears a more sophisticated attempt to defend the equality of all sins by arguing that sins differ in the *amount* of sins involved but not in *kind.* Supposedly this would account for calling some sins greater (being greater in quantity but not in quality) and for making some punishments worse than others. But if this were so, some serious consequences would follow. Five little lies would be

[16] John 19:11; Matthew 23:23; 22:37, 38; 5:22; 12:32 [Emphases added].
[17] 1 Corinthians 13:13; 1 Timothy 1:15; Romans 2:6.

worse than one big murder. If sins differ only in quantity but not quality, then stealing an apple five times would be worse than committing adultery once or twice, and so on. Surely, such a ridiculous position is to be emphatically rejected. Sins do differ in kind and quality. Some things are intrinsically worse than others. Likewise, some acts are intrinsically better than others. And in every situation one ought to do what is the morally best thing to do. Certainly those who allegedly believe in the equality of all sins would rather have someone take their money many times over than take their life once.

In a kind of inexplicable "last ditch" stand for the equality of all sins, it has been contended that one sin is worse than another (even though it is equal in kind) because this sin will involve or lead to a greater amount of sins. But the apparent plausibility of this position fades quickly when applied to the facts. The facts are that some very *big* sins do not necessarily entail many other sins, and some very *little* sins often do entail many more of their kind and worse. Examples of the former are easy to find. Betraying Christ (which, incidentally, Jesus said was a great sin) [18] did not lead to many sins. It led to a few more (e.g., Pilate's, the crucifier's, etc.), but not many. In fact most of the sins it led to ended rather quickly when Christ died. It did not lead to many more sins in Judas, perhaps only one big one (suicide). [19] In any event, betraying Christ should have been (if all sins are equal) a relatively small sin, not entailing too many more sins. But Jesus declared it to be one of the *worst* of all sins. He implied it was greater than Pilate's sin, and he said of Judas, "It would have been good for that man if he had not been born." What a sin! And what is true of Judas' sin is true of many of the best-planned and most malicious murders. They do not really lead to many more sins, especially if the murderer is apprehended. But some of these kinds of quiet murders are among the most heinous crimes men have committed.

On the other hand, few sins are as contagious as the "harmless" little lie. One lie leads to another in an endless way. One little lie leads to many more little lies. But often the sum total of little lies does not equal one brutal bullet which strikes down a great civil rights leader. Surely a hundred "white" lies are not as bad as assassinating one dedicated young president.

In brief, there is simply no evidence from Scripture or from human experience that all sins are equal in kind and differ only in the amount of sins they entail. Nor is there any indication that all virtues are equal in quality and differ only in quantity. Certainly it should not be argued that giving a dollar each to one hundred beggars is equal to

---

[18] Matthew 26:24.

[19] In fact, betraying Christ led, strangely enough, to the greatest good men have ever known, salvation from their sins.

the intrinsic value of sacrificing one's life for a friend. Jesus said, "*Greater* love has no man than this, that a man lay down his life for his friends." [20] He certainly did not mean that such an act had a great *quantity* of love in it. Love is a quality, not a quantity, and this is the greatest *kind* of love one can exercise.

B. *How Can a Norm Be Transcended and Still Be Universal?*

Another criticism which is often leveled at ethical hierarchicalism is that it wants to have its cake (of ethical absolutes) and eat it too (i.e., be able to break them for higher norms). How can a norm such as truth-telling be unbreakable if it is sometimes to be broken in order to save a life? Either the norm of truth-telling is not really universal but has exceptions or else it should never be broken. "Unbreakable norms which can be broken" is a contradiction in terms.

This is a serious criticism, and it deserves a straightforward answer. In brief, the answer is this. When one obeys a higher norm in favor of a lower and opposing one, he is not really breaking the lower one but transcending it. He is not making an exception to the lower norm but getting an exemption from it in view of a superior obligation. And even when it is transcended, the lower norm remains intact as a universal.

1. *Higher Norms Transcend But Do Not Abolish Lower Norms* — The most direct answer as to how a norm can be unbreakable when it can be broken in favor of a higher norm is to point out that it is not really *broken;* it is *transcended.* When one's obedience to God necessitates disobedience to his parents, he is not really breaking the law of filial piety. The law is still there; it still holds at all times and places. It is simply that on occasions a higher law overshadows this lower law. But when the lower law is overpowered by a higher, the former is not abolished; it is merely surpassed. Likewise, when the love of God clashes with the love of man, then the latter must be suspended for the former. But when a lower principle or norm is suspended, it is not really broken. The higher dethrones the lower but it does not destroy it.

There are several senses in which the lower norm is not really *broken* by higher norms. First of all, the strength and validity of the lower norm is there before, during, and after the conflict. That is precisely what occasions the conflict. If the lower norm did not maintain *its own* universal validity, then there would be no tension with the higher norms. This means that it is always wrong to disobey the lower principle *as such.* However, this does not mean that the lower norm, without sacrificing its own validity *as such,* cannot be sacrificed *as superseded* by a higher norm. In other words, the lower norm is universal in its own domain, as far as that goes. The lower norms

[20] John 15:13.

are absolutely binding on the relationship they cover, as long as that relationship does not overlap with another binding relationship. And when there is such a conflict of binding relationships, then the *most* binding relationship ought to prevail. But each universal ethical norm is absolutely and universally binding in its own sphere unless it is transcended by a higher norm.

2. *There Are Exemptions From Lower Norms But No Exceptions to Them* — Another way to answer the problem as to how lower norms may be transcended by higher norms without destroying the universal validity of the lower norms is to point out the difference between an *exemption* and an *exception*. The generalist, it will be remembered, argued that there are exceptions to norms. Norms are not really universal because there are times when they do not really apply. Not so for ethical hierarchicalism. The absolute norms always apply; there are no exceptions. They are truly universally binding on that particular relationship as such. But what is universally binding on a given relationship as such does not preclude the possibility that there may be a pre-emptory relationship which conflicts with it. And it is in view of the possibility (and actuality) of conflicting human relationships that the hierarchical arrangement of norms is necessary. But in the hierarchy of duties exceptions are not made to lower duties when the exemptions are given. One is exempt *if and only if* there is a higher, overriding responsibility which temporarily excuses him from his lower duty. The lower duty is still there, and there are no exceptions to it. One must always follow even the lower norm as such.

An example may help to clarify this point. When Bucher lied to save the lives of his crew, the norm of truth-telling was not broken by the norm of life-saving. It is *always* wrong to tell a lie as such. It is always wrong, i.e., *unless* some other responsibility transcends it. A lie in itself is never right; it is never justifiable. But a lie necessitated by the duty to save lives is justified.

It must be pointed out here that this is *not* what is commonly meant by "the end justifies the means." Ethical hierarchicalism is not a utilitarian ethic; it is a deontological ethic built on intrinsic values. A lie should never be told simply because of the supposed good results one can foresee it should bring. The end does not justify the means in a utilitarian sense of the word "end." The means (e.g., lying) is not justified by the end (i.e., the saved lives). The lives may not be saved; the lie might not work. It is not utilitarian *ends* which can justify lying, but hierarchical *norms* can justify it. That is, one should never break an ethical norm representing an intrinsically valuable act for the mere intrinsic value of bringing more pleasure to more men. But one should break a norm representing a lower value in favor of a norm representing a higher value when the two are in irresolvable conflict. So the *end* does not justify the means of breaking norms, but higher *norms* do justify the means of superseding lower norms.

3. *Absolute Norms Are Universal Only in Their Context* — If lower ethical norms can be transcended by higher ones without incurring guilt for not following the lower ones, then it follows that these lower norms are not universal in the broadest sense of the word. They are universal only in their context. They cover everything *in their area*. That is, lower ethical norms cannot be universally universal but only locally universal. They are valid *on their particular relationship* but not on all relationships. There are no legitimate exceptions to an ethical absolute, but not all absolutes are absolutely absolute. Some are only relatively absolute, i.e., absolute relative to their particular area. Obviously, there can be only one thing which is absolute in the full and final sense of that word (viz., God). However, this does not mean that there are not many norms (from God) which can be absolute *in a given context*. In fact, this is precisely what ethical hierarchicalism is, a form of contextual absolutism. However, it is not a non-conflicting contextual absolutism which holds that the contexts never overlap. [21] According to hierarchicalism, there are some irresolvable conflicts of contexts which can be resolved by the fact that different contexts or relationships are higher or lower than others.

Let us be a bit more specific. Within the context of a truth relation with other persons one ought never to lie. That is, as far as the truth relation is concerned, it is final. But when by the interjection of a life relation a conflict is engendered, then one is no longer dealing with single relationships. In this event, what is binding so far as a single relationship is concerned is not binding outside of that single relationship. Truth-telling is an inviolable obligation so far as that single relationship is concerned. But when there is an intermingling of relationships, then one ought to obey the higher one. Or, to take another example, *insofar as* one's relationship to his neighbor's property goes, he ought not take it without permission. But if by grabbing the neighbor's water hose without permission he can save his children from burning to death, who would say he has done an evil? On the contrary, by fulfilling his duty to his children he has done a greater good, even though he took his neighbor's water hose without permission. Likewise, one ought never intentionally take the life of another human being *insofar as* he has a single uncomplicated relation with that person. If however, that person is threatening the lives of innocent children and there is no other way to dissuade him, then it is morally justifiable to take the would-be murderer's life.

[21] Non-conflicting absolutism was discussed in chapter five.

In summary, ethical hierarchicalism holds that there are no exceptions to ethical absolutes, even though there are some exemptions in view of higher obligations. Each absolute norm is universal in its own context as to the particular relationship it covers. But contexts do conflict, and a hierarchical arrangement of values is the way to resolve those conflicts without having to hold the individual morally responsible for something he could not avoid.

III. ETHICAL HIERARCHICALISM: A SYNTHESIS OF THE OTHER POSITIONS

In view of the above explanation of the hierarchical position as compared to the other positions on ethical norms, it should be apparent that there are significant similarities. In fact, each one of the other positions stresses an essential truth which finds its best exemplification in the hierarchical position. No one of the other positions is without some truth, and the essential truth of each of the other views is best synthesized in ethical hierarchicalism.

A. *Antinomianism: Stressing Personal Responsibility*

The existential antinomians (see chapter two) were wrong insofar as they denied objective norms, but they were right in emphasizing both freedom and personal responsibility. Without freedom there is no individual responsibility. Because man is free he can be held accountable for his own choices. And not only is man responsible for his own choices but he is responsible to choose for others. Since man is free he should respect not only his own freedom but also the freedom of others. This would mean that others should be treated as subjects and not objects, and that is the heart of the Christian love ethic. If carried through consistently, the existential stress on personal freedom and responsibility would be identical to the hierarchical position on the value of persons over things.

The mistake among some existentialists, however, is in assuming that men do not have an ethical *obligation* to choose for others or to treat them as ends and not means. For if men have no moral *duty* to love others as themselves, they will not be bound to do it. And without the binding responsibility to love others there can be no accountability when men hate each other. And without accountability for moral negligence, society is not possible. Love cannot be forced but it can be enforced. That is, men cannot be forced against their will to love someone else, but they can be penalized when they do not love others (at least in the negative and overt senses of the word love). Love cannot be compelled, but it is commanded. Men *ought* to love one another whether they *choose* to or not. That is, love is an objectively imposed duty and not, as some existentialists say, a mere subjectively chosen desire or project.

B. *Situationism: Stressing the Absolute Duty of Love*

That love is the one absolute norm for conduct is stressed most emphatically by situationism (see chapter two) and rightly so. Certainly agapic love is the only ethical norm which is truly ultimate, consistent, and not eventually self-destructive. Love is absolute and beyond moral appeal. And unless men love each other as persons they cannot really relate as persons at all. For love is the only personal way to relate to other persons. Treating persons as things is a travesty of personhood. So the love situationist is right: there is really only one thing which is ultimate and absolute — *love* (and, it may be added, love is of God, for God is love).

What the situationist does not perceive, however, is that love has *many* relationships and that each of these is binding in its context. For example, love may be related to things, to potential persons, to incomplete persons, to complete persons, and to infinite personhood. Each of these relationships in and of itself is binding and inviolable. But when there is a conflict among these love relations, then the latter (i.e., higher) love relationships transcend the former (i.e., lower) ones. For instance, on the first ethical norm men ought to love things only as means but never as ends. And when the love for some thing becomes either an end in itself, or when it conflicts with love for some person (who *is* an end in himself), then the latter norm supersedes the former. The same holds true right·on up the whole hierarchy of norms: the higher love relationship always surpasses the lower one. So love relationships are absolute and binding in themselves wherever they are found, and higher love relationships always transcend lower ones whenever there is a complexity of duties. Hence, the hierarchical love scale best explains love's conflicting duties.

C. *Generalism: The Struggle for Universal Norms*

Within generalism can be witnessed the struggle to attain universal norms. From the normative function of the end (i.e., the greatest good for the greatest number) in determining which means are best, to the normative function of the "fund" of human experience in determining what the end or results might be, there is an evident move toward ethical norms. Furthermore, the finality of the end and the alleged unbreakability of some norms manifests a tendency in the direction of some universal norms. Despite the fact that the norms offered even by the rule-utilitarians were really less than truly universally representative of intrinsic values, there is evidenced both a marked tendency toward some kind of intrinsic values and toward some principles which ought never be broken.

Another point at which generalism is tangential to the hierarchical synthesis appears when it speaks of defining the legitimate exceptions to ethical norms. For it is only an indefinable or unspecifiable exception to a rule which is really an exception. Exceptions which are definable in advance are not really exceptions at all; they are merely specifications as to precisely how far the context of the rule really extends. In other words, a well-defined relationship which has no unspecified exceptions would be just as universal as hierarchical norms which are held to be universal only *in their context*. So the point at which generalists are seeking for norms which are so well-defined that they admit of no further exceptions and the point at which hierarchicalists posit norms which are universal in context are not so distant from each other as may first appear. The basic difference at this point is that hierarchicalism sees that universal norms represent acts which are universally valid *because they have intrinsic value*. This is a much firmer foundation for universal norms than the mere utilitarian fact that these particular acts are always *found* by experience to bring better results. Experience may change and exceptions may yet be found, and then the norm is no longer universal. A deontological norm, on the other hand, is always right to follow as such because that is always a valuable act to perform. And we may assume that because it is a valuable act it will bring the greatest good in the long run.

D. *Pluralistic Absolutism: Maintaining Absolute Norms*

Common to the three pluralistic absolutisms discussed above (chapters five, six, and seven) is the desire to maintain (consistently) many universal norms. Non-conflicting absolutism attempts to do this by defining the various norms so that they never actually overlap. But as helpful as definition is to understanding the true context of a given norm, there are two reasons why this solution is not as adequate as hierarchicalism. First, even after a reasonable redefinition of norms, there are still irresolvable conflicts among norms, as has been amply illustrated already. Second, if one continues to redefine until there is no conflict at all, he soon discovers that there is no norm left, either. In other words, the unbreakable norm is defined away so that it will not be found in conflict with other unbreakable norms. In brief, the absolute norms suffer in this way an eventual death by a thousand qualifications.

The ideal absolutists, also to be commended for their attempt to maintain many absolutes, recognize rightly that there are conflicts between ethical norms no matter how carefully they are defined. However, their attempt to resolve the conflict by appealing to results as a guide in determining which norm-breaking is a lesser evil has two problems. First, if this is meant in a utilitarian sense, then they have departed from a deontological stand on intrinsically good acts to a utilitarian quest for extrinsically good ends. It would be far more consistent to resolve the conflict between norms by judging which norm is intrinsically higher than the other norm. But the very thing which makes this solution better is its hierarchical arrangement of values. In other words, when ideal absolutism becomes consistent with intrinsic values, it becomes ethical hierarchicalism.

This leaves but one basic difference between these two remaining kinds of pluralistic absolutism. Ideal absolutism holds the individual morally guilty for breaking lower ethical norms in order to keep higher ones and ethical hierarchicalism does not. The former contends that when universal norms conflict, one should do the lesser evil, and the latter holds that it is not an evil at all; it is the greatest good. In this difference the hierarchical position is preferable since it shows how the universality of the norms can be preserved, and, what is more, i retains the fact of moral responsibility. In other words, hierarchicalism both maintains the many inviolable relationships of love and at the same time holds that the most loving thing to do is the morally *right* course of action. No one is held morally guilty, as in ideal absolutism, for performing the most loving act possible under the circumstances. Thus hierarchicalism is the best synthesis of the tendencies and emphases of the other positions.

PART TWO
ETHICAL ISSUES

The first section of this book examined the basic alternatives in ethics and opted for a Christian ethical position built on the hierarchical arrangement of the many relationships of love. This position was founded both on a general intuitive basis, and on the revelation of the Christian Scriptures.

Assuming the Christian ethic of many absolute duties of love, the second section of this book will attempt to face some of the major contemporary ethical issues. Throughout this section an effort will be made to unfold the social implications of the basic ethical position of ethical hierarchicalism as revealed in the Christian Scriptures.

What is the role of self-love in Christian ethics? Is war ever the loving thing to do? What is the Christian's social responsibility? Is abortion ever morally justifiable? How does the Christian love ethic apply to sexual relationships? What implications does the Christian love ethic have for race relationships? For ecology? These are some of the pressing ethical questions which call for an answer. The following pages suggest how a Christian might respond.

8 / The Christian and Self-Love

There are several reasons for beginning this section with an analysis of the ethic of self-love. First, the topic has assumed greater significance because of the contemporary emphasis on self-love as the basis of a sound psychological and even social life. Second, because the Christian teaching of self-denial and self-hatred has come under attack for promoting many of today's psychological and social problems. Third, at the heart of the Christian ethic is the fact that he is commanded: "Love your neighbor *as yourself.*" Does this imply a Christian should love himself and then love others as he loves himself? If so, then why are selfishness and lovers of self condemned in Scripture? Is not self-love a form of pride which is man's most basic sin?

Caught somewhere between the extremes of selfish egoism and selfless altruism, the Christian ethic struggles to discover the role of self-love. What is a Christian ethic of self-love? Is there any legitimate role for self-love? To focus the problem it will be profitable first to survey the spectrum of opinion on self-love which makes the issue so crucial for contemporary Christian ethics.

I. THE SPECTRUM OF OPINION ON SELF-LOVE

The one thing on which much of ethical opinion is in agreement is that there is a legitimate sense of self-love. The variation of opinion is on the sense in which self-love is right and on the *reason* one ought to love himself. On the humanistic end are those who stress the ultimate value of the individual as the reason for self-love. Opposed to this is the Christian teaching on the depravity of man which is often

139

taken to be the basis on which a man should hate his sinful self. There are several other positions which shade off in between these two extremes. The positions outlined here will begin at the egoistic extreme and will be classified on the basis of the reason given for a legitimate kind of self-love. We will begin with one of the more radical egoisms of our day, the ethic of self-interest represented by Ayn Rand.

A. *Ayn Rand: Loving One's Self for Its Own Sake*

Traditionally moralists argued over whether one should sacrifice his life for God or for other men, says Rand. "And no one came to say that your life belongs to you and that the good is to live it." No one saw that "by the grace of reality and the nature of life, man — every man — is an end in himself, he exists for his own sake, and the achievement of his own happiness is his highest moral purpose." The purpose of morality is not to teach one to suffer for others and die, but to enjoy himself and to live. [1]

1. *No Obligation to Others* — What moral obligation does one have to other men? "None — except the obligation I owe to myself, to material objects and to all of existence. . . . It is only with their mind that I can deal and only for my own self-interest, when they see that my interest coincides with theirs." Self-interest — enlightened reasonable self-interest — is the ultimate norm of interhuman relations. Man is not his brother's keeper. He owes his neighbor nothing. The neighbor owes him nothing. "I seek or desire nothing from them [i.e., neighbors]," says Rand, "except such relations as they care to enter of their own voluntary choice." Men are not duty-bound to help each other. [2]

But "so long as men desire to live together, no man may initiate . . . the use of physical force against others." If there are aggressors, then the enlightened self-interest of individuals may justifiably lead them together in mutual self-defense. Such a mutual compact is not a moral duty but a voluntary choice, engaged in not to help others but to protect one's own self-interest. Hence, "the only proper purpose of a government is to protect man's rights, which means: to protect him from physical violence. A proper government is only a policeman, acting as an agent of man's self-defense. . . ." [3]

2. *Sacrificing for Others Is a Morality of the Immoral* — "The creed of sacrifice is a morality for the immoral — a morality that declares its own bankruptcy by confessing that it can't impart to men any personal stake in virtues or values. . . ." Why is it immoral to produce a value and keep it, but moral to give it away? asks Rand, "And if

---

[1] Ayn Rand, *For the New Intellectual,* New American Library, 1961, pp. 120, 123.

[2] *Ibid.,* p. 133.

[3] *Ibid.,* pp. 134, 183.

it is not moral for you to keep a value, why is it moral for others to accept it?" For "if you are selfless and virtuous when you give it, are they not selfish and vicious when they take it?" [4]

There is no virtue in sacrifice as such. "Who is the conqueror of physical reality," Rand asks, "the man who sleeps on a bed of nails or the man who sleeps on an innerspring mattress?" The triumph of man's spirit is not a germ-eaten hovel on the Ganges but a skyline apartment on the Atlantic. Suffering for others has no value. One has no duty to sacrifice for other men. The only time it is right to help other men is "if such is your own desire based on your own selfish pleasure in the value of his person and his struggle." Man is not "a sacrificial animal who exists for the pleasure of others. Fight for the value of your person. Fight for the virtue of your pride," [5] she urges.

3. *Help Only Those Who Deserve and Pay for Your Help* — Suffering as such has no value; only the fight against suffering is valuable. "If you choose to help a man who suffers, do it only on the ground of his virtues . . .; then your action is still a trade, and his virtue is the payment for your help," Rand writes. "But to help a man who has no virtues, to help him on the ground of his suffering as such, to accept his faults, his need, as a claim — is to accept the mortgage of a zero on your values." [6] We are not morally indebted to any man. Whatever help is offered to others is voluntary and ought to be given only if we are repaid for it with some pleasure or value for ourselves.

No value is higher than self-esteem. All who esteem others better than themselves are fighting for a creed of self-destruction. The very fact that even those who hold to a creed of self-sacrifice manifest a need for self-esteem is a testimony within their soul for the truth of the virtue of selfishness. The only things or persons for which one ought to sacrifice or pay are worthy or valuable ones. One should not help another person for nothing, especially an unworthy person. [7]

4. *One Should Love Only What Has Value* — Rand criticizes traditional morality as one which divorces love from values and gives to a vagrant, not in response to his worth, but in response to his need. It is wrong to give alms instead of a reward. One ought to make payments for virtues, but one ought not give blank checks on vices. A man should be loved for his virtues, nothing else.

Just "as there can be no causeless wealth, so there can be no causeless love or any sort of causeless emotion." And "the man who tells you that it is possible to value without values, to love those whom you appraise as worthless, is the man who tells you that it is possible to

---

[4] *Ibid.*, pp. 141, 144.
[5] *Ibid.*, pp. 180, 192.
[6] *Ibid.*, p. 180.
[7] *Ibid.*, p. 176.

grow rich by consuming without producing and that paper money is as valuable as gold." Value is the cause of love. Things and persons are to be loved if they have value and for no other reason. [8]

5. *One's Self Is His Most Basic Value* — The most basic value a man possesses is his own self. The belief in the superiority of others is the beginning of faith in the supernatural. "When a mystic declares that he feels the existence of a power superior to reason, he feels it all right," says Rand, "but that power is not an omniscient super-spirit of the universe, it is the consciousness of any passer-by to whom he has surrendered his own." [9] Whether superiority is attributed to a supposed God or to other men makes little difference; both are wrong. One's own autonomous, rational self is his most basic value. Self-love is not only morally right but morally required. The self is good and valuable and, therefore, ought to be loved.

Rand singles out the doctrine of original sin for special criticism in contrast to her belief in the value of human nature. "A sin without volition is a slap at morality and an insolent contradiction in terms: that which is outside the possibility of choice is outside the province of morality." For "if man is evil by birth, he has no will, no power to change it; if he has no will, he can be neither good nor evil; a robot is amoral." Further, "to hold, as man's sin, a fact not open to his voice is a mockery of morality. To hold man's nature as his sin is a mockery of nature." And "to punish him for a crime he committed before he was born is a mockery of justice. To hold him guilty in a matter where no innocence exists is a mockery of reason." Furthermore, to hide behind the evasion that man is born with a free will but also with a tendency to evil is cowardly. "A free will saddled with a tendency is like a game with loaded dice." For "it forces man to struggle through the effort of playing, to bear responsibility and pay for the game but the decision is weighed in favor of a tendency that he has no power to escape." In brief, "if the tendency is of his choice, he cannot possess it at birth; if it is not of his choice, his will is not free." [10]

Man ought to love himself because the self is intrinsically valuable. Man is an end in himself. Therefore, man ought to love himself for his own sake. There is virtue in self-love, because there is virtue in the rational self. And one ought to love the value in his own self above all else.

B. *Erich Fromm: Loving the Self As a Representative of Mankind*

Erich Fromm, as opposed to Rand's loving oneself for the sake of loving oneself, contends that one should love himself as a represen-

[8] *Ibid.*, p. 147.
[9] *Ibid.*, p. 161.
[10] *Ibid.*, pp. 136-137.

tative of mankind. Fromm sees this as the essence of a humanistic religion, which in opposition to traditional authoritarian religions, affirms mankind (but not the individual man) as the object of religious commitment.

1. *Authoritarian Versus Humanistic Religion* — According to Fromm, "the study of man permits us to recognize that the need for a common system of orientation and for an object of devotion is deeply rooted in the conditions of human existence." Consequently, "there is no one without a religious need, a need to have a frame of orientation and an object of devotion." Therefore, "the question is not *religion or not* but *which kind of religion*, whether it is one furthering man's development, the unfolding of his specifically human powers, or one paralyzing them." [11]

Basically, there are two kinds of religions, authoritarian and humanistic. The difference between them is not simply that the former stresses that man is controlled by a higher power outside himself. "What makes it so is the idea that his power, because of the control it exercises, is *entitled* to 'obedience, reverence and worship.'" Fromm stresses the word "entitled" to show that the reason for the worship in authoritarian religions is not in the moral qualities of the deity (as love or justice) but in the fact that it has power to force man to worship. So "the essential element in authoritarian religion and the authoritarian religious experience is surrender to a power transcending man." The main virtue of authoritarianism is obedience and the cardinal sin is disobedience. For Fromm authoritarianism is not teaching humility but humiliation; it is masochistic and self-destructive to one's humanity. Man must not be made more dependent; he must become more independent. Fromm sees two basic fallacies in authoritarian religion: (1) man's indulging in a sense of dependence on forces outside him, and (2) positing a power beyond man simply because man has an ineradicable longing to transcend himself. [12]

Humanistic religion, on the contrary, views God as a symbol of man's higher self and not an outside being. "God is not a symbol of power over man but of man's own power." For "in humanistic religion God is the image of man's higher self, a symbol of what man potentially is or ought to become. . . ." So "man's aim in humanistic religion is to achieve the greatest strength, not the greatest powerlessness; virtue is self-realization, not obedience." Hence, the prevailing mood of humanistic religion is not guilt and sorrow but joy. [13]

2. *Self-Love Is Basic to Humanistic Religion* — Since God is the symbol of man's higher self, not a being external to man, the love of

[11] Erich Fromm, *Psychoanalysis and Religion*, New Haven: Yale University Press, 1967, p. 26.

[12] *Ibid.*, pp. 34-35, 53-54.

[13] *Ibid.*, pp. 49, 54, 87.

God is a symbol for the love of man. In Fromm's words, "God's love is a symbol for love out of strength and not out of weakness (i.e., to love from the fullness of one's personality)." So the real question is not atheism vs. theism but the love of mankind under the symbol "God" or surrender to a supernatural sovereign. The former is a truly humanistic religion, and the latter is idolatry. The true love of "God" is the love of mankind, i.e., the love of the highest and best that is man's. So "the command to 'Love thy neighbor as thyself' is, with only slight variation in its expression, the basic principle common to all humanistic religions." [14]

To love "God" is to love man. But one is to love other men *as he loves himself*. That means that self-love is at the very basis of the religious experience. "Furthermore, anyone who loves his neighbor but does not love himself shows that the love of his neighbor is not genuine." For "love is based on an attitude of affirmation and respect, and if this attitude does not exist toward oneself, who is after all only another human being and another neighbor, it does not exist at all." In other words, if one cannot love himself, then he cannot love another man, for humanity is found just as truly in himself as it is found in other men. The failure to love oneself is at the basis of unhappiness and mental illness. Therefore, "sin is not primarily sin against God but sin against ourselves." Unless a man has a sense of responsibility for other men built on a healthy respect for his own person, he is not fulfilling his religious duty. [15]

3. *Loving Oneself for Humanistic Reasons* — For Fromm, the reason for loving oneself is not the same as it is for Rand. One is not to love his self merely for its own sake; one is to love himself as a representative of mankind. That is, the individual self is not an ultimate end in itself. It is only part of a collective whole, the highest of which is to be respected as "God." It is selfish and wrong for the individual to consider himself an ultimate end. However, insofar as the individual is a part of mankind and insofar as mankind is a worthy object of religious devotion, a man ought to love himself as a concrete example of his worth. For "if it is a virtue to love my neighbor as a human being it must be a virtue — and not a vice — to love myself since I am a human being too." [16] To deny the value of manhood anywhere — in oneself or in another — is a sin against humanity, yes, a sin against "God." To affirm the value of oneself as a part of the totality of humanity is to affirm what is of ultimate value (viz., the human). That is to say, in loving one's own humanity one is loving "God," for "God" is by definition that which is ultimately valuable in mankind.

14 *Ibid.*, pp. 113, 114, 86.
15 *Ibid.*, pp. 86, 87, 88.
16 Erich Fromm, *Man for Himself*, Rinehart, 1947.

In brief, for Fromm self-love is not only an exercise in therapeutic psychology; it is also a manifestation of religious devotion. For in loving oneself, one is loving a representative of "God." Self-love, then, is not an end in itself. One is loving himself, not for the sake of loving himself; one is loving himself because, thereby, he is loving mankind representatively.

C. Paul Tillich: Loving Self as an Affirmation of Being

Basically, Paul Tillich agrees with Fromm that "the right self-love and the right love of others are interdependent, and that selfishness and the abuse of others are equally interdependent." [17]

1. Self-Love Is Self-Affirmation — True self-love and love of others are interrelated because it is a virtue to affirm oneself. However, it must be recognized, said Tillich, that "self-centeredness is not selfishness, self-determination is not sinfulness." It is time to end the moral indignation at every word which has "self" in it. In fact, "even moral indignation would not exist without a centered self and ontological self-affirmation." That is, when one affirms himself he is affirming being or reality. And everyone who lives creatively affirms himself as a participant in the meaning of reality. "He affirms himself as receiving and transforming reality creatively." For example, "the scientist loves both the truth he discovers and himself insofar as he discovers it. . . ." [18]

What a man affirms in self-love is his own being. "We have defined courage," Tillich wrote, "as the self-affirmation of being in spite of non-being. The power of this self-affirmation is the power of being which is effective in every act of courage." Of course, this "self-affirmation in spite of the anxiety of guilt and condemnation presupposes participation in something which transcends the self." That is, man is not affirming himself as Being itself. The individual is not all there is to reality. Being transcends man's being. But in affirming his own being — i.e., by having the courage to be — man is affirming his participation in being itself. [19]

2. Self-Love Is Not Selfishness — Despite Tillich's approval of an ontological self-love — i.e., an affirmation of one's being by participation in being itself — Tillich desired to avoid the morally bad connotations of selfishness. True self-love or self-affirmation is a guarantee against selfishness. "And if this self-love does not exist, we become 'selfish,' because selfishness and disgust toward oneself are one and the same thing." On the other hand, "the right self-love is self-affirmation, in the sense in which God sees us, or the sense in which we are

[17] Paul Tillich, The Courage to Be, New Haven, Conn.: Yale University Press, 1952, p. 22.
[18] Ibid., pp. 87, 46.
[19] Ibid., pp. 172, 165.

essentially created." In other words, the proper kind of self-love of oneself as a creature of God, as a participant in being. [20]

There is a wrong kind of self-love. In fact, the wrong kind of self-love is so common that Tillich was led to say in later years (in contrast to his own earlier usage of it): "The term 'self-love' I reject completely." Following Augustine, he made a distinction between ordered and unordered self-love. "Unordered self-love is what we would call selfishness today, and ordered self-love is what I call 'self-affirmation' simply in order to avoid a very misleading term. . . ." Tillich quotes Jesus' command to love others *as oneself,* saying, "This means that he presupposes, without saying it directly, that there is a natural self-affirmation in a person which should not prevent the affirmation of others. . . ." In brief, loving oneself should not be done at others' expense; that would be selfish. As a matter of fact, the highest form of love toward oneself is not mere self-affirmation but self-acceptance. This is "self-acceptance in spite of." It means to have the right love toward oneself. In order to avoid confusion, says Tillich, "I would not call it self-love, but self-acceptance, because it is the acceptance of being accepted." This is not attained naturally but by "faith." [21]

3. *Self-Love and Humanism* — This does not mean that humanism is necessarily contrary to faith or to a proper kind of self-love. If one's faith is in actual, finite man as he is, then this kind of humanism is contrary to faith. "However, if faith is understood as the state of being ultimately concerned about the ultimate, humanism implies faith." That is, humanism is compatible with faith if man is taken in an ideal sense in his true essence. In this sense, "for humanism the divine is manifest in the human; the ultimate concern of man is man." The humanist finds the depth of his concern within man and not beyond his world as the mystics do. Hence, the humanist's faith is called "secular" as opposed to "religious." [22]

The important thing for Tillich, however, is not whether the object of one's faith or ultimate concern is within man or beyond man but whether the object is truly ultimate. No finite reality should be the considered ultimate. This would be idolatry. Only what is infinite or truly ultimate is worthy of an ultimate affirmation. In other words, no finite man should be the object of our ultimate concern, whether this finite object be oneself or others. Self-love is legitimate only if it affirms the self (or others) as participating in what transcends the limited. [23] To affirm oneself (or others) as more than a finite participant in the infinite is improper self-love or selfishness. In other words,

[20] Paul Tillich, *Ultimate Concern,* pp. 48, 206.
[21] *Ibid.,* p. 206.
[22] Paul Tillich, *Dynamics of Faith,* pp. 62, 63.
[23] Paul Tillich, *Ultimate Concern,* pp. 12, 24.

Tillich believes that a man ought to love himself as a finite participant in being but not as Being itself.

D. Sören Kierkegaard: Loving Oneself Selflessly

Self-love has a curious status in the thinking of the Danish father of existentialism. One ought to love himself, according to Kierkegaard, but he ought to love himself in an unselfish way. In and of itself, self-love is selfish, and the biblical command to love others *as oneself* is really directed at eliminating self-love.

1. *Loving Oneself the Wrong Way* — Kierkegaard admits that the command, "'Thou shalt love thy neighbor as thyself,' . . . contains *the presupposition that every man loves himself.*" However, he asks, "Could anyone misunderstand this, as if it were the intention of Christianity to hold self-love in honor?" "On the contrary," he writes, "it is its intention to strip us of our selfishness. This selfishness consists in loving one's self." Indeed, the very reason for including "as thyself" in the command is to wrench all selfishness from one's hand. When the commandment is rightly understood, it says, "'Thou shalt love thyself in the right way.' If anyone, therefore, will not learn from Christianity to love *himself* in the right way, then neither can he love his neighbor." For "to love oneself in the right way to love one's neighbors are absolutely analogous concepts, are at bottom one and the same." And "when the 'as thyself' of the commandment has taken from you the selfishness which Christianity, sad to say, must presuppose as existing in every human being, then you have rightly learned to love yourself." Hence the law is this: "You shall love yourself as you love your neighbor when you love him as yourself." [24]

2. *Loving Oneself the Right Way* — But what is the *right* way to love oneself? When all of the dialectical subtleties of Kierkegaard's restatement of the commandment are unwound, the answer in one word is "unselfishly." The selfish man wastes time on vain and unimportant projects. He frivolously abandons himself to the folly of a moment. The selfish person may even wish, in a moment of melancholy, to be done with life. Some selfish men even torment themselves, thinking their torture is a divine service. In brief, a man ought to love *himself*, for this command is inextricably related to the command to love others (there is only one "thou" and two objects in the command). But a man ought to *love,* not ruin, himself. That is, he ought to have a proper love for himself. [25]

But is this loving others as one ought to love himself really the highest form of love? "Would it not be possible to love a man *better than oneself?*" asks Kierkegaard. The answer is no. The desire to love others *more* than self is mere poetic enthusiasm. Men *sing* about

24 Sören Kierkegaard, *The Works of Love,* pp. 284, 285, 289.
25 *Ibid.,* pp. 289, 290, 285, 286.

such love but we are not commanded to do it. Indeed, this great love they praise is secretly self-love, for "this foolishness pleases the poet beyond all measure, it is delicious in his ears, it inspires him to sing." But "Christianity teaches that this is blasphemy." For "there is only One whom a man may with the truth of the eternal love better than himself, that is God." This is why the Scriptures say to love other men *as oneself* but to love God *with all one's* heart and soul and mind. "A man must love God in *unconditional obedience* and love Him in adoration." And "it would be ungodliness if any man dared to love himself in this way, or dared to love another man in this way, or dared to permit another man to love him in this way." [26]

Loving oneself and other men as one ought to love means to love oneself and others as creatures of God, not as ultimate. Furthermore, it means to will the best for them whether this is what they want or not. For "if you can better perceive his best than he can, then you will not be able to excuse yourself by the fact that the harmful thing was his own wish, was what he himself asked for." Indeed, giving a man what is harmful to him simply because he wishes it is a perverse kind of loving him *more* than oneself. It is "*obediently* doing it because he asked it, or *adoringly,* because he wished it. But this you simply have no right to do." [27]

Consequently, Kierkegaard concludes "as thyself" is a fatal blow to false love both of oneself and of others. It would keep one from loving himself more than others and from loving others more than God. It is most ingeniously designed to teach men to love the way they *ought* to love.

E. *A Summary of Self-Love*

Other opinions could be added to the spectrum on self-love, but this is not necessary. Basically, views on self-love may be classified under three headings: (1) self-love for its own sake, (2) self-love for others' sake, and (3) self-love for God's sake. In each case there is agreement about the *need* for self-love, only the *reason* for self-love differs. Loving oneself for one's own sake is egoistic; loving self for others' sake is humanistic, and loving oneself for God's sake may be called altruistic.

There are many variations possible within these basic categories, but enough has been said by way of introduction. The task now is to examine the biblical data in search of a solution to the question: Is there a legitimate role of self-love in a biblical approach to Christian ethics?

[26] *Ibid.,* pp. 285, 286.
[27] *Ibid.,* p. 287.

II. Examining the Biblical Data on Self-Love

The Biblical data on the subject of self-love fall into two broad categories: (1) those verses indicating that man is sinful and ought to hate himself, and (2) those verses which imply that man is valuable and ought to respect himself. Let us look first at the verses "against" self-love.

A. *Self-Love As Condemned in Scripture*

The basis in Scripture on which a man ought not love his "self" is that it is a sinful self. Hence, it is a misdirected and unworthy love. Passages which depict man as sinful are numerous. A significant sampling of these is sufficient to illustrate the point.

1. *Man Is Sinful by "Nature"* — From the very beginning, "the Lord saw that the wickedness of man was great in the earth, and that every imagination of the thoughts of his heart was only evil continually" (Gen. 6:5). The prophet said, "The heart is deceitful above all things, and desperately corrupt" (Jer. 17:9). The psalmist indicated that man is sinful from birth, writing, "Behold, I was brought forth in iniquity, and in sin did my mother conceive me" (Ps. 51:5). Or again, "The wicked go astray from the womb, they err from their birth, speaking lies" (Ps. 58:3).

The sinfulness of man is not only natal, it is natural. Men are depicted as being sinful by "nature." Paul wrote, "We were by nature the children of wrath, like the rest of mankind" (Eph. 2:3). "For there is no distinction; since all have sinned and fall short of the glory of God . . . " (Rom. 3:23). As it is written, "None is righteous, no, not even one. No one understands, no one seeks for God . . . no one does good, not even one," and, "There is no fear of God before their eyes" (Rom. 3:10, 12, 18).

It is because men are sinful by "nature" and by birth that Jesus told Nicodemus the Pharisee, "That which is born of the flesh is flesh, and that which is born of the Spirit is spirit. Do not marvel that I said to you, 'You must be born anew'" (John 3:6, 7). On another occasion Jesus told some men, "You are of your father the devil, and your will is to do your father's desires" (John 8:44). John the apostle echoes this truth, saying, ". . . and the whole world is in the power of the evil one" (1 John 5:19).

Elsewhere the New Testament speaks of the Christian possessing a carnal or "earthly" nature. Paul urged the Colossians: "Put to death therefore what is earthly in you," and he reminded them that as Christians they "have put off the old nature with its practices and have put on the new nature . . . " (Col. 3:5, 10, 11). This old, sinful "nature" is also called the "flesh" which wars against the Spirit. "For the desires of the flesh are against the Spirit, and the desires of the Spirit are against the flesh" (Gal. 5:17). This sampling of Scripture is sufficient to suggest the basis for the view that naturally man is intrinsically evil. And if this is the case, it is not difficult to see why men are urged to deny and even hate this evil within their selves.

2. *Man Ought to Hate His Sinful Self* — A number of biblical passages may be cited to illustrate the contention that since man is evil by "nature" he ought not love his "self" but even to hate it. Jesus said, "If any man would come after me, let him deny himself and take up his cross daily and follow me" (Luke 9:23). Likewise, Paul urged the Roman Christians, "So you also must consider yourselves dead to sin . . ." (Rom. 6:11). He said, "I have been crucified with Christ; it is no longer I who live, but Christ who lives in me" (Gal. 2:20). This is why Paul exhorted the Colossians: "Put to death therefore what is earthly in you" (Col. 3:5).

In fact, the Scriptures urge one to hate his own life. Jesus said, "He who loves his life loses it, and he who hates his life in this world will keep it for eternal life" (John 12:25). Again he said, "If any one comes after me and does not hate his own father and mother . . . , yes, and even his own life, he cannot be my disciple" (Luke 14:26). Paul warned Timothy against men who will be "lovers of self" (2 Tim. 3:2). Indeed, throughout the Scriptures there are repeated condemnations of the proud and selfish. [28] The apostle summed up the reason for hating one's evil "self" when he said, "For I know that nothing good dwells within me, that is, in my flesh." Therefore, he exclaimed, "Wretched man that I am! Who will deliver me from this body of death?" (Rom. 7:18, 24).

In summary, the Scriptures declare natural man to be sinful by "nature" and urge Christians to deny and even hate their "selves." In view of human depravity, then, how can it be maintained that men should love themselves? What role could self-love possibly have in a biblical ethic?

B. *Self-Love As Commended in Scripture*

Before we are in a position to answer this question there are other scriptural passages to examine. If the above type of verses against self-love were the *only* ones, then our conclusion might be somewhat different. But in the balance of Scripture the weight of truth is not all in favor of hating oneself. Besides the above passages which clearly condemn self-love, there are two kinds of verses which imply that one ought to love himself.

1. *Man Has Intrinsic Value* — The first class of biblical data which implies a self-love is that group which teaches that man is in some sense good, even fallen man. The refrain of the creation story is il-

---

[28] Cf. 1 John 2:16; Proverbs 16:8.

lustrative of the fact that man is essentially valuable. After a day's work of creation God viewed the results and said, "It is *good*." And after reviewing the whole process, including the creation of man, "God saw everything that he had made, and behold, it was *very good*" (Gen. 1:31). What was good about man? Man was good by nature because "God created man in his own image . . ." (Gen. 1:27). Man was like God. Paul quotes with approval the poet who wrote that all men are "the offspring of God" and adds that this implies we are like God (Acts 17:28, 29). Indeed, there are indications elsewhere in Scripture that God holds Fatherhood over all His creation which, therefore, bears some resemblance to Him (cf. Mal. 2:10; Eph. 3:14, 15; Ps. 19:1, etc.).

Even after man sinned, the image of God remained in man. It was marred with sin to be sure, but there was still something about man which was good and like God. The image of God in fallen man is effaced but not completely erased. This is the reason given for the wrongness of murder, viz., "for God made man in his own image" (Gen. 9:6). Murder, of all men, even fallen sinful men, is wrong because it is like killing God in effigy. Man is like God and it is wrong to destroy this good godlike resemblance which is in man. Even cursing another man is evil, implies James, because men "are made in the likeness of God" (James 3:9). Surely both murder and cursing other men would not be forbidden unless there were some value or good in even the most sinful men.

There are many other verses declaring men to be good by nature insofar as they are the creation of God. Paul told Timothy, "Everything created by God is good . . ." (1 Tim. 4:4). To Titus Paul wrote, "To the pure all things are pure . . ." (Titus 1:15). Not only are men good by nature but even evil men can *do* good things. Jesus said, "If you then, who are evil, know how to give good gifts to your children, then how much more will your Father who is in heaven . . ." (Matt. 7:11).

Furthermore, Paul testified of his sinful self, "I can will what is right, but," he added in complaint, "I cannot do it" (Rom. 7:18). Nonetheless, he felt a good will within him. "For I delight in the law of God, in my inmost self . . . ," he noted. In other words, despite his sinful tendencies and inability to do all the good things he wanted to do, the apostle recognized within his sinful self an "inmost self" which could at least "will what is right." That is, there is some remnant of the image of God, some tendency to good within men which must be called good. [29] And if there is a good nature or ten-

---

[29] Cf. also Paul's teaching that all men have a conscience which urges them to do good (Romans 2:6-8, 12-16).

dency within man, then surely this is not to be despised or denied but affirmed and loved.

2. *Man Ought to Love Himself* — If self-love is not directly commanded anywhere in Scripture, it is at least implied in many places. First of all, that one ought to love himself is implied in the command, "You shall love your neighbor *as yourself*" (Lev. 19:18; Matt. 22:39). If this often-repeated ethical norm does not command self-love, it at least seems to imply that self-love is right. It appears to be saying that self-love is the basis of loving others, that one cannot even love others unless he loves himself. For if one does not respect the good God created in himself, then how can he be expected to respect the good of God's creation elsewhere?

The teaching of Paul would seem to confirm this interpretation of the command to love others *as oneself*. He wrote, "For no man ever hates his own flesh, but nourishes and cherishes it . . ." (Eph. 5:29). There is nothing wrong with this. Everyone ought to care for himself. Self-respect is morally necessary. A man has no more right to hate God's created good in himself than anywhere else. In other words, men *do* love themselves, and there is a basic sense in which they *ought* to do this.

But if men ought to love themselves, then why does the Bible not command them to do so in so many words? At best, the scriptural commands seem to imply that self-love is a *fact* but do not seem to enjoin it on men as a command. The answer to this may be twofold. First, perhaps there is a command to self-love implied in the love norm. Maybe it is saying, "You ought to love others as you [*ought to*] love yourself." Second, even if it is saying, "You ought to love others as you [*do in fact*] love yourselves," there is still a tacit approval of self-love. Indeed, man is so constructed that it is *unnecessary* to command self-love. Men do it without having to be commanded to do it. In any event, proper self-love is approved by Scripture. Men ought to respect their lives and the divine image within them. There is at least a remnant of good in the unregenerate person which should be esteemed by others and by himself.

III. A Synthesis and Solution

Now that the basic biblical data has been exposed, how can it be reconciled? For on the one hand, men are condemned for being lovers of self; on the other hand there is a sense in which they are supposed to love themselves. On the one hand, there is allegedly no good in men; on the other hand, they are bearers of the image of God. Men are told both to hate themselves and to love themselves; they are urged to deny themselves because of evil and to affirm their own good as creatures of God.

The nature of fallen man is evil and corrupted, but it is not beyond redemption. Even in his sinful condition man has value as a creature of God who can become a son of God by redemption. The image of God is not lost in fallen man. There is value in the unredeemed because he is not unredeemable. And, therefore, there is a sense in which this value should be loved or respected.

A. Man's Nature Is Not Totally Corrupted

The doctrine of total depravity is sometimes misunderstood. It is not to be understood in a metaphysical sense. That is, fallen men are not totally deprived of all good in their nature, for if this were true they would have no nature there at all. Augustine gave one of the strongest defenses of the position that every nature as such is good. He argued that God is the supreme good and "... from Him is everything that by nature is good. Thus every nature is good, and everything good is from God." [30] He contended that "no nature, therefore, as far as it is nature is evil." [31]

What we call evil has no nature of its own; rather it is a diminution of a nature. "For evil has no positive nature; but the loss of good has received the name 'evil.'" [32] Evil is a privation of a good nature or being. Evil is an ontological parasite. It is not a good but the lack of a good which belongs to a certain thing. In other words, evil is not a substance but the corruption of a substance. Like rust or rot, evil cannot live on its own. It exists only in another nature. Evil is a lack which ought to be there like the lack of sight in the blind or the lack of a limb in the maimed. [33]

It does not follow from this that no natures are evil or corrupted. There obviously are imperfect natures which lack many perfections they ought to have. However, there are no totally corrupted natures. There are no cars which are totally rusted, for if they were they would no longer be cars. There are no trees which are totally rotted, for then they would no longer be trees. There are no garments which are totally moth-eaten, for then there would be no garment there at all. Likewise, there are no men who are totally deprived of their good natures which make them in God's image, for if they were then they would no longer be men. Surely it cannot be argued with biblical support that fallen human beings are no longer human. Therefore, it follows that there is some good in the most sinful of men.

What is called an evil nature, then, is not totally evil but a corrup-

[30] Augustine, *Against the Epistle of the Manicheans*, XL, 46, *The Nicene and Post-Nicene Fathers*, ed. Philip Schaff (Grand Rapids: Wm. B. Eerdmans Publishing Company, 1956), Vol. IV.
[31] Augustine, *On the Nature of the Good*, XVII, XVIII, XXXVIII.
[32] Augustine, *The City of God*, XI, 9.
[33] Augustine, *Against the Epistle of the Manicheans*, XXXV, 39.

tion or privation of some of the good in a perfectly good nature which God originally created. "Nature," said Augustine, "which has been corrupted, is called evil for assuredly when incorrupt it is good: but even when corrupt, so far as it is corrupted it is evil." [34] So, then, what is called the sinful "nature" in fallen men is nothing but a corruption of the good nature which God created. It is surely not some new (but evil) nature which man or the devil created. Rather, it is a privation of a perfectly good nature which God made. In other words, the image of God is effaced but not erased in fallen men. It has been distorted but not destroyed. In fact, only the grace of God can repair the damage which sin has done to his nature. Man cannot by any effort on his own restore the good of which his nature has been deprived by sin. Fallen man is beyond human repair (Eph. 2:8, 9; Titus 3:5-7 etc.).

Man's inability to redeem himself does not make him unredeemable. The fact that sin has made a wreck of man does not place him beyond divine repair. Indeed it does not leave man without redeeming value. The wreck of sin is salvagable. There is value even in fallen man which must be respected. Only in hell is man without redeemable value and this of man's own choice because he refuses restoration through God's grace. [35] Short of hell there can be found some salvagable good in the most wicked of men. On the other hand, the corrupting influence in human nature should not be loved. Men should hate that which distorts and diminishes their value as creatures of God.

Just what is this evil "self" in man which he is to hate? It is that evil tendency in man, growing out of the corruption of his nature due to Adam's sin, to love himself more than he ought to love himself. It is selfishness and self-centeredness rather than unselfishness and God-centeredness. Sinful man by nature sets himself in the place of God. He worships the creature more than the Creator. It is this basic tendency in his corrupted nature which a man ought to hate, deny, and crucify. This self-centeredness is an improper self-love. It is a rearrangement of the hierarchy of values established by God. For in his egoism man affirms that a finite person is more valuable than the infinite person. Certainly this is a misdirected love which affirms its own finite value over the infinite value of God. This fundamental desire to be God on the part of what is not God but only mortal and sinful man should be hated and despised. Men should hate their own selfish and self-centered attitudes. [36]

[34] Augustine, *On the Nature of the Good*, IV.
[35] Cf. Matt. 25:41f.; 2 Thess. 1:7-9.
[36] *That* improper self-love (viz. pride) is man's basic sin is supported by a host of Scriptures. *Why* all men inevitably love themselves in this improper way is part of the mystery of depravity. That all rationally and morally mature men

What is the origin of this evil propensity in man? Whence come these evil desires and decisions? If all selves are good by nature, then why does a self ever want to disturb its proper relation to others or to set itself up as God when it is merely a creature? The answer is found in freedom. Persons are free and freedom is a good thing. It is good to be free, as all who have tasted of it can attest. However, with this good thing called freedom comes the possibility of having evil relations, i.e., of freely rejecting God's hierarchy of values. For example, man can freely choose to put himself in place of God, to consider his own self ultimate rather than God. Without this kind of freedom men would have no assurance that they were more than puppets; they would never be sure they were really free. But with this kind of freedom comes the possibility of evil, the possibility that men will make themselves God. Hence, evil results when men use their good freedom to consider their good selves to be better than they are. That is, evil arises when creatures consider themselves to be the Creator. Loving oneself as a creature is good, but exalting oneself as the Creator is evil. And this tendency to love creatures in an improper way is the evil "self" which the Bible exhorts men to hate. [37]

B. *Loving the Good in Oneself*

Men are to hate the selfish tendencies in themselves, but they are to love themselves. That is, improper love of self should not hinder the proper love of oneself. Loving oneself as ultimate (as God) is improper; loving oneself as a creature of God is proper and good. This legitimate self-love is clearly implied in Scripture's command to "Love your neighbor *as yourself.*"

There are several reasons why fallen men ought to love themselves. First, men ought to love themselves because *they are like God.* The Scriptures teach that man is made in the image and likeness of God. To hate oneself is to hate God in effigy. Even if the image of God is not perfect. God is good, and He declared His creatures good and even sinful men have not lost all this good. Hence, to hate one of God's creatures (even if it be oneself) is to hate God in an indirect way.

Second, men ought to love themselves because *it is the basis of their* love for others. The love of others is based on one's love of self. If one does not properly love himself, he cannot properly love others.

sin is the clear teaching of Scripture. How this tendency to sin can be reconciled with the ability not to sin is the subject of another study which will not be attempted here. It will be sufficient for the present to note that there is no contradiction in affirming that men are able (by God's grace) to resist each particular sin they encounter even though it is inevitable that they will not resist *all* of them. That is, even though men inevitably *will* commit some sin, nonetheless, there is no reason they *must* commit any particular sin. Enabling grace is available.

[37] Luke 9:23

Conversely, failure to love others rightly is based on a failure to love oneself in a proper way. Since the Bible commands the Christian to love others and since love of self is the basis for loving others, then there is the clear implication that one ought to learn to love himself correctly. Of course, the Christian must not love himself merely for the sake of loving himself; that would be egoism. The Christian should also love himself *for the sake of loving others;* this is a form of altruism. That is, one of the reasons for cultivating self-love is that it will enable one to love others better, which is what God commands.

Thirdly, since the Bible teaches that to love others is to love God, one should learn a proper self-love so that he can love others more and, thereby, *love God better.* Jesus said, "As you did it [showed love] to one of the least of these my brethren, you did it to me" (Matt. 25:40). John wrote, "If any one says, 'I love God,' and hates his brother, he is a liar" (1 John 4:20). While loving others is not necessarily the only way one can love God, nonetheless, it is one way. Indeed, a proper self-love as a basis for loving other men can be a way of increasing one's love for God. This is, perhaps, the highest motivation for self-love, viz., loving self for the sake of loving God.

Finally, a Christian should love himself *because God loves him.* God loves man (even as fallen creature) and wishes to redeem him and reconcile man to Himself. [38] Lost, sinful men are the "pearl of great value" for which Christ sacrificed all to purchase. [39] Lost, sinful men are not only redeemable but valuable to God. God loves fallen mankind and sent His Son to be the sacrifice for their sins. [40] And if God so loves sinful men for the redeemable value in them, then we ought to love these men too, (including ourselves among them), and both work and pray for their redemption.

In summary, men ought to love themselves (1) for their own sakes as God's creatures, (2) for the sake of others as responsible creatures, (3) for God's sake and because God loves them and has provided redemption for them through Christ. And when there is a conflict between any of these levels of love, then the latter transcend the former. They must be arranged in an ascending order of priority. For many persons (viz., others) are of more value that one person (viz., oneself) and the infinite Person (God) is of more value than finite persons (men). Men are ends in themselves but not *ultimate* ends. Only God is to be loved for His own sake in an ultimate and final way. All other persons are to be loved as *immediate* ends which may become means to the ultimate end of loving God.

---

[38] Cf. Rom. 5:8; 1 Tim. 1:15f; 1 Peter 3:18.
[39] Cf. Matt. 13:45.
[40] Cf. John 3:16; Mark 10:45; Rom. 3:24-25; 1 John 2:2.

SELECT READINGS FOR CHAPTER EIGHT: SELF-LOVE

Augustine, *City of God, Book* XIV, Garden City, New York: Image Books, A Division of Doubleday & Company, Inc., 1958.

Fromm, Erich, *Man for Himself*, New York: Premier Books, 1968.

Kierkegaard, Sören, *Works of Love*, trans. by Lillian and Marvin Swenson. Princeton University Press, 1946.

Lewis, C. S., *Four Loves*, New York: Harcourt Brace Jovanovitch, 1960.

Rand, Ayn, *The Virtue of Selfishness*, New York: A Signet Book, 1961.

Tillich, Paul, *The Courage to Be*, New Haven, Conn.: Yale University Press. 1952.

9 / The Christian and War

What is the Christian's attitude toward war? Is it ever right to take the life of another person under the command of one's government? Is there a biblical basis for engaging in war? These questions have found varying responses among Christians. Basically, there are three views taken by Christians on the question of whether one should be involved in war to the point of taking the lives of others. First, there is *activism* which holds that the Christian ought to go to *all wars* in obedience to his government because government is ordained of God. Second, there is *pacifism* which contends that Christians should participate in *no wars* to the point of taking the lives of others, since God has commanded men never to take the lives of others. Finally, there is *selectivism* which argues that Christians should participate only *some wars,* viz., the just ones, since to do otherwise is to refuse to do the greater good God has commanded.

I. ACTIVISM: IT IS ALWAYS RIGHT TO PARTICIPATE IN WAR

The argument of activism that a Christian is duty-bound to obey his government and participate in every war has two different kinds of arguments: biblical and philosophical or social. The biblical data will be examined first.

A. *The Biblical Argument: "Government Is Ordained of God."*

The Scriptures seem emphatic on this point. Government is of God. Whether it be in the religious realm or the civil realm, God is the God of order and not of chaos.[1]

[1] Cf. I Corinthians 14:33, 40.

1. *Old Testament Data on God and Government* – From the very beginning the Scriptures declare that man is to "have *dominion* over . . . every living thing that moves upon the earth" (Gen. 1:28).[2] Man was to be king over all the earth. After the fall the woman was told, "your desire shall be for your husband, and he shall *rule* over you" (Gen. 2:16). When Cain killed Abel it is implied that he failed to realize that he was his "brother's keeper" (Gen. 4:10). Finally, when the whole predeluvian civilization had become corrupt "and the earth was filled with violence," God destroyed it and instituted human government. God said to Noah and his family after the flood, "For your lifeblood I will surely require a reckoning . . . ; of every man's brother I will require the life of man." For whoever sheds the blood of man, by man shall his blood be shed; for God made man in his own image" (Gen. 9:5, 6).

In brief, God ordained government. Adam was given the crown to reign over the earth, and when evil became rampant Noah was given the sword to rule in the earth. Government is of God both because order is from God and because disorder must be put down for God. Men have the right from God to take the lives of unruly men who shed innocent blood. Government is invested with divine power. The sword which was given to Noah was used by Abraham when he engaged in war against the kings of Genesis 14 who had made aggression against Abraham's nephew Lot. As Carroll Stegall notes, this passage indicates "that God approves wars which are for the protection of the peaceful from the aggressor."[3]

Although the specific form of government changed throughout the Old Testament, there is a reiteration of this principle that goverment is of God. In the Mosaic theocracy the powers of government are very explicit: "You shall give life for life, eye for eye, tooth for tooth, hand for hand, foot for foot, burn for burn, wound for wound, stripe for stripe" (Ex. 21:25). Even when Israel set up its monarchy contrary to God's plan for them (1 Sam. 8:7), God nevertheless anointed their choice of a king. God said to Samuel the prophet, "Hearken to their voice, and make them a king" (1 Sam. 8:22). Later Samuel said, "Do you see him whom the Lord has chosen?" (1 Sam. 10:24). David, even before he was king, was commanded to fight against the Philistines who were robbing Israel (1 Sam. 23:1).

As far as the governments of gentile nations were concerned, the Old Testament declares "that the Most High rules the kingdom of men, and gives it to whom he will" (Dan. 4:25). And from the rest

---

[2] Throughout this chapter all of the emphases added in the scriptural quotations will be our own.

[3] Carroll R. Stegall, "God and the USA in Vietnam," *Eternity*, March, 1968, p. 15

of Daniel's prophecy it is clear that God ordained the great Babylonian Medo-Persian, Grecian, and Roman governments (cf. Dan. 2, 7). In fact, the indication is that God ordained government wherever it is found. And since government is given of God, it would follow that to disobey government is to disobey God. If, therefore, one's government commands one to go to war, a biblical activism would argue that one must respond in obedience to God. For God has ordained the government with the sword or the power to take lives.

2. *New Testament Data on God and Government* – The New Testament confirms the view of the Old Testament that God has ordained government. Jesus is quoted as saying a man ought to "render therefore to Caesar the things that are Caesar's . . ." (Matt. 22:21). That civil authority is God-given was further acknowledged by Jesus before Pilate when he said, "You would have no power over me unless it had been given you from above" (John 19:11). Paul admonishes Timothy to pray and give thanks "for kings and all who are in high positions . . ." (1 Tim. 2:2). Titus is exhorted about the Cretans, "Remind them to be submissive to rulers and authorities, to be obedient . . ." (Tit. 3:1). Peter is very clear: "Be subject for the Lord's sake to every human institution, whether it be to the emperor as supreme, or to governors as sent by him . . ." (1 Pet. 2:13, 14).

The most extensive passage in the New Testament on the relation of the Christian to government is found in Romans 13:1-7. The first verse makes it clear that all government is divinely established. "Let every person be subject to the governing authorities. For there is no authority except from God, and those that exist have been instituted by God," wrote Paul. "Therefore he who resists the authorities resists what God has appointed, and those who resist will incur judgment" (v. 2). The further reason given for obeying a ruler is that "he is God's servant for your good . . . . He is the servant of God to execute his wrath on the wrongdoer" (v. 4). Further, wrote Paul, "For the same reason you also pay taxes, for the authorities are ministers of God, attending to this very thing" (v. 6). In view of this, the Christian is urged to "pay all of them their dues, taxes to whom taxes are due, revenue to whom revenue is due, respect to whom respect is due, honor to whom honor is due" (v. 7).

What is specially significant about this passage of Scripture is that it is the New Testament's reiteration of the power of government to take a human life. The Christians are urged to obey the existing governor or king, "for he does not bear the sword in vain" (v. 4). That is, government with its power over life is ordained of

God. And whoever resists His government is resisting God. It would follow from this, according to biblical activists, that one ought to respond to the call of his government to war because God has given the authority of the sword to the governing authorities.

B. *The Philosophical Argument: Government Is Man's Guardian*

Activism is not supported merely with biblical data. One of the most forceful arguments ever written for this position came from the pen of Plato. He offers three explicit reasons (and two more implied) as to why a man should not disobey even a government which is unjustly putting him to death. The scene is the prison where Socrates awaits his death, having been charged with impiety and sentenced to drink the cup of poison. Socrates' young friend, Crito, urges him to escape and evade the death penalty. In Socrates' reply are given five reasons for obeying an unjust government, even to the point of death.

1. *Government Is Man's Parent* — One ought not disobey even an unjust government. "First, because in disobeying it he is disobeying his parents." By this Socrates means that it was under the sponsorship of that government that the individual was brought into the world. He was not born in lawless jungle but he came into this world under the parentage of Athens. It was this state which made his very birth more than barbaric—a birth into a state of civilization, not anarchy. In brief, just as a parent spends months in preparation and anticipation for a child, so many years have been spent in maintaining the state which makes a civilized birth possible, and these years may not be lightly regarded later because one finds himself at odds with his government. It was that government (or some government) which made his free birth possible. If one were to disobey government, said Socrates, would it not reply, "In the first place did we not bring you into existence? Your father married your mother by our aid and begat you. Say whether you have any objections to urge against those of us who regulate marriage? None, I should reply." [4]

2. *Government Is Man's Educator* — Socrates offers another reason for obedience to one's government. "Second, because it is the author of his education." The implication here is that the very education which makes one to be what he is today (including his knowledge of justice and injustice) was given to him by his government. He was a Greek and not a barbarian, not only by birth but by training. And both the birth and training were made possible by the government which was now demanding his life. What can one reply against governments which "after birth regulate the nurture and education of children, in which you were also trained? Were not

4 *Crito,* pp. 101, 102.

the laws, which have charge of education, right in commanding your father to train you in music and gymnastic? Right, I should reply."[5] From this it follows that government could say to us, "Since you were brought into the world and nurtured and educated by us, can you deny in the first place that you are our child and slave, as your fathers were before you?" And if this is true, man is not on equal terms with his government. Man has no more right to strike back at it and revile it than one does to his master or father. Even if government would destroy us, we have no right to destroy it in return. If one thinks he does, he has "failed to discover that his country is more to be valued and higher and holier far than mother or father or any ancestor . . . ." In brief, government is not only prior to the individual citizen (first argument), but it is superior to him. Government not only precedes the individual life but it takes precedence over his life.

3. *The Governed (i.e., Citizen) Has Covenanted to Obey His Government* — The third reason Plato gives for a man's obeying his government is that "he has made an agreement with it that he will duly obey its commands." That is, the consent of the governed to make that government his government by pledging his allegieance to it binds him to obey its laws or suffer the consequences. By the very fact that a man makes a given country *his* country he has thereby made a tacit covenant to be obedient to its commands. "And when we are punished by her [our country], whether with imprisonment or stripes," wrote Plato, "the punishment is to be endured in silence; and if she lead us to wounds or death in battle, thither we follow as is right." For if one is to accept the privileges of education and protection of his government, then he has thereby implicitly agreed to accept the responsibilities (and penalties) of his government to obey its laws and even to go to war for it.

4. *The Governed Is Not Compelled to Remain Under His Government* — There are at least two other implied arguments which Plato uses to support his case that one ought not disobey his government. "Any one who does not like it and the city, may go where he likes . . . . But he who has experience of the manner in which we [i.e., rulers] order justice and administer the State, and still remains, has entered into an implied contract that he will do as we command him." Plato makes it clear, however, that whatever emigrating one is going to do must be done *before* he is indicted or drafted by his country. For to flee in the face of one's responsibilities to his government is "doing only what a miserable slave would do, running away and turning your back upon the compacts and agreements which you made as a citizen." In other words, if one is not

[5] *Ibid.*

willing to obey his country, he should find another country he can obey. But if a man assumes the protection and privilege of a country by his constant presence there as a citizen, then he must not seek exile simply because his country's demands on him are undesirable.

5. *Without Government There Would Be Social Chaos* — Another reason one should not disobey his government is implied in Plato's question, "And who would care about a State which has no laws?" An unjust law is bad, but no law is even worse. Even a bad monarchy is to be preferred to anarchy. Any government is better than no government at all. And if men disobey their government in what they feel is unjust or undesirable, then social chaos would result. For if obedience to government is determined individually or subjectively, then no law would be immune from some citizen's disapproval or disobedience. The result would be chaotic. To borrow a phrase from the Scriptures, to have no laws which are binding on all citizens would be for "every man to do that which was right in his own eyes." And such would not really be a society but a social chaos. Even a government closed to its citizens would be better than one open to revolution among its peoples.

In these five arguments Plato stated the major arguments used as a basis for activism. A man should always obey his government because it is his guardian. Government—even one that seems to be unjust — must be obeyed even to the point of going to war. For without government man would be no better than a savage, living in a state of ignorance and anarchy. Hence, no matter how undesirable one's responsibilities to his government may be, nevertheless, he is obliged to obey it as his parent and master.

Contemporary writers have not added many major points to the biblical and classical arguments in favor of activism. One over-all argument not explicitly included in the five listed above is that it is a greater evil not to resist an evil aggressor than to fight against him. This is reminiscent of the famous line: "All that is necessary for evil to triumph is for good men to do nothing." If good men will not resist evil men, then evil men will prevail in the world.

Of course, there is a basic problem with the activist's position which pacifists are quick to point out, and it is this: in most wars *both* sides claim to be in the right. Often each country claims the other is the aggressor. The "enemy" is always wrong, but both countries are "enemies," each being the enemy of the other. At this point the total activists seem obliged to admit that both parties (or countries) in a war are not always right. But even when one country is unjustly engaged in war, its citizens are duty bound to respond to its military draft, for disobedience to government (even an evil one) is a greater evil than obedience to it in an unjust war.

To disobey any government leads to revolution and anarchy which is a greater evil than participating in a war where one form of order is vying with another for which form of order will be dominant. In brief, the complete activist can argue that it would be better to fight on the side of an order which is more evil than another order than to contribute, by disobedience, to total disorder and chaos. And if one were in doubt as to which government was the best or most just, then he could content himself with obedience to his own government on the ground that it is *his* guardian and educator. And whether his own country were the most just or not, he could fight for it, believing that the outcome of the war would reveal in which way justice will triumph.

II. Pacifism: It Is Never Right to Participate in War

There are many reasons pacifism rejects the activist's arguments. The reasons given by the pacifist may serve both as a critique of total activism and as the other half of the dialogue on war which forces the Christian to examine both his Bible and his conscience for a conclusion to a vexing problem. The arguments for pacifism may be divided into two basic groups, the biblical and the social.

A. *The Biblical Arguments*: *War Is Always Wrong*

There are many points to the Christian pacifist's argument against all wars but there are several basic biblical premises behind all of them. One of these premises is stated in the biblical injunction, "You shall not kill" (Ex. 20:13), and the other in Jesus' words, "Do not resist one who is evil" (Matt. 5:39).

1. *Killing Is Always Wrong* — At the very heart of pacifism is the conviction that intentionally taking another human life is always wrong. Intentional life-taking, especially in war, is basically and radically wrong. The scriptural prohibition, "You shall not kill," includes war. War is mass murder. But murder is murder whether it is done within one's own society or on men in another society.

Since this conclusion is *prima facie* at odds with the many cases in Scripture, which seem to be commanding war, the Christian pacifists must offer an explanation as to why the Bible appears sometimes to command war.

Various answers have been given by different pacifists. (1) First, the wars of the Old Testament which God is represented as "commanding" (e.g., Joshua's) were not really commanded by God at all. They represent a more barbarous state of mankind in which wars were justified by attaching divine sanctions to them.[6] (2) An-

---

[6] This option seems clearly to reject the authority of the Old Testament and is not a viable alternative for an evangelical Christian. Perhaps the most serious objection to this critical view of the Old Testament is that it rejects the authority

other explanation is that these wars were unique in that Israel was acting as a theocratic instrument in the hands of God. These were not really Israel's wars at all but God's wars, as is evidenced by the special miracles God performed to win them (cf. Jos. 6; 10; Psalm 44). (3) Finally, it is sometimes argued that the wars of the Old Testament were not God's "perfect" will but only His "permissive" will. That is, God is represented as "commanding" war in the same secondary and concessive sense that He is said to have "commanded" Samuel to anoint Saul king, even though God had not chosen Saul but David to be king (1 Sam. 10:1). Or, wars are "commanded" by God in the same sense in which Moses "commanded" divorce, viz., because of the hardness of men's hearts (Matt. 19:8). It was not that God really desired and commanded war any more than He likes disobedience or divorce. God has a better way than that and it is obedience and love. God could have accomplished His purposes in Israel and Canaan without war, had they been more obedient to Him.[7]

No war as such is ever God's command. What God commands clearly and unequivocally is, "You shall not kill." This command applies to all men, friends or enemies. All men are made in God's image and, therefore, it is wrong to kill them. The Old Testament clearly teaches that one should love his enemies (cf. Lev. 19:18, 34; Jonah 4), and Jesus reaffirmed this, saying, "Love your enemies and pray for those who persecute you . . ." (Matt. 5:44). War is based in hate and is intrinsically wrong. Taking the life of another person is contrary to the principle of love and is, therefore, basically unchristian.

2. *Forcefully Resisting Evil Is Wrong* — Closely connected with the first basic premise of pacifism that killing is wrong is another, viz., evil should never be resisted with physical force but rather with the spiritual force of love. Did not Jesus say, "Do not resist one who is evil. But if one strikes you on the right cheek, turn to him the other also" (Matt. 5:39)? Did not Christ also teach in this passage, "If any one forces you to go one mile, go with him two miles" (v. 41)? The Christian is not to retaliate or pay back evil with evil. Vengeance belongs to God (Deut. 32:35). Paul wrote, "Beloved, never avenge yourself, but leave it to the wrath of God . . . . No, if your enemy is hungry, feed him; if he is thirsty, give him drink . . . . Do not be overcome by evil, but overcome evil with

of Christ who personally verified the basic authority and authenticity of the Old Testament. See *General Introduction to the Bible,* Chapter 6, N. L. Geisler and W. E. Nix.

[7] That is, God could have intervened and accomplished His purposes without war, such as He did in the fall of Jericho or in the other miracles wherein Israel won without really fighting.

good" (Rom. 12:19-21). The Christian is to "repay no one evil for evil. . . . If possible, so far as it depends on you, live peaceably with all" (vv. 17-18).

The story of Jesus' driving the money-changers from the temple is not incompatible with this position, argue some pacifists. For physical force (i.e., the whip) was used only on the animals, not the people. Furthermore, the authority Jesus used was that of His own person and that of Scripture, not that of a strong-armed band of disciples (cf. John 2:15-16). Finally, the kind of physical force used by Jesus in the temple falls far short of proving that Jesus would sanction using extreme physical force to the point of taking human life.[8]

Further, Jesus' statement, "I have not come to bring peace, but a sword," cannot be used to support war. For Jesus commanded Peter, "Put your sword back into its place; for all who take the sword perish by the sword."[9] Jesus was not defining the *purpose* but the *result* of His ministry, viz., that the effect of allegiance to Him would "set a man against his father, and a daughter against her mother . . ." (v. 35). That is, the *effect* of Christ's ministry is often to divide families as if by a "sword" (Luke 12:51 uses the word "division" instead of "sword"), even though this is not the *intent* of His coming.

Pacifism is committed to the premise that it is essentially wrong to use physical force, at least to the point of life-taking, in order to resist evil. This does not mean that the pacifist repudiates all force. It means only that he believes in affirming the greater force of spiritual good in the face of the forces of physical evil. Pacifists believe basically that "we are not contending against flesh and blood, but against . . . the spiritual hosts of wickedness in heavenly places" (Eph. 6:12).

When pressed to the wall by a militant activist as to whether he would kill a would-be murderer of his wife, the complete pacifist sometimes retorts with a devastatingly simple answer. Why kill a wicked murderer and send his soul to judgment, when permitting the murderer to kill his wife will result in his sending her to heaven and still leave a chance to win the murderer? The less simplistic pacifist (or perhaps any pacifist with a non-Christian wife) might argue that wounding or disarming the murderer would be sufficient but that one should never aim to kill even a murderer.

3. *Public and Private Ethics Are the Same* — Another basic premise of pacifism is that there is no real distinction between what one should

[8] It is consistent with the pacifist's position to hold that some physical force can be used to restrain evil but that it should never be exercised to the point of taking the life of another human being.

[9] Matthew 10:34; 26:52.

do as a private citizen and what one should do as a public official. What is wrong for a person to do in his own neighborhood (e.g., killing) is wrong in any other neighborhood of the world. Putting on a military uniform does not revoke one's moral responsibility. Dietrich Bonhoeffer asked the crucial pacifistic question in this regard. "Am I ever acting only as a private person or only in an official capacity? Am I not always an individual, face to face with Jesus, even in the performance of my official duties?" He answers this question, saying, "But this distinction between person and office is wholly alien to the teaching of Jesus . . . . He addresses his disciples as men who have left all to follow him and the precept of non-violence applies equally in private life and official duty."[10] A double standard ethic — one for the private citizen and another for the public official — is foreign to the teaching of Scripture. The Bible pronounces, "Woe to those who decree iniquitous decrees, and to the writers who keep writing oppression, to turn aside the needy from justice. . . ." The prophet asked them, "What will you do on the day of punishment, in the storm which will come from afar?" (Isa. 10:1-3). David was held guilty when he initiated the death of Uriah in order to take his wife, Bathsheba, even though the death happened in a battle while Israel was at war (2 Sam. 12:5-7).

No man is exonerated from God's command not to kill simply because he is acting as a servant of the state. The moral command against murder is not abrogated by one's obligation to the state. We are to render to Caesar what is his, but Caesar does not hold the power of life and death—only God does. The powers of state are social but not capital. The right to take a life belongs only to the Author of life Himself (cf. Job 1:21). No human authority has the right to transcend the moral law. Indeed, what authority government has it derives from the moral law. And the moral law applies without respect to person or office.

B. *The Social Arguments: War Is Always Evil*

There are strong social arguments against war. It is not the best way to settle human disputes. A river of human blood has been left in the wake of wars down through history. Evils of all kinds result from war: starvation, cruelty, plagues, and death.

1. *War Is Based on the Evil of Greed* — As far back as Plato's *Republic* it was recognized by thinking people that the desire for luxury was the basis of warfare. He wrote, "We need not say yet whether war does good or harm, but only that we have discovered

[10] Dietrich Bonhoeffer, *The Cost of Discipleship*, trans. by R. H. Fuller, New York: The Macmillan Company, 1963, p. 159, 160.

its origin in desires [for wealth] which are the most fruitful source of evils both to individuals and to states."[11] In another place Plato said, "All wars are made for the sake of getting money."[12] There are several passages of Scripture which agree with Plato's analysis. James wrote, "What causes wars, and what causes fightings among you? Is it not your passions that are at war in your members? You desire and do not have; so you kill. And you covet and cannot obtain; so you fight and wage war" (James 4:2). Paul warned Timothy, "For the love of money is the root of all evils" (1 Tim. 6:10). So the covetous craving for wealth is the basis of all kinds of evil and particularly of one of the worst evils known to man, viz., war.

2. *War Results in Many Evils* — The many evils of war are well known and need not be dwelt upon here. The concomitant of war is death and destruction. Famine and pestilence often result from warfare as well. Perhaps there is no way to estimate the sorrow, pain, even cruelty and torture usually connected with war. The general sequence of war is illustrated well in the sixth chapter of the Apocalypse. After the "white horse" of war ". . . went out conquering and to conquer" there followed the "red horse" of blood-shed, the "black horse" of famine. After this John said, "And I saw, and behold, a pale horse, and its rider's name was Death, and Hades followed him" (vv. 1-8). Such are the evil results of war.

3. *War breeds More War* — One of the worst results of war is that it breeds more war. No war to the present has really made the world free from wars. Subdued enemies often rise to retaliate against their conquerors. Some wars continue over long periods with only brief interruptions. Sometimes "hot" wars end, but "cold" wars follow them for lengthy periods. There seems to be nothing intrinsic to war which really provides a permanent settlement to disputes. Rather than bringing men together, war seems to solidify the tensions and excite the spirit of retaliation and the possibility of renewed conflict.

Perhaps it is this sense of futility about war which has led so many contemporary thinkers into the pacifistic position. Slogans like, "Make love not war," "Ban the Bomb," and the popularity of the peace sign and the "dove" symbol depict a growing dissatisfaction with war as a means of dealing with other nations. Even some who are not pacifists by conviction are willing to risk total unilateral disarmament in the hope it may elicit a similar response from the enemy. "It cannot fail any worse than war has," they cry out in a desperate attempt at peace.

[11] Plato, *Republic* II, 374, trans. by Francis M. Cornford.
[12] Plato, *Phaedo* 66 c.

In summary, the pacifists argue that war is both unbiblical and anti-social. It is forbidden by God under the prohibition against murder and it is becoming increasingly repugnant to men who are showing signs of battle fatigue under the continued inhumanities of man to man.

III. SELECTIVISM: IT IS RIGHT TO PARTICIPATE IN SOME WARS

Not all men are content with the blind patriotism of activism which would kill upon their government's request while shouting, "My country, right or wrong!" Neither are all men satisfied with a naively passive attitude which would permit a Hitler to attempt genocide without lifting a gun in resistance. Even the previously pacifistic Bonhoeffer finally concluded that Hitler should have been assassinated. Out of dissatisfaction with the "easy" solutions of declaring *all* wars just or *no* war justifiable is emerging a growing number of adherents to selectivism, which holds that *some* wars are jutifiable and some are not. It is this view which seems to us to be the most satisfactory alternative for the Christian.

A. Biblical Basis for Selectivism

Both activism and pacifism claim the support of Scripture. Is selectivism just a third way to interpret the same biblical data? To answer this, we suggest that both activism and pacifism are right (at least in part) and that the sense in which they are both right is the essence of selectivism. In other words, selectivism is a synthesis of activism and pacifism. The truth of pacifism is that some wars are unjust and Christians ought not participate in these. The truth of activism is that some wars are just and Christians ought to fight in these. Selectivism, then, is committed to the position that one ought to participate only in a just war.

In fact, there is a point of agreement (at least theoretically) with all three views. All could assent to the following ethical proposition: One should not participate in an unjust war. The pacifist, of course, feels that *all* wars are unjust. The activist holds that *no* war is unjust (or at least if there are some unjust wars participation in them is not wrong). And the selectivist contends that in principle some wars are unjust and some are just. Hence, to support a Christian selectivism one must show both that (1) at least some wars are just in principle (thus showing that total pacifism is wrong) *and* (2) that some wars are unjust in principle (thus showing that activism is wrong).

1. *Some Wars Are Unjust* — The rejection of total activism is supported by the Scriptures. For the Bible teaches that it is not always right to obey one's government in everything it commands and particularly when its commands contradict higher spiritual laws

of God. There are clear instances of this in the Bible. The three Hebrew youths disobeyed the king's command to worship an idol (Dan. 3). Daniel broke a law commanding him not to pray to God (Dan. 6). The early apostles disobeyed orders not to preach the Gospel of Christ (Acts 4 and 5). And in a very clear case of divinely approved disobedience to civil law the Hebrew midwives in Egypt disobeyed the command to kill all the male babies born. It is written, "The midwives feared God, and did not do as the king of Egypt commanded them, but let the male children live.... So God dealt well with the midwives; and the people multiplied and grew very strong." Further, "because the midwives feared God he gave them families" (Ex. 1:17,19-21). This passage clearly teaches that it is wrong to take the life of an innocent human, even if the government "ordained of God" commands it. The government which commands it can be ordained of God, but their morally unjustifiable command was not ordained of God. The parents of Jesus evidenced the same conviction that government has no rights over the life of an innocent human being, since, under God's direction, they fled Herod's attempt to kill the Christ-child (Matt. 2:13-14).

We may easily conclude from these Scriptures that government is *not* always to be obeyed, especially when its command conflicts with the higher laws of God regarding the taking of innocent human lives. And since government is not sovereign in its commands regarding life-taking, it follows that not all wars waged by one's government are just. Indeed, even within a just war there may be unjust commands given which should be disobeyed. But if there are times when one should not obey his government's command to kill, then total activism is wrong. That is, not all wars nor all acts of war are morally justifiable on the grounds that one is acting in obedience to his government. This was the conclusion of the Nuremberg trials following Word War II and has been used again in the Viet Nam My Lai incident. The moral principle applied in both cases is that no individual member of the armed forces of any country should be excused for engaging in a war crime simply because he has been ordered to commit the act by his superior officer. Evil is evil whether a government commands it or not. The Bible is clear on the point that one should not *always* obey government.

2. *Some Wars Are Just* — The Scriptures also teach that not all wars are necessarily evil. That is, contrary to pacifism, some wars are just. Life-taking is often clearly commanded by God, both within a nation and between nations. Not all life-taking is murder. Sometimes God delegates the authority to take a human life to other

humans. This was clearly the case with the power of capital punishment given to Noah after the flood (Gen. 9:6), which was restated by Moses in the law to Israel (Ex. 21:25), and which was reaffirmed by Paul as residing in the emperor of Rome (Rom. 13:4), and was even implied by Jesus before Pilate (John 19:11). It is evident from these passages that every government, even apart from the special theocratic government of Israel, was given divine authority to take the life of one of its citizens guilty of a capital offense.

There is another somewhat neglected quotation of Jesus which may lend support to the claim that an individual has the right to wield a sword in his own defense. It is well known that Jesus admonished his disciples not to spread the Gospel with the sword (Matt. 26:52) and also not to resist religious persecution with physical force (Matt. 5:39). But it is sometimes overlooked that Jesus commanded His disciples to buy a sword (for their own protection). He said to them, "And let him who has no sword sell his mantle and buy one" (Luke 22:36). Since swords were forbidden by Jesus either for the purpose of supporting the preaching of the Gospel or for defense against being persecuted for the Gospel (cf. John 18:11), what possible purpose lay behind Jesus' command for the disciples to sell their outer garments and to buy a sword? If swords were excluded by Jesus on religious grounds we may assume that they are included by Jesus on civil grounds. That is, swords are not valid weapons to fight *spiritual* battles but they are legitimate tools for one's *civil* defense. Herein seems to be the sanction of Jesus to the justifiable use of an instrument of death in defense against an unjust aggressor. That is, Jesus commanded the use of the sword as a means of self-defense.[13]

The story of Abraham's battle against the kings of Genesis 14 lends support to the principle that unjust national aggressors should be resisted as well as unjust individual aggressors (cf. also 1 Sam. 23:1f). Nations as well as individuals can be robbers and murderers. And it would be a faulty logic to argue that one should resist a murderous man with the sword but let a murderous country run roughshod over thousands of innocent people.

Further support for the position that defensive military power is sometimes justifiable may be deducted from the life of the apostle Paul. When his life was threatened by unruly men he appealed to his Roman citizenship and accepted the protection of the Roman army (Acts 22:25-29). On one occasion certain men dedicated themselves to kill Paul, but he was taken under the protection of a small army of soldiers (Acts 23:23). There is no reason to believe that the apostle

---

[13] To interpret this command metaphorically or ironically, as some pacifists do, is contrary to the fact that the disciples fetched two literal swords and Jesus acknowledged them (v. 38).

did not consider it his right as a citizen to be protected by the army from unjust aggression against his life. On the contrary, his actions clearly demonstrate that as a Roman citizen he demanded this protection. And the principle of using military power in self-defense can be extended to a nation as well as to individuals. For, as pacifists acknowledge too, there is not in the New Testament a double standard of morality, one rule for the individual and another for the country. After all, countries are made of many individuals. In brief, not all killings or wars are unjust. God sometimes commands that men use the sword to resist evil men.

Perhaps a word should be said here about the pacifist's unacceptable way of explaining God's "commands" as purely cultural or as concessions to human sinfulness. For this kind of hermeneutic would undermine the Christian's confidence in all the commands of Scripture. When a command is conditional or cultural the Scriptures reveal it to be such. For example, Jesus pointed out that Moses had not really *commanded* divorce but merely allowed it (Matt. 19:8). Likewise, the Bible clearly indicates that God's order to anoint Saul king over Israel was a concession and not God's desire for Israel (cf. 1 Sam. 8:6-9). However, there is no such indication that God wanted Israel to "make love not war" with the Canaanites. They were past winning; they were incurably wicked and God ordered them to be exterminated (cf. Lev. 18:27, 28; Deut. 20:16, 17). Neither is there any indication that capital punishment was used on murderers simply because the prevailing culture taught this or because the people didn't love the murderer enough. The implication of Scripture is that capital punishment is the very thing that God wanted to be done for such murderers (cf. Gen. 9:6; Rom. 13:4).

So, too, were the commands to Israel to wage war on Canaan really ordered by God. We read continually in the book of Joshua statements like this, "He left none remaining, but utterly destroyed all that breathed, *as the Lord God of Israel commanded*" (Josh. 10:40). Even before Israel entered Canaan they were told, "But in the cities of these people that the Lord your God gives you for an inheritance, you shall save nothing that breathes, but you shall utterly destroy them . . ." (Deut. 20:16, 17). But with regard to all cities outside of Canaan they were told, "When you draw near to a city to fight against it, offer terms of peace to it. And if its answer to you is peace and it opens to you, then all the people who are found in it shall do forced labor for you and serve you. But," it continues, "if it makes no peace with you, but makes war against you, then you shall besiege it; . . . you shall put all the males to the sword, but the women and the little ones, the cattle and everything else in the city, all its spoil, you shall take as booty for yourselves" (Deut. 20:10-17). In this case waging war was conditional but this was not so with the command of God to wage war on the Canaanites.

From this passage it may be concluded that God not only sanctioned the war of exterminating the Canaanites but also approved other just wars against peoples who would not accept a just peace but "came out fighting." In brief, God's command to engage in just wars cannot be limited to the theocratic purposes of God to exterminate the wicked Canaanites. Even in the later monarchies God is said to have commanded Israel to war against its aggressors (cf. 2 Chron. 13:15, 16; 20: 29). Indeed, throughout the Old and New Testaments, God ordained war as an instrument of the cause of justice. Even apostate Israel herself, despite her special covenant relation to God, became the victim of governments raised up by God to defeat her (cf. Deut. 28:25ff; Dan. 1:1, 2). Nebuchadnezzar (Dan. 4:17), Cyrus (Isa. 44:28), and even Nero are described as servants of God empowered with the sword. Paul wrote of the latter, "But if you do wrong, be afraid, for he does not bear the sword in vain; he is the servant of God to execute His wrath on the wrongdoer" (Rom. 13:4). From this it is evident that Gentile rulers of both Testaments were given the sword to promote good and resist evil.

Hence, total pacifism on the alleged grounds that one should never take another human life is unbiblical. The prohibition is against *murder*, not against life-taking. Not all life-taking is murder, according to the Bible. Capital punishment is not murder. War in defense of the innocent is not murder. And a war against an unjust aggressor is not murder. The total pacifist is not looking fairly at *all* the data of Scripture. Rather, he clings to the prohibition against murder, overlooks the verses where God commands the life-taking of wicked men in defense of the innocent, and naively presupposes that all life-taking is murder.

B. *Moral Basis for Selectivism*

Selectivism can be defended on other than biblical grounds. There are strong moral arguments which can be urged in its favor as well. Two such moral reasons for selectivism are now offered.

1. *Both Pacifism and Activism Are Moral "Copouts"* — To hold to either complete pacifism or total activism is the morally easy way out of a difficult ethical position. It is very easy for one to let his country decide for him that all wars are just. That absolves the individual citizen of any struggle to decide whether the war to which he is being drafted is just or unjust. It does not really matter, for obedience to government is always right; the government is responsible for the war. The soldier is not acting as an individual but as an officer of the state. What he does while "in uniform" is not his ethical responsibility. So goes activism's ethically easy way of resolving the individual's

moral responsibility to do what is morally right regardless of what rulers command. In this respect, pacifism is a corrective of the ethical ease of activism by reminding the activist that one cannot divorce his private and public ethic. There is no moral reason to support exempting a person from responsibility for an unjust killing simply because he does it as a public official and not as a private citizen. (This applies to the police as well as to soldiers.)

On the other hand, pacifism is also an ethically easy way out of facing the real moral problem. The real problem is this: is this or that particular war a just one? (Or, is this or that particular act of war a just one?) The pacifist doesn't need to struggle for an answer. His position has conveniently eliminated in advance the need even to raise the question of the justice of this or that war. The total pacifist rests comfortably on the naive presupposition that *no* war could possibly be just. The reason this position is said to be naive will be given below, but even apart from these reasons, it should be clear that it is ethically much easier to say that *all* war is wrong and *all* life-taking is murder. The pacifist, like the activist, enjoys the comfort and simplicity of his general theory without looking at the difficulty and complexity of the particular facts.

2. *Evil Should Be Resisted* — Another fallacy in the non-selectivisms is the premise that evil should not be resisted. On the contrary, it is morally unjustifiable *not* to resist evil. To permit a murder when one could have prevented it is wrong. To allow a rape when one could have hindered it is an evil. To watch an act of cruelty to children without trying to intervene is morally inexcusable. In brief, not resisting evil is a sin of omission, and sins of omission can be just as evil as sins of commission. In biblical language, "Whoever knows what is right to do and fails to do it, for him it is sin" (James 4:17). And certainly it is right to protect the innocent and to thwart evil aggressors. The pacifist fails to protect the innocent from unjust aggressors and the activist fails to thwart evil aggressors by participating in their unjust wars.

Pacifism is really ethical non-involvism. It refuses to use realistic and appropriate means of protecting the innocent. Anyone who would not shoot a madman strangling his wife or children is morally insensitive to the rights of the innocent. Likewise, the able citizen who would not defend his country against an evil aggressor is morally remiss. Or, the larger power which would not help defend the rights of less powerful countries being overrun by bigger states is morally unrealistic. The total pacifist can easily find himself aiding an evil cause by failing to defend a good one. Thus, complete pacifism is at best morally naive and at worst morally delinquent.

Another sidelight on the evil of pacifism is that it leads to political "copoutism." That is, the pacifist tends to become disengaged with the whole body politic. Sometimes pacifists refuse to pay taxes because that would be supporting a war the country wages. Other more complete Christian pacifists infer that no Christian should assume any official post where he would wield political, police, or military power over non-Christians. The assumption behind this conclusion is that a Christian ought not exert any other force than the spiritual force of love and that this spiritual force is incompatible with the exercise of political power. The fallacy of this reasoning should be evident. It assumes wrongly that government is not of God and that morality is essentially incompatible with government.

Activism, too, can be guilty of not resisting evil. By blind obedience to government on the fallacious ground that all of a government's *decisions* must be of God because its *authority* is of God, one can contribute to an evil cause. Many who followed Hitler in his attempt at genocide came to see the evil of blind activism. Unless the citizen takes the time to determine whether or not the commands of his government are morally right, he may find himself "patriotically" defending the cause which is morally wrong. Or, unless a citizen determines whether or not his country is taking its rightful place *under* God, he may be giving his government the place *of* God. [14] Such would be idolatry, and idolatry is wrong whether the idol is material or governmental. When anything less than God, such as government is, becomes the object of an ultimate commitment (such as "My country, right or wrong"), then one has become a "patriotic" idolator. The Christian patriot pledges allegiance to his country only "under God." He places his country under God and does not replace God within country.

Selectivism avoids the dilemma of pacifism's non-involvism as well as activism's idolatrous patriotism. The selectivist is committed to resisting evil wherever it is found with whatever appropriate means are available. If this means taking up arms to resist an evil aggressor, the selectivist is willing to do so. And because selectivism is committed to defending actively what is morally right, it is a more difficult position than those of the non-selectivisms. It is more difficult because it is actively dedicated to resisting evil with whatever force is appropriate to the evil, spiritual evil with spiritual force, political evil with political force, and even military evil with military force. Further, selectivism is more difficult because the individual must decide in the light of the moral law *which* wars are just and which wars are not. Admittedly, this is not an easy task.

Finally, pacifism is not only moral "copoutism" but in its consistent

[14] See further discussion of this in chapter nine.

form it leads to political "dropoutism."[15] For the body politic by its very nature is committed to the use of political, police, and even military force — all of which are inconsistent with the premise that evil should not be resisted with anything but a moral force. Therefore, personal participation in the body politic would commit the complete pacifist to the use of the kind of force in resisting evil which his major premise does not allow. But to assume that a Christian should not be in government, the police force, or the army is contrary to both the example and teaching of Scripture. It is a strange logic to conclude that even though government is ordained of God as an instrument of justice (Rom. 13:1, 2), and even though Christians are told to pray for governors (1 Tim. 2:1), nevertheless, Christians are themselves forbidden to fulfill God's ordination and their own prayers.

C. *Selectivism and Nuclear War*

What has been said in defense of selectivism thus far applies to limited wars but not to global wars involving macro-nuclear military weapons. Tactical nuclear weapons are a conceivable part of a limited war but megaton nuclear power is so devastating as to make such a war automatically unjust. The same could be said of macro-chemical bombs. Any weapon so devastating as to eliminate whole sectors of the civilian populace cannot be morally justified. For weapons to qualify for a just war they must be limited and applicable to military targets. Megaton nuclear weapons are an irrational and immoral implement of warfare.

In effect, then, when it comes to all-out nuclear war Christian selectivism might be called a nuclear pacifism. The purpose of war is to deter the aggressor, not to destroy him completely. Its aim is to overpower not annihilate one's foes. For a war to be just it must envisage securing a peace which establishes with moral order some meaningful community in its wake. If this cannot be the reasonable anticipation of warfare, as it cannot be in total nuclear war, then allowing evil aggression would be better than total annihilation. Saving the race is more important than winning the war, whatever "winning" could mean in that kind of situation. In brief, selectivism applies only to limited warfare aimed at freeing a people from evil aggression and preserving an on-going community after the war. Since all-out nuclear war cannot do this it is, ipso facto, an unjust war. At the point of universal war and destruction selectivism and pacifism meet. At the point of limited warfare for a just cause selectivism and activism join.

D. *Selectivism and Hierarchicalism*

In the first section of this book (in chapter seven) it was argued

---

15 This point was made by William E. Nix in his article "The Evangelical and War," *Journal of the Evangelical Theological Society*, Vol. XIII, Part III (Summer, 1970), p. 138.

that there is a hierarchy of ethical norms such that whenever there is a conflict one should obey the higher norm and break the lower. The principle of higher and lower ethical laws can be seen in operation in the position of selectivism. For the Christian selectivist acknowledges that government is ordained of God and that the Christian should *always* submit to his government under God (1 Peter 2: 13). However, the Christian selectivist recognizes a higher obligation than the one binding him to government. He acknowledges that government is to be obeyed only *under* God but not when government takes the place *of* God. In the event of a conflict between God and government, the selectivist is ready to obey God rather than man. He recognizes that there is a difference between what is Caesar's and what is God's and that what is God's is of higher value than what is Caesar's. For Caesar's powers are delegated by God and are transcended by God. That is, one's direct obligation to God is greater than his indirect relation to God through government. For government is ordained of God to *represent* Him in the social and political area of life, but government was not intended to *replace* God by completely dominating man's moral and religious life. When the lower laws (of government) conflict with the higher laws (of God), then one ought to obey God rather than man.

SELECT READINGS FOR CHAPTER NINE: WAR

Bainton, Roland H., *Christian Attitude Toward War and Peace*, New York: Abingdon Press, 1960.

Bennet, John C., *Foreign Policy as a Problem for Christian Ethics*, New York: Charles Scribner's Sons, 1966.

Bonhoeffer, Dietrich, *The Cost of Discipleship*, trans. by R. H. Fuller, New York: The Macmillan Company, 1963.

Clouse, R. G., et. al. (eds.), *Protest and Politics: Christianity and Contemporary Affairs*, Greenwood, S. C.: Attic Press, 1968.

Finn, James (ed.), *A Conflict of Loyalities: The Case for Selective Conscientious Objection*, New York: Pegasus, 1969.

MacGregor, G. H. C., *The New Testament Basis of Pacifism*, New York: The Fellowship of Reconciliation, 1942.

Nagel, William J. (ed.), *Morality and Modern Warfare: The State of the Question*, Baltimore, Maryland: Helicon Press, Inc., 1960.

Plato, *Crito* in *The Collected Dialogues of Plato*, ed. by Edith Hamilton and H. Cairns, New York: Random House, Inc., 1961.

Ramsey, Paul, *The Just War: Force and Political Responsibility*, New York: Scribners, 1968.

10 / The Christian and Social Responsibility

It was the conclusion of the first part of this book that a Christian's basic ethical position include several norms. Two of these form the basis for the Christian's social responsibility: (1) other men should be respected as persons (i.e., ends) and not used as things (i.e., means); (2) many persons are of more value than one person. In biblical language this means that (1) the Christian should love his neighbor (Matt. 22:39) and (2) that every other person, friend or enemy, is our neighbor (Matt. 5:43, 44; Luke 10:29ff). In brief, the Christian has a responsibility to his neighbors, and the whole world of persons are his neighbors. All men are God's offspring or children [1] and, therefore, they are natural brothers of each other, made in the image and likeness of God (Acts 17:26, 28). And in this fraternity of created persons God has charged each with the responsibility for the others. Love demands that we be our brother's keeper.

I. THE CHRISTIAN'S SOCIAL RESPONSIBILITY IN GENERAL

That man is responsible for his fellowman is clearly taught in Scripture. What is apparently not obvious to some Christians is that this responsibility extends to social as well as to spiritual ones. A survey of Scripture will support the position that the Christian's duty to love includes the social as well as the spiritual dimensions of love.

A. Responsibility for Other Persons

It is apparent thoughout Scripture that men do have a responsibility to others. The answer to Cain's question, "Am I my brother's keeper?"

---

[1] All men are "children" of God by creation, even though they must be born again to become God's children by redemption (John 3:3ff).

178

the christian and social responsibility / 179

is a clear "Yes." Even before Cain, Adam was given the responsibility for his wife, a point implied in the fact that the command for both Adam and Eve was addressed to Adam alone (Gen. 2:16, 17). Later, when murder and violence filled the earth, God gave to men authority to administer capital punishment in order to curb violence (Gen. 9:6). This responsibility of men for one another through government is seen throughout the rest of the Old Testament (cf. Dan. 4:17) and in the New Testament as well (cf. Rom. 13:1-7).

The responsibility is not merely to protect innocent lives; it also includes doing positive good for others. According to Jesus, it is the teaching of the Old Testament, too, that a man is responsible to love his neighbor as himself. Jesus said that love is the essence of the moral law (Matt. 22:39). He even said that the whole of Old Testament morality could be reduced to the Golden Rule (Matt. 7:12). Specific examples of what it means to love others are not lacking either in the life or teachings of Christ. Jesus' healing of the lame, the lepers, and the blind illustrate His own concern, and His story about the Good Samaritan demonstrates the love all men should have to others (Luke 10:30ff).

The epistles of the New Testament abound with exhortations to Christians to care for one another and for others. Paul wrote, "Let each of you look not only to his own interests, but also to the interests of others" (Phil. 2:4). Again, "Bear one another's burdens, and so fulfill the law of Christ" (Gal. 6:2; cf. verse 10). The first epistle of John is very explicit about the Christian's responsibility to love others (cf. 3:17-18), as is James (cf. 1:27). In brief, man is morally responsible for other men. He is his brother's keeper.

B. *Responsibility for the Whole Person*

What sometimes escapes Christians is the fact that the responsibility to love other persons extends to the *whole* person. That is, man is more than a soul destined for another world; he is also a *body* living in this world. And as a resident of this time-space continuum man has physical and social needs which cannot be isolated from spiritual needs. Hence, in order to love man as he is — the whole man — one must exercise a concern about his social needs as well as his spiritual needs.

Some of the neglect of the "whole man" stems from a non-Christian platonic stress on the duality of man. This emphasis was imbibed by Christians in the Middle Ages and has been passed on to the present. [2] In essence it contends that man is essentially a spiritual being and only functionally connected with a body which at best is a hindrance and at worst a great evil. The corrective of this

[2] Platonic philosophy stems from Plato's emphasis on the other heavenly world of true forms of which this material world is at best a shadow and image. See *Republic*, Book VII.

error is found in the biblical teaching of the essential unity of man and the goodness of the physical and bodily creation of God (cf. Gen. 1:31). Both the unity of man and the goodness of the body are made evident in the Christian doctrine of the resurrection, a fact repugnant to the Greek mind (cf. Acts 17:32). The resurrection of the body would not make good sense if men were complete without their body (cf. 1 Cor. 15:53f; 2 Cor. 5:4) or if the body were evil. On the other hand, if man is essentially and permanently to be a souled body, then the neglect of either aspect is a serious mistake. If man is to be loved as man, then one must love him as he is (and as he will be) viz., as a physical and social creature as well as a spiritual one.

Even if one rejects the doctrines of the unity of man and the immortality of the body, it is short-sighted to show concern for only his spiritual dimensions in this life. For men in this life do have bodies and cannot live here without them. Therefore, if they are to be reached for the next world — if we are to save their "souls" — then this must be accomplished through their bodies. Starving bodies are not likely to be impressed by the message about the bread of life if we refuse to give them food for this life. Jesus fed the hungry multitude with physical bread before He preached to them about spiritual bread (John 6:11ff). Men are not as likely to feel the thirst for the water of life when they are overwhelmed by bodily thirst. In other words, if Christians show no concern for the basic physical and social needs of men, then they cannot expect much of a positive response from them to their spiritual message.

II. The Christian's Social Responsibilities in Particular

A better way of showing that Christians do have a social responsibility is by a discussion of the particular exhortations of Scripture in this regard. There are many areas of need for which the Christian is held responsible in love. The first and most basic area is the responsibility for one's own.

A. *Social Responsibility to One's Own*

The responsibility of a person to provide for his own self and for his own family is his basic social responsibility. In a socialistic type of society it is easy to forget that society does not owe the able a living; rather, it owes him an opportunity to make a living. It is in this sense that there is truth in the slogan, "I fight poverty; I work." [3]

1. *Providing for One's Self* — There is a sense in which self-love is at the very basis of social responsibility. [4] A man is to love his

---

[3] However, if a man is not able to work or not able to find work, he should be helped by society.

neighbor *as* himself. Paul said, "For no man ever hates his own flesh, but nourishes and cherishes it . . ." (Eph. 5:29). However, not every one loves himself in a *proper* way. The proper way to love oneself is to provide the basic needs for one's own existence. It will not be possible to live and love others unless one loves and provides for his own life. "But we exhort you brethren," wrote Paul, "to mind your own affairs, and to work with your hands, as we charged you; so that you may command the respect of outsiders, and be dependent on nobody" (1 Thess. 4:11, 12). In his second epistle to the Thessalonians the apostle reminds them of his own example: "We were not idle when we were with you, we did not eat any one's bread without paying, but with toil and labor we worked night and day, that we might not burden any of you" (3:7, 8). And he left this command with them: "*If any one will not work, let him not eat*" (3:10).[5]

So one of the most basic things each able-bodied man can do for others is to make his own living. For if each man who could do so would become independent, then there would be fewer men dependent on others for their basic social needs. That is, the fundamental social good a man can perform for others is providing for himself so that others do not need to provide both for themselves and also for those who won't provide for themselves. In this sense self-love is one of the first and most fundamental social goods one can perform.

2. *Providing for One's Family* — Of course, not everyone is able to provide for himself. There are children, dependents, widows, orphans, and other indigent people. If any of these happens to be in one's immediate family or among his relatives, then it is his social responsibility to provide for them. On this point the Bible is very plain: "If any one does not provide for his relatives, and especially for his own family, he has disowned the faith and is worse than an unbeliever" (1 Tim. 5:8). Further, "if any believing [man or] woman has relatives who are widows, let [him or] her assist them; let the church not be burdened, so that it may assist those who are real widows" (v. 16). The point is that the primary social obligation for the poor and needy does not fall on the church or the state but on the immediate family. This does not mean, of course, that one cannot fulfill his social responsibility to relatives indirectly through state aid which his taxes support. It does mean that the able individual must provide for his own relatives somehow, whether through the state or on his own.

On the other side of the issue, it is implied that able-bodied

[4] See chapter eight on self-love for further elaboration of this point.
[5] Emphasis added.

persons, whether they are widows or not, will provide for themselves so that relatives, church, or state will not have to provide for them. Paul would not permit widows under sixty years of age to be placed on the welfare rolls of the church, and then only those who had previously helped others were enrolled (1 Tim. 5:9, 10). Younger widows were encouraged to keep busy and to remarry (v. 14). The rule implied throughout is that one ought to provide for his own, unless they are not able to provide for themselves. If one fails to provide for indigent relatives, he has failed in his basic Christian responsibility to his own family.

3. *Providing for One's Fellow Believers* — According to the Scriptures one's next social responsibility is to other believers. Beyond his own family, it is the basic needs of other believers which should be the Christian's concern. Paul urged the Galatians, "So then, as we have opportunity, let us do good to all men, and *especially to those who are of the household of faith*" (6:10). Paul himself was very active in taking an offering for the poor saints at Jerusalem (cf. Rom. 15:26). John, likewise, stressed providing for the needs of the brethren, writing, "But if any one has the world's goods and sees his brother in need, yet closes his heart against him, how does God's love abide in him?" (1 John 3:17).

James is equally strong on the emphasis of providing for the brethren: "If a brother or a sister is ill-clad and in lack of daily food, and one of you says to them, 'Go in peace, be warmed and filled,' without giving them the things needed for the body, what does it profit?' (James 2:15, 16). Faith without works is dead. As John put it, "If any one says, 'I love God,' and hates his brother, he is a liar; for he who does not love his brother whom he has seen, cannot love God whom he has not seen" (1 John 4:20). And the most basic mark of Christian love is the love of the brethren. Jesus said, "By this all men will know that you are my disciples, if you have love for one another" (John 13:35). The Christian's social responsibility of love beyond his own family begins with the family of God. This truth is implied also in the care of the early church for its own widows (Acts 6:1; 1 Tim. 5:9ff).

It does not follow from this that Christians should not be socially concerned about non-Christians. Far from it. The Bible is full of evidence that believers should do good to *all men*. The Christian's social concern should *begin* with his own family and other believers but it should not *end* there.

B. *Social Responsibility to All Men*

The exhortation, "Do good to all men," is repeated in kind throughout the Bible. Of the rich Paul wrote, "They are to do good, to be rich in good deeds, liberal and generous . . ." (1 Tim. 6:18).

Indeed, Christian love leads people to give "according to their means" and can even prompt some to give "beyond their means, of their own free will" (2 Cor. 8:3). But every Christian is obliged to the poor to give "as God has prospered him" (1 Cor. 16:2, A. V.). The writer of Hebrews reminds those believers, "Do not neglect to do good and to share what you have, for such sacrifices are pleasing to God" (13:16). Often the Christian is challenged as follows, "Whatever you do, in word or deed, do everything in the name of the Lord Jesus . . ." (Col. 3:17; cf. 1 Cor. 10:31). It is fair to conclude that the question is not *whether* a Christian has a social responsibility to all men; rather, the question is *what* is this social responsibility? In order to answer this question it will be necessary to look first at the precise areas of social responsibility outlined in Scripture. From this may be drawn some general principles which may be applied to other more complex societies.

1. *Social Responsibility to the Poor* — Jesus said, "You always have the poor with you . . ." (Matt. 26:11). By this He described the inevitability of poverty as a social phenomenon, not its desirability. Indeed, Jesus said, "When you give a feast, invite the poor . . . and you will be blessed, because they cannot repay you" (Luke 14:13-14). To a man whose sin was love of money Jesus said, "One thing you still lack. Sell all that you have and distribute to the poor . . ." (Luke 18:22). When Zacchaeus was converted he said, "Behold, Lord, the half of my goods I give to the poor" (Luke 19:8).

The first church at Jerusalem asked Paul to "remember the poor, which very thing," said he, "I was eager to do" (Gal. 2:10). In fulfillment of this Paul wrote, "Macedonia and Achaia have been pleased to make some contribution for the poor among the saints at Jerusalem" (Rom. 15:26). Even before this time, when there was a famine in Jerusalem, "the disciples determined, everyone according to his ability, to send relief to the brethren who live in Judea" (Acts 11:29). It was an assumed part of Christian social responsibility from the very beginning that those who were able should give to the poor. That God has special regard for the poor is taught also in the book of James (cf. 2:5).

The Old Testament abounds with exhortations about the poor. The law of Moses commanded that the corners and gleanings of the fields be left for the poor and for strangers (Lev. 19:9). It was further commanded, "If your brother becomes poor, and cannot maintain himself with you, you shall maintain him" (Lev. 25:35; cf. Deut 15:15). Special blessing is promised those who give to the poor: "He who is kind to the poor lends to the Lord, and he will repay him for his deeds" (Prov. 19:17). Again, "Blessed is he who considers the poor!" (Ps. 41:1). On the other hand, those who oppressed the poor were singled out for definite judgment. The Psalmist said, "I know that the Lord maintains the cause of the afflicted, and executes justice for the needy" (140:12). The prophets were champions of the poor. Isaiah wrote, "Woe to those who decree iniquitous decrees, . . . to turn aside the needy from justice and to rob the poor of my people of their right . . ." (10:1-2). Amos warned, "Hear this, you who trample upon the needy, and bring the poor of the land to an end, . . . The Lord has sworn by the pride of Jacob: 'Surely I will never forget any of their deeds'" (8:4, 7).

Briefly stated, the Bible teaches that it is morally wrong to exploit the poor and morally right to help the poor. Whether their need is food, clothes, or shelter, the believer is morally obliged to help fill it. In fact, what one does for the poor he is doing to Christ. "Truly, I say to you, as you did it to one of the least of these my brethren, you did it to me," for "I was hungry and you gave me food, I was thirsty and you gave me drink, I was a stranger and you welcomed me, I was naked and you clothed me . . ." (Matt. 25:40, 35-36).

2. *Social Responsibility to Widows and Orphans* — The Scriptures have numerous references to widows and orphans. God said, "You shall not afflict any widow or orphan. If you do afflict them, and they cry out to me, I will surely hear their cry" (Ex. 22:22, 23). There was a prohibition against taking a woman's garment in pledge (Deut. 24:17). When fields were reaped, all the forgotten sheaves were to be left for widows and fatherless (Deut. 24:19). Every third year the tithe of produce went to widows, orphans, and so-journers (Deut. 26:12-13). This latter point seems to establish the basis for taxation to support the needy. For it was not a voluntary offering but a required tithe that was to be used for the needy. In brief, God prounounced special blessing on the needy (cf. Ps. 146:9), a curse on those who exploited them (Deut. 27:19), and an obligation on all to support them.

The New Testament, likewise, stresses the Christian's social obligation to the fatherless and widows. Jesus warned, "Beware of the scribes . . . who devour widow's houses . . ." (Mark 12:40). Jesus singled out a widow for special attention because of her sacrificial giving (Luke 21:2). The early church ministered to widows (Acts 6:1), and Paul reminded Timothy, "Honor widows who are real widows" (1 Tim. 5:3). The church had a welfare roll for widows who were too old to work or who could not remarry (1 Tim. 5:9f). Perhaps the strongest passage in the New Testament on the subject is in the book of James, where it is written, "Religion that is pure and undefiled before God and the Father is this: to visit orphans and widows in their affliction . . ." (James 1:27). The biblical concept of "visitation" meant far more than pay a call on them; it meant to help relieve their affliction. Unless one is doing this, says James, his religion is not pure.

The obligation which Christians have toward widows and orphans can be applied by extension to other needy persons such as the handicapped, the homeless, and the helpless. The principle of social responsibility is that there is an obligation to help others who cannot help themselves. If they are without a home, hospitality is to be shown them (Heb. 13:2). If they are without clothes, clothes should be given (James 2:15). If they are without friends, they should be visited (Matt. 25:36). In a word, whatever basic social need — food, clothes, shelter, etc. — one may have, the Christian is obliged to try to meet it.

3. *Social Responsibility to Slaves and Oppressed* — Christians are to defend the oppressed and enslaved. The Bible has no prohibition against voluntary servanthood, but it does oppose forced slavery. The term "voluntary servant" is just another way of describing an employee, and there is nothing wrong with willingly working for another. A willing submission to another is not socially or morally wrong. If it were, then marriage would be the greatest social evil, for wives are constantly urged to submit to their husbands (Eph. 5:21; Col. 3:18; 1 Pet. 3:1).

At first glance, the Scriptures may seem to condone forced slavery. The children of Israel made slaves of their enemies (Josh. 9:23). New Testament Christians had slaves (cf. Philemon). Paul wrote, "Slaves, be obedient to those who are your earthly masters, with fear and trembling, in singleness of heart, as to Christ" (Eph. 6:5). However, it should be noticed that the Bible does not *command* slavery; at best it only *permitted* slavery. In like manner, the Scriptures do not *advocate* divorce but only *allowed* it because of the hardness of men's hearts (cf. Matt. 19:8). Indeed even the Old Testament says clearly, "For I hate divorce, says the Lord God ..." (Mal. 3:16). Jesus said of marriage, "What therefore God has joined together, let no man put asunder" (Matt. 19:6). But are there any indications that God hates slavery, even though He sometimes has permitted it along with other sins of men's hard hearts? The answer is a clear yes. Everything the Scriptures say about the essential equality of men and the wrongness of oppressing others is indicative of God's attitude about slavery.

Moses commanded, "You shall not give up to his master a slave who has escaped from his master to you . . . [and] you shall not oppress him" (Deut. 23:16). One of the most complete passages on social justice in the entire Bible speaks out against all kinds of oppression. Ezekiel wrote,

If a man is righteous and does what is lawful and right — if he . . . does not oppress any one, but restores to the debtor his pledge, commits no robbery, gives his bread to the hungry and covers the naked with his garment, does not lend at interest or take any increase, withholds his hands from iniquity, executes true justice between man and man . . . — he is righteous, he shall surely live, says the Lord God (Ezek. 18:5-9).

Among other things, this passage shows that God is against economic slavery as well as social slavery.

Although there are numerous references against oppression in the Old Testament (e.g., Ex. 22:21; Jer. 30:20; Mal. 3:5), one of the strongest indications that God opposes political and social slavery is the deliverance of Israel from Egypt. The Lord said, "I have seen the affliction of my people who are in Egypt, and have heard their cry because of their taskmasters; I know their suffering, and I have come down to deliver them out of the hand of the Egyptians. . . . I have seen the oppression with which the Egyptians oppress them" (Ex. 3:8-9). When the king of Egypt set taskmasters over Israel, afflicted them with heavy burdens, and forced them to build cities, God sent Moses to deliver them (Ex. 1:11-13). God is strongly opposed to institutions of human slavery. Whether the slavery be political or economic, God is saying, "Let my people go."

The New Testament is as opposed to slavery as the Old Testament is. Paul pointed out that "there is neither Jew nor Greek, there is neither slave nor free . . . for you are all one in Christ Jesus" (Gal. 3:28). "Masters," he warned, "treat your slaves justly and fairly, knowing that you also have a Master in heaven" (Col. 4:1). When the converted runaway slave, Onesimus, returned to his master, Philemon, it was "no longer as a slave but more than a slave, as a beloved brother . . . both in the flesh and in the Lord" (Philemon 16). Hence, by showing that slave and master were brothers under one Master — that they were one in Christ — the New Testament eroded the foundation of slavery built on any alleged essential inequality of men.

It is true that Paul urged every man to continue after his conversion what he was before he became a Christian, whether circumcised or uncircumcised. "Every one should remain in the state in which he was called," he wrote (1 Cor. 7:20). However, to the slaves, he added, "were you a slave when called? Never mind. But if you can gain your freedom, avail yourself of the opportunity. For he who was called in the Lord as a slave is a freeman of the Lord" (vv. 21, 22).

If there is any point on which the Bible is emphatic it is that all men are created in the image of God and that they should be treated as persons (ends in themselves) and not used as things (means to ends), i.e., not enslaved to others. Hence, in a word, the Christian's obligation to slaves is to help free them from their oppressors, political, economic, or whatever.

The myth about Negroid slavery falsely based on Noah's curse on Canaan in Genesis 9:25-27 has been amply exposed. The Canaanites were not Negroes, and they were cursed and subjected to the Israelites when Joshua captured the land of Canaan. There is no indication in this passage that God pronounced the Negroes slaves.

4. *Social Responsibility to Rulers and Governors* — The Christian has a social responsibility not only to other citizens but also to rulers. It is a three-fold duty; he must (1) obey them, (2) honor them, and (3) pay taxes to them. Jesus verified that one should pay taxes to whom taxes are due, revenue to whom revenue is due, respect to whom respect is due, honor to whom honor is due" (Rom. 13:7). In the same passage Christians are told, "Let every person be subject to the governing authorities. For there is no authority except from God, and those that exist have been instituted by God" (v. 1). About the Christians at Crete Paul said to Titus, "Remind them to be submissive to rulers and authorities, to be obedient . . ." (Titus 3:1). Peter, likewise, wrote, "Be subject for the Lord's sake to every human institution, whether it be to the emperor as supreme, or to governors . . ." (1 Pet. 2:13-14).

There are some obvious reasons for obeying the government: (1) it is ordained of God (Rom. 13:1); (2) government restrains evildoers (v. 3); (3) government rewards good men (v. 3); (4) disobedience to government incurs its wrath (v. 4); (5) it is a good testimony for Christ (v. 5). In brief, it is a great social service to oneself and other men to obey one's government. By submitting to government, one is doing good and resisting evil; he is promoting order and preventing chaos. The question arises, however, whether it is ever one's social responsibility to disobey government. The answer to this question seems to be yes.

Several instances of divinely approved disobedience to government illustrate that they all have one common denominator. The Hebrew midwives disobeyed the king when he commanded them to *kill innocent children* (Ex. 1:16f). The three Hebrew youths disobeyed government when it demanded that they *worship an idol* (Dan. 3). Daniel refused the order of the king *not to pray to the true God* (Dan. 6). The apostles would not agree with the Jewish authorities who demanded that they *never again preach the Gospel* of Christ (Acts 4:18; 5:29). Peter said to these rulers, "We must obey God rather than men." When Jesus said, "Render therefore to Caesar the things that are Caesar's, and to God the things that are God's" (Matt. 22:21), the implication is that not everything is Caesar's.

In plain view of Peter's statement and the example of the other saints' disobedience, the following principle may be deduced: one should always obey government when it takes its rightful place *under* God, but one should never obey government when it takes the place *of* God. Only God has the right to demand the sacrifice of human lives, for God alone is the Author and Owner of all life (Deut. 32:39). Only God has the right to be worshiped or to expect prayer to be exclusively to Himself. For a ruler to assume any of these roles is to overstep his authority *under* God and to assume the authority *of* God.

Governors are called the ministers or servants of God (Rom. 13:4), but they are not God. To play God is not only a dangerous role for a ruler but it is an unjustified one. No Christian has a *social* obligation to obey a government which assumes the place of God. On the contrary, the Christian has a *spiritual* obligation to disobey such a government. To do otherwise would be idolatry. For whatever is given the sovereign place of God — whether a relic or a ruler — is an idol.

A specific example of how an oppressive government can assume the place *of* God rather than taking its place *under* God is that of the Egyptian king who refused to let Israel go. Moses had requested that Pharaoh let Israel go that they might serve God (Ex. 4:23) and sacrifice to the Lord (5:17). But Pharaoh hardened his heart and refused to let Israel go (7:14, 22). Since Pharaoh would not stop playing God to Israel, it was necessary for them to disobey the king and go anyway. [6] There were several ways that Egyptian kings had assumed the role of God: (1) they commanded the mid-wives to take innocent human lives (Ex. 1:16f); (2) they forbade Israel to worship and serve God the way God had commanded (Ex. 4:23; 5:17); (3) they put Israel into forced slavery (Ex. 1:11-14); (4) they did not permit Israel to leave the country when they requested (Ex. 7:14, 22). The first two reasons were spiritual (violating their responsibility before God) and the last two were social (violating their rights as creatures of God).

From these latter two reasons we may deduce the following rule: a government is wrongly assuming the role of God rather than taking its rightful place under God when it either (1) oppresses its citizens in a forced kind of slavery, or (2) does not respect the principle of governing by the consent of the governed. Even in

[6] It is true that Pharaoh temporarily changed his mind and said Israel might leave Egypt (Exod. 9:28), but when Israel finally left, it was not with the Pharaoh's approval as is obvious from his pursuit of them (Exod. 14:10ff).

Plato's arguments used to support the activist's position, two of the reasons given were that one has consented to obey his government and if he doesn't like his government he can go elsewhere. [7] However, when a government is forcing people into slavery against their will and refuses to let them leave the country, then it is assuming the role of God. It is violating the rights of creatures to be treated as persons and not to be used as things. No one has the social obligation to obey a government which is not treating persons as persons (i.e., ends) but is using them as things (i.e., means to an end). In fact, it may be one's moral obligation to refuse to obey such an oppressive government in those matters that violate basic human rights.

One further point should be made in this regard and that is that it is never morally justifiable to rebel against a government which is not assuming the role of God. *Under* God, government has full authority. Absalom's rebellion against David was unjustified (2 Sam. 15), as was Jeroboam's revolt after Solomon's death (1 Kings 12). Both were politically motivated, and no revolution is justified for a Christian on *purely political grounds,* i.e., in preferring one form of government under God over another one. [8] Of course, one can and should work within his government to improve it politically, but there is no biblical justification for working to overthrow one's government unless it assumes the role of God (and this is a moral or spiritual reason, not a purely political one).

5. *Responsibility to Promote Peace and Morality* — It is for the good of all men as social beings that society be peaceful and godly. To this end Christians are charged with a special responsibility to all men. "First of all, then," wrote the apostle, "I urge that supplication, prayers, intercession, and thanksgiving be made for all men . . . that we may lead a quiet and peaceable life, godly and respectful in every way" (1 Tim. 2:1, 2). Elsewhere Paul adds, "Live in harmony with one another. . . . If possible, so far as it depends upon you, live peaceably with all" (Rom. 12:17, 18). Jesus said, "Blessed are the peacemakers" (Matt. 5:9). The Christian, then, is to do whatever he can to be an ambassador of peace in society. Whatever mediative role he may assume to bring men together, whether by intercession with God or by negotiation with men, the Christian should pursue. And whatever influence for moral good a Christian can exert in his community or in the world, surely he should be active in exerting. As the salt of society, the Christian may have to

---

[7] See chapter nine where this is discussed.

[8] "Purely political" should not be understood here as having no religious overtones, but as not having any justifiable religious grounds. A justifiable religious ground for disobedience is the government's taking the place of God, as already described.

place himself in some of the most rotten spots where his preserving influence can be most effective. Wherever there is some good to do in society the Christian should be on the front line, remembering the injunction of Scripture, "So then, as we have opportunity, let us do good to all men" (Gal. 6:10).

A word of summary is now in order. The Bible teaches that a Christian has a social responsibility to (1) give to the poor, (2) help widows and orphans, (3) work for the release of slaves and other oppressed people, (4) obey rulers under God, and (5) promote peace and morality wherever he can. The Christian's social responsibility begins with his own family and extends to all men and is to be measured according to his resources. This, then, is *what* the Christian should do, but it leaves two other questions unanswered, viz., *how* and *why* should a Christian exercise these social responsibilities?

III. The Motive and Method of the Christian's Social
     Responsibility

Should a Christian do social good only for the sake of gaining an opportunity for doing some further spiritual good? Or, should social good be done for its own sake?

A. *The Motives for Doing Social Good*

There is more than one reason for a Christian's social responsibility. The reasons listed here are not necessarily exclusive of each other. Some of them overlap and some may be different ways of saying almost the same thing.

1. *Social Benevolence Is a Good Testimony for Christ* — In several places in the New Testament it is implied that the Christian ought to perform social good as a good testimony of his faith. This is implied in Paul's reasons for obeying rulers. He said, "Therefore one must be subject . . . for the sake of conscience" (Rom. 13:5). Peter wrote, "Be subject for the Lord's sake. . . . For it is God's will that by doing right you should put to silence the ignorance of foolish men" (1 Pet. 2:13, 15). To refuse to do good in Christ's name is to bring reproach on Christ by default.

2. *What Is Done for the Needy Is Done to Christ* — Not only is a social good to be performed *for* Christ but it should be done as *to* Christ. Jesus said, "As you did it to one of the least of these my brethren, you did it to me" (Matt. 25:40). Feeding the hungry, clothing the naked, visiting the needy is doing these things to Christ Himself. And failing to do these social goods is failing to do them to Christ, for "as you did it not to one of the least of these, you did it not to me," Jesus said (Matt. 25:45). The Christian, then, should perform social good out of the motive that he is doing it for Christ.

With this agrees the apostle's statement, "Whatever your task, work heartily, as serving the Lord and not men, knowing that from the Lord you will receive the inheritance as your reward; you are serving the Lord Christ" (Col. 3:23, 24).

3. *Social Good Can Help Win Men to Christ* — There are clear indications in Scripture that social good can be used as the means to reach men with the spiritual good of the Gospel. The apostle wrote, "I try to please all men in everything I do . . . that they may be saved" (1 Cor. 10:33). In another context he said, "I have become all things to all men, that I might by all means save some" (1 Cor. 9:22). It makes good sense that men will be more receptive to the spiritual bread of life if they are given some physical bread for their bodies. Christian rescue missions and medical missionaries have shown the effectiveness of this reasoning.

4. *Doing Social Good for Its Own Sake* — It appears that social good should be done for Christ, unto Christ, and to win men to Christ, but should it ever be done for its own sake? Must the Christian always have an evangelistic reason for doing social good? Must everything be directed toward winning men to Christ or getting a reward from Christ? If the example of Christ is followed, then the answer is clearly no. Jesus did social good for its own sake. He healed ten lepers knowing that only one would return to give thanks (Luke 17:13ff). Further, Jesus urged that one do good to his enemies who would not return the favor (Matt. 5:43, 44), and to the needy who could not repay the kindness (Luke 14:12, 13). The Christian, following Christ, should do whatever good he can simply because it is a good, whether or not any one appreciates it or is won to Christ through it. Jesus' love of Judas, even though he knew Judas would betray him, is exemplary in this regard.

But if the Christian ought to do good — social or spiritual — for its own sake, then why all the emphasis on doing good for Christ and for reward? Are not doing good for rewards and doing good for its own sake mutually exclusive? Is not working for rewards selfish, or at least less than the highest motivation? Not necessarily. If the reward is the enlarged capacity to do more good, then working for rewards is not selfish. It is not incompatible to do good for the sake of doing good and for reward if the reward is the ability to do more good. Nor is it necessarily wrong to do one good (say, social) with the *hope* that it may open the opportunity to do another good (say, spiritual). Working for Christ and working for needy men are not mutually exclusive, since Jesus said that whatever is done to them is done to Him. The Christian can perform social good for its own sake, for Christ's sake, and for the Gospel's sake all at the same time. And he *need not* tie a tract to his CARE package to demonstrate the connection between these; good is *of* God and *for* God in whatever form it may come (cf. James 1:17). Good speaks for itself; it is self-perpetuating. Doing good naturally tends to make more opportunity for performing good work.

B. *Method of Doing Social Good*

Generally speaking, the Christian's social responsibility is clear: he should do his best to help provide for the basic needs (including food, clothes, shelter, etc.) of those who cannot provide for themselves. The problem is not in knowing *what* to do but in knowing *how* best to do it. If the Christian follows Jesus' words, "Give to him who begs from you," literally and simplistically, he may be doing more social harm than good. For example, should a Christian give money to a skid row alcoholic simply because he asks? Would this not contribute to the already great social ill of alcoholism? Likewise, should America give its excess wheat to the hungry of India? Does this not keep more hungry people alive who produce more hungry children which makes the problem of hunger worse than it was? How can the Christian exercise the love principle in a complex society? According to 1 Corinthians 13, it is not necessarily loving to give all of one's possessions to the poor (v. 3). Rather, as Phillips translates verse four, love ". . . looks for a way of being constructive." It may be far more loving to help the poor find a job than to put him on charity.

1. *Helping Others Help Themselves* — If a man can earn his own living, then he can both feed himself and preserve his own dignity as a human being. In this way a constructive love gains a double benefit, that of taking the burden of one man off another plus developing the personhood of another man by making him self-supporting. Further, it may be more loving for the United States to teach the underdeveloped nations how to help themselves rather than playing Santa Claus to the world. It is not always the most loving thing for a country or person to give a "handout." The "haves" are morally obligated to help the "have nots," but they are not bound to empty their closets or bank accounts to equalize the social status of all men. [9] Society does not owe the poor a living; it owes them a way of making a living. Hence, it would be far more *constructive* for love to find ways of employing men than simply to continue supporting them. And since education is crucial to em-

---

[9] Economic communism is a biblical possibility, though not necessarily the ideal. The early Christian communism (Acts 2:44) was not taught as an ideal nor is there any indication in the New Testament that it was any more than a temporary arrangement rising out of the peculiar circumstances of those early Christians, e.g., poverty, persecution, etc.

ployment, it follows that a very basic way for love to be constructive is to help educate the needy.

2. *Helping Others to Not Hurt Themselves* — Not every man knows what is best for himself. The skid row drunk should not be given money; he should be given a meal. He would probably use money to compound his problem with more alcohol. The loving thing to do is to refuse to give money or anything (alcohol, drugs, weapons) to anyone who would thereby add to the problems of society, his own or others'. Of course, it is not always easy to know when something is or is not going to be more harm than help, but the principle is clear and a judgment must be made.

This raises the question of censorship which cannot be treated in detail here. The moral principle behind the right of parents or even society to censor may be stated here. [10] One has the right to censor other beings for whom he is socially responsible when what they are doing is clearly harmful to themselves and/or to others. The problem, again, is not with the moral principle but with one's knowledge of the facts and judgment as to whether the given things are or are not harmful.

3. *Helping One's Own to Help Others* — Furthermore, it is not necessarily selfish to see to it that one gets an education and a job for himself and to seek the same for his family. For the responsibility of love *begins* with oneself. If a man does not love and care for himself and for his own, then someone else will have to do it. Therefore, it will not be ipso facto selfish for a man to care for his own social needs *first*. It may be selfish if he goes no farther than his own household or if he cares for his own luxuries without being concerned about the survival of others. On the other hand, if a man spends his time caring for his own so that some one else does not have to and, in addition, so that his own may be able in turn to help others, then he is performing a definite good for society at large.

C. *Social Responsibility and Hierarchical Ethics*

The conclusion to part one of this book was that there is a hierarchy of ethical principles. Among the basic ethic principles concluded were these: (1) persons are of intrinsic, value, and (2) many persons are of more value than one person. [11] These two norms are at work in the Christian's social ethic. They are both implied in the love principle, as is obvious from Jesus' answer to the lawyer's question, "And who is my *neighbor?*" (Luke 10:29). Jesus replied by telling the story of the Samaritan who was *neighborly*

[10] On censorship see Plato's views in *Republic* Books II and III. John Milton wrote against censorship in his *Areopagitica*.

[11] See chapter seven for further information on the hierarchical position.

to the man who was robbed and beaten by thieves (cf. vv. 36, 37). Although Jesus' answer relates to one's responsibility to be neighborly, the clear implication is that one should love *any fellow human being in need.* That is, the commandment to love one's neighbor is not intended to be taken in the singular. Everyone is my neighbor. Hence, one is really commanded to love his neighbor*s*. The responsibility to love must be maximized among as many human beings as possible. This would imply that loving so as to benefit many persons rather than a few is morally preferable.

Another indication that the principle of love is not provincial is found in the Sermon on the Mount. 'You have heard that it was *said* [i.e., by false interpretors of the law, for it is nowhere *written* in the law], 'you shall love your neighbor and hate your enemy.' But I say to you," affirmed Jesus, "Love your enemies and pray for those who persecute you" (Matt. 5:43-44). Jesus rejected any subtle distinction between one's "neighbor" and his "enemy." One is not obligated merely to love his neighbors, and free, therefore, by implication to hate those who were not his immediate neighbors. This, Jesus declared, is a sophisticated evasion of what was clearly intended in the command to love all men as oneself. The Jews should have understood that the Old Testament did not limit love to one's friends or countrymen by the command to love strangers (Deut. 10:19), by God's dealing with Jonah (cf. 4:1, 2), and His redeeming interest in Gentiles in general (cf. Isa. 49:22; Joel 3:9; Mal. 1:11).

The conclusion, then, is this. The Bible teaches that one should love his neighbors, i.e., all men. And this implies that one should love in such a way as to benefit the most men possible, not just his immediate neighbors. This is to say the same thing as expressed by the hierarchical principle that love for many persons is more valuable than love for only one. When love is distrubuted in this way among the most men possible, the love norm becomes a constructive social ethic. Without this, it can be a destructive provincialism.

It does not necessarily follow, of course, that one should "spread" his love so thin that all men receive an equal amount. For in this event no one would receive a significant amount of love. Indeed, the best way to love most men in the long run may well be to love one's immediate family and friends the best he can. Love is contagious. It spreads like a disease if one gets "infected" with enough of it. Christian love is concerned with all men, but it *begins* with those under one's own roof, it goes out to those next door, then it extends to those across the street, and finally it reaches out to those beyond the sea.

the christian and social responsibility / 195

SELECT READINGS FOR CHAPTER TEN: SOCIAL RESPONSIBILITY

Anderson, John B., *Between Two Worlds: A Congressman's Choice,* Grand Rapids, Mich,: Zondervan Publishing House, 1970.

Bennett, John C., *Christian Ethics and Social Policy,* New York: Charles Scribner's Sons, 1946.

————. *Christian Social Ethics in a Changing World,* New York: Association Press, 1966.

Clouse, R. G., *et al.* (eds.), *Protest and Politics: Christianity and Contemporary Affairs,* Greenwood, S. C.: Attic Press, 1968.

Collins, Gary, *Our Society in Turmoil,* Carol Stream, Illinois: Creation House, 1970.

Grounds, Vernon C., *Evangelical and Social Responsibility,* Scottdale, Penn.

Henry, Carl, *Aspects of Christian Social Ethics,* Grand Rapids, Mich.: William B. Eerdmans Publishing Company, 1964.

Hutchison, John A., (ed.), *Christian Faith and Social Action,* New York: Charles Scribner's Sons, 1953.

Moberg, David, *Inasmuch:Christian Social Responsibility in the Twentieth Century,* Grand Rapids, Mich.: William B. Eerdmans Publishing Company, 1965.

Niebuhr, Reinholdt, *Moral Man and Immoral Society,* New York: Charles Scribner's Sons, 1932.

Wirt, Sherwood E., *The Social Conscience of the Evangelical,* New York: Harper and Row, 1968.

11 / The Christian and Sex

Sex is one of the most important interpersonal relations in which individuals engage. It is one of the most powerful and yet most perverted forces in the world. Perhaps one of the reasons for its perversion is its power. If power tends to corrupt, then great power tends to corrupt greatly. On the other hand, much of the misuse of sex may result from a misunderstanding of it. What is a Christian view of sex? What do the Scriptures really teach about sexual activity?

I. THE BIBLICAL BASIS FOR SEX

Basically, the Bible says three things about sex: (1) sex is good, (2) sex is powerful, and therefore, (3) sex needs to be controlled. In fact, the very first references to sex in Scripture imply all three of these factors.

A. *The Nature of Sex*

Sex is intrinsically good; it is not evil. The Scriptures declare that "God created man in his own image . . . ; male and female [that is sex!] he created them" (Gen. 1:27). And when He had finished, "God saw everything that he had made, and behold, it was very good" (v. 31). Sex is good. God made it and it somehow reflects His own goodness. Perhaps it is because of the creative power of sex that it resembles an aspect of the being of God. Or, maybe it is in its force to bring about the strongest bond of unity and oneness. In whatever other way we are supposed to understand that sex is good like God, it is plain that fundamentally sex is good because God made it and declared it good.

196

1. *Sex Is Essentially Good* — Sex is good in and of itself because it is part of the creation of God. Unlike many non-Christian philosophies (of Gnostic and Platonic varieties), the Bible declares matter and the physical universe (including man's body and bodily organs) to be good. After each day's creation it is written again and again, "And God saw that it was *good*" (Gen. 1:10, 12, 18, 21, 25). After the final day it reads, ". . . and behold, it was *very good*" (v. 31). Sex was an integral part of this very good creation. The Bible confirms this view elsewhere saying, "Everything created by God is good . . ." (1 Tim. 4:4). If sex seems impure to some, we are reminded that "to the pure all things are pure, but to the corrupt and unbelieving nothing is pure" (Titus 1:15).

Speaking specifically of sex, the writer of the epistle to the Hebrews declared, "Let marriage be held in honor among all, and let the marriage bed be undefiled" (Heb. 13:4). Marriage is an honorable state. Marriage could hardly be considered honorable unless sex is good, since sex is an integral part of marriage. So holy is sex that it is used in Scripture to illustrate the most intimate union one can have with God. Paul wrote, "For this reason a man shall leave his father and mother and be joined to his wife, and the two shall become one. This is a great mystery, and I take it to mean Christ and the church" (Eph. 5:31, 32).

The intrinsic goodness of sex may be deduced, as well, from the fact that God has commanded sexual union. God said to the first pair, "Be fruitful and multiply, and fill the earth . . ." (Gen. 1:28) — a command which the race is fulfilling very well! When Eve had her first child she declared, "I have gotten a man with the help of the Lord" (Gen. 4:1), thus acknowledging God's approval of the sexual process. Surely, judging by the numerous references throughout the Scripture to the blessing of children (cf. Ps. 127:4, 5; Prov. 17:6), God judges sex to be good.

2. *Sex Is Powerful* — Not only is sex essentially good but it is very powerful. This was implied in the fact that it could be used to "multiply" people and "fill" the earth (Gen. 1:28). The power of sex is not only dramatically demonstrated by its ability to reproduce in abundance but by the kind of creature it is producing. The children of human parents are generated in the image of God. Adam was made in God's image, and "he became the father of a son in his own likeness, after his image . . . " (Gen. 9:6; James 3:9). Hence, by the process of human sexuality are produced not only many beings but many little "gods." Jesus quoted Psalm 82:6 which says, "I say, 'You are gods, sons of the Most High, all of you.'" (John 10:35). When the nature of the human creature produced through sex is fully appreciated, it

is probably no exaggeration to consider sex one of the most significant powers on earth.

When a human male sperm and a female ovum unite, a little "god" is in the making. All things being equal, the result of that conception will be a creature which both resembles and represents God on earth. [1] Without deciding here the question about whether the unborn embryo or fetus is truly human, [2] it is an indisputable fact that, given the proper circumstances, it definitely will become an immortal creature. Humans are immortal, never-dying persons. They will live forever. [3] Surely, this is no ordinary power given to the sons of men that is capable of conveying into the world a never-dying person, made in the likeness of God Himself. Therefore, human sex is not only good by nature but great in power. It is great both by virtue of how much it can produce and also by virtue of what kind of creature is the product, viz., a never-dying person.

3. *Sex Needs to be Controlled* — It goes without saying that anything as powerful as sex needs to be controlled. No one in his right mind would let immature children play with dynamite. Nor would any responsible agents make atomic weapons available to the general public. And yet sex is in many ways more potent than either dynamite or atomic power. The only reasonable position to take with regard to any force as potent as sex is that it must be controlled or regulated. There must be means of channeling and directing the power of sex for the good of men. For, like atomic power, if sex power is not harnessed for good purposes, then its abuse may threaten to destroy mankind.

According to the Bible, the God-ordained means of directing and regulating the good and great power of sex is known as *marriage*. From the very beginning God declared, "Therefore a man leaves his father and his mother and *cleaves* to his wife, and they become one flesh" (Gen. 2:24). Jesus added, "So they are no longer two but *one*. What therefore God has *joined together*, let no man put asunder" (Matt. 19:6). That is to say, marriage which joins male and female in a unique and abiding relationship is the channel established by God in order to regulate the power of sex.

Of course, sex is not only a power to procreate; it is also a power for pleasure. But whatever kind of power sex is, it needs to be con-

[1] The words "image" and "likeness" may be parallel, but in context they imply that man both represents God (as images do) and resembles Him (as likenesses do).

[2] See chapter twelve for a discusion of the nature of an unborn child, whether it is truly human or not.

[3] The New Testament does not speak of an immortal soul, but it does teach the immortality of a souled body (cf. 2 Tim. 1:10; 1 Cor. 15:51ff; 2 Cor. 5:6-10; 1 Thess. 4:13-18; John 5:28).

trolled. No passion should go unbridled. [4] Rape and sadistic sexual crimes cannot be justified on the mere grounds that they bring pleasure to the abuser. Even if it were true that only pleasures are intrinsically good, it does not follow that *all* pleasures are good. Some pleasures are harmful to oneself and/or others. For example, the pleasures some get from being cruel or unjust or hateful are not good pleasures. Further, not all pleasures are equally good; some are higher than others. Hence, one cannot justify an uncontrolled exercise of sex merely on the grounds that it is pleasureful. All pleasures must be controlled, and there are higher spiritual satisfactions than the mere physical pleasures of sex. According to the Scriptures, the channel for controlling the pleasure power of sexual intercouse (as well as its procreative power) is marriage. This conclusion is amply supported by a study of the function of sex within the Scriptures.

B. *The Function of Sex*

The function of sex may be viewed from several different vantage points: (1) before marriage, (2) within monogomous marriage, (3) outside of marriage, (4) within polygamous marriage, (5) and for divorcees.

1. *The Role of Sex Before Marriage* — So far as the Bible is concerned, there is no role for premarital sexual intercourse. Intercourse *is* a marriage. Any conjugal relationship is a marriage in God's eyes. It is not necessary a lawful or rightful union, but it is a union. The first reference to marriage declares that man and woman become "one flesh" (Gen. 2:24), implying that marriage occurs when two bodies are joined. That sexual intercourse is marriage is even clearer from the common way of describing the act as a man "lying" with a woman. Moses commanded, "If a man is found lying with the wife of another man, both of them shall die . . . " (Deut. 22:22).

The New Testament further confirms this by using the words "marriage" and "marriage bed" in parallel (Heb. 13:4). In fact, there are no explicit condemnations of premarital sex in the Old Testament. For if an unbetrothed couple engaged in intercourse, the fellow was obliged to pay the marriage fee to the father and to assume the girl as his wife (Deut. 22:28). And when a man goes in to a harlot the Bible considers this a "marriage." Paul wrote, "Do you not know that he who joins himself to a prostitute becomes one body with her," quoting as his proof that the Scriptures say, "The two shall become one" (1 Cor. 6:16). In brief, there is no such thing as premarital intercourse in the Bible. If the couple were not married, then intercourse made them married. If they were already married, then inter-

---

[4] As Plato observed long ago, uncontrolled passions have a despotic effect on the individual as well as on his society. Cf. *Republic* IX, 576 - 579.

course with another person constituted a second, adulterous marriage for them. Harlotry is considered an illegitimate marriage.

An engaged couple who have intercourse have thereby consummated their marriage before God and ought to legalize it before the state as soon as possible, because God commands citizens to be obedient to governmental regulations (Rom. 13:1; 1 Peter 2:13). Engaged couples, according to Paul, should either control their sexual drives or else marry. He wrote, "If any one thinks that he is not behaving properly toward his betrothed, if his passions are strong, and it has to be, let him do as he wishes: let them marry — it is no sin" (1 Cor. 7:36). On the other hand, "whoever is firmly established in his heart, being under no necessity but having his desire under control, and has determined this in his heart, to keep her as his betrothed, he will do well" (v. 37). That is, intercourse is not proper for engaged couples. They should either keep their emotions in check or marry. And when they do engage in intercourse, then they are married in God's eyes and should legalize it before the state, if it is the law of the land to so do.

As to premarital sex relations among those who are not ready to marry the answer is no. If one is not ready to assume the responsibilities of a wife and family then he should not play with sex. The exhortation of Solomon is applicable here: ". . . an adulteress stalks a man's very life. Can a man carry fire in his bosom and his clothes not be burned" (Prov. 6:26, 27). One should not "make out" unless he is prepared to go all the way. And he should not go all the way until he is married, for intercourse is marriage in God's eyes.

As far as autosexuality is concerned (i.e., masturbation), it is generally wrong. Sublimation (draining sexual energy through exercises) and natural nocturnal emissions are considered to be legitimate ways to burn up excess sexual energy. Masturbation is sinful (1) when its only motive is sheer biological pleasure, (2) when it is allowed to become a compulsive habit, and/or (3) when the habit results from inferior feelings and causes guilt feelings. Masturbation is sinful when it is performed in connection with pornographic images, for as Jesus said, lust is a matter of the interests of the heart (Matt. 5:28). On the other hand, masturbation can be right when it is used as a limited, temporary program of self-control to avoid lust before marriage. If one is fully committed to leading a pure life until marriage, it may be permissible on occasion to use autosexual stimulation to relieve one's tension. As long as it does not become a habit nor a means of gratifying one's lust, masturbation is not necessarily immoral. In fact, when the motive is not *lust* but *self-control,* masturbation can be a moral act (cf. 1 Cor. 7:5; 9:25). The biblical rule is that whatever can be done to the glory of God, whatever does not enslave the doer (1 Cor. 10:31; 6:12) is to that extent moral. Masturbation used in moderation without lust for the purpose of retaining one's purity is not immoral. [5]

2. *The Role of Sex in Marriage* — There are several basic functions of sex in marriage, and all of them indicate why marriage is the God-ordained way to regulate these functions. Three positive roles of sex within marriage are: (1) to bring about a unique, intimate *unity* of two persons; (2) to provide *ecstasy* or pleasure for the persons involved in this unique relationship; (3) to bring about a *multiplicity* of persons in the world by having children. Respectively, the three basic functions of sex in marriage are unification, recreation, and procreation.

First, marriage is aimed at bringing two human beings into the closest possible human relationship. "The two shall become *one*" is repeated over and over in Scripture (Gen. 2:24; Matt. 19:5; 1 Cor. 6:16; Eph. 5:31). So unique is this marital union brought about by sex that the Bible uses it to illustrate the mystical union a believer has with Christ (Eph. 5:32). And it is the unique one-of-a-kind nature of the sex relation which calls for a man to sustain it with only one woman. It is not really possible to have two one-of-a-kind relations at once. Marriage — in fact, monogomous marriage — is the only controlled way to maintain a continuously unique relationship between husband and wife. In polygamy there is the ever-present threat of jealousy and the question of who is the "favorite" wife. Indeed, it is not possible to have two "favorite" wives in the same sense. Therefore, it is possible for a man to have a unique relation with one wife only. Monogamous marriage is God's ideal of attaining this ideal relationship between two persons.

The second function of marriage is recreational. Sexual intercourse is literally a re-creation of the bliss of the native nuptial unity. It is a sacramental reminder of the joy of one's first love. Sexual union is the happy reunion of those who were made one by marriage. The satisfaction sex provides is the pleasure gained from reaffirming the original pledge of mutual love. In this regard, the re-creational and reunificational functions of marriage are inseparable. For the real pleasure of sex is that gained from the reaffirmation and re-enforcement of the unique union marriage brought about at the beginning. So the attempt to have the pleasure of sex without the unique and abiding relationship of marriage is illusory. The real joy comes only with the real union, and the real union comes only if there is a unique and abiding relation between two persons of the opposite sex.

[5] The discussion here is summarized from a recent book by Herbert J. Miles, *Sexual Understanding Before Marriage*, Grand Rapids, Zondervan Publishing House, 1971, pp. 137f.

The third role of marriage is procreation. The fruit of unity in matrimony is multiplicity of offspring. Of course, children are the natural but not necessary fruit of marriage. [6] Although marriage is the natural thing to do, it is not necessary to marry. One single person may choose not to marry, without sinning (cf. Matt. 19:12; 1 Cor. 7: 7, 8). Likewise, a married couple may decide not to have children, without sinning (cf. 1 Cor. 7:5), even though it is natural to have them. When children do result from marriage they are a further reason for maintaining marriage as a unique and abiding relation between parents. Children need loving discipline (Prov. 22:15; Eph. 6:4; Col. 3:21). They need the unity and security provided by a happy marriage of their parents. Neither polygamy nor divorce nor anonymity nor community of parents have proven to be strengthening factors in the personalities of children. Scarcely anything is superior to an abiding unity between mother and father for the rearing of healthy, happy children.

A word of summary is now necessary. The function of sex within marriage is threefold: unification, recreation, and procreation. All of these roles demonstrate the need for marital fidelity. Whenever the unique relationship of marriage is broken by extra-marital intercourse one has both destroyed the unique unity of marriage and lessened the true pleasure possible, to say nothing of weakening the basis of stability for any offspring from this union.

From these three positive functions of sex in marriage one negative role may be deduced. Sex within marriage is the way to satisfy what would be lust and lead to promiscuity outside marriage. "Because of the temptation to immorality, each man should have his own wife and each woman her own husband," wrote the apostle (1 Cor. 7:2). All single persons should keep themselves under sexual self-control, "but if they cannot exercise self-control, they should marry. For it is better to marry than to be aflame with passion" (1 Cor. 7:9). Likewise, to the young Thessalonian Christians Paul wrote, "For this is the will of God, your sanctification: that you abstain from immorality; that each one of you know how to take a wife for himself in holiness and honor, not in the passion of lust like heathen . . ." (1 Thess. 4: 3-5). In a word, along with the three positive purposes of sex within marriage is one negative reason, viz., that marriage will provide a preventive channel for the sexual drive so that one can avoid immorality.

3. *The Role of Sex Outside Marriage* — With the purposes of marriage in mind one can more easily understand the strong prohibitions in Scripture about illicit extra-marital relations. Adultery, fornication, harlotry, and sodomy (homosexuality) all come under strong con-

---

[6] Birth control will be discussed in chapter twelve.

demnation. Each one of these sins in its own way violates a divinely ordained inter-personal relationship.

Adultery and harlotry are wrong for two basic reasons, viz., they are multiple marriages. First, they are attempts to carry on *many* most-intimate relationships at once. In each case one is cheating on the one he really loves the most and probably lying to the one(s) he does not love the most. The second reason fornication is wrong is that it is intended to be only a temporary union whereas God desires a sexual union to be abiding and permanent (Matt. 19:6). There is no way to assure the highest pleasure in a marital union unless it is found within the context of a mutual life-long commitment of love.

The Bible is emphatic: "You shall not commit adultery" (Ex. 20: 14). In the Old Testament the adulterers were to be put to death (Lev. 20:10). The New Testament is also emphatically against adultery. Jesus pronounced it wrong even in its basic motives (Matt. 5: 27, 28). Paul called it an evil work of the flesh (Gal. 5:19), and John envisioned in the lake of fire some of those who practiced it (Rev. 21:8).

The word "fornication" is often used in Scripture of illicit sexual relations outside of marriage, although the general understanding is that it implies that at least one member of the relationship was not married. The Jerusalem apostles urged all Christians to abstain from fornication (also called unchastity) (Acts 15:20). Paul said that the body is not for fornication and that a man should flee it (1 Cor. 6: 13, 18). The Ephesians were told that fornication should not be even once named (or spoken of) among them (5:3). Fornication is evil because it, too, is a "marriage" outside of marriage, because it joins persons in an illicit way without their intending to carry through the abiding and unique implications of their relationship.

Homosexualty is not in the same class with the heterosexual sins of adultery, harlotry, and fornication. Homosexuality is unlike these three in that no intercourse in the strict sense of the word occurs and no births can result from it. However, homosexuality in the sense of sexually stimulating and manipulating a person of the same sex is definitely forbidden in Scripture. In the Old Testament this sin was called sodomy, after Sodom, that wicked city which was destroyed on account of this perversity (Gen. 19:5-8, 24). Later, the law of Moses forbade any "sodomite" (A.V.) [7] from being part of the community of Israel (Deut. 23:17). Later, during the reforms of King Asa, "he put away the male cult prostitutes out of the land . . ." (1 Kings 15:12). There are many references to the sins of Sodom (cf. Isa. 3:9; Ezek. 16:46). The New Testament is equally clear on the

---

[7] The Revised Standard Version renders "sodomite" by the words "cult prostitute."

subject. Romans chapter one speaks of homosexuality as that which "exchanged natural relations for unnatural . . . " (v. 26). It is a "shameless act" which results from vile passions (v. 27). In another passage Paul wrote, "Do not be deceived; neither the immoral, nor idolaters, nor adulterers, nor homosexuals . . . will inherit the kingdom of God" (1 Cor. 6:9). These are all a perversion of the proper use of sex. Hetereosexual acts are wrong outside marriage because they set up a husband-wife relation between those who are not husband and wife. Homosexual acts are wrong because they set up a unique husband-wife relation between those who cannot be husband and wife, since they are both of the same sex.

Of course, the biblical prohibitions on homosexuality do not refer to close friendships (with physical affection) between those of the same sex. Such friendships are both normal and beautiful. David and Jonathan are a classic example. The Scriptures say, "The soul of Jonathan was knit to the soul of David, and Jonathan loved him as his own soul" (1 Sam. 18:1). Intimate friendship is one thing; illegitimate and unnatural sexual encounters are quite another thing.

4. *The Role of Sex in Multiple Marriages* — There is little question that polygamy was permitted by God in biblical times. Even some of the great saints had several wives (cf. Abraham, David, Solomon). The real problem is not whether God *permitted* polygamy but whether He *planned* it. That is, was polygamy, like divorce, something God tolerated but did not really desire?

There is ample evidence, even within the Old Testament, that polygamy was not God's ideal for man. That monogamy was His ideal for man is obvious from several perspectives. (1) God made only one wife for Adam (Gen. 2:18ff), thus setting the ideal precedent for the race. (2) Polygamy is first mentioned as part of the wicked Cainite civilization (Gen. 4:23). (3) God clearly forbade the kings of Israel (leaders were the persons who became polygamists) saying, "And he shall not multiply wives for himself, lest his heart turn away again" (Deut. 17:17). (4) The saints who became polygamists paid for their sins. 1 Kings 11:1, 3 says, "Now King Solomon loved many foreign women. . . . He had seven hundred wives, princesses, and three hundred concubines; and his wives turned away his heart." (5) The greatest polygamist of the Old Testament, Solomon, gave testimony to the fact that he had only one true love, for whom he wrote "The Song of Songs." The Canticles stand as the greatest polygamist's greatest rebuke to polygamy. Even Solomon with his 1,000 wives had only one true love. (6) Polygamy is usually situated in the context of sin in the Old Testament. Abraham's marriage of Hagar was clearly a carnal act of unbelief (Gen. 16:1f). David was not at a spiritual peak when he added Abigail and Ahinoam as his wives (1 Sam. 25:

42, 43), nor was Jacob when he married Leah and Rachel (Gen. 29:23, 28). (7) The polygamous relation was less than ideal. It was one of jealousy among the wives. Jacob loved Rachel more than Leah (Gen. 29:31). Elkanah's one wife was considered a "rival" or adversary by the other, who "used to provoke her sorely, to irritate her . . ." (1 Sam. 1:6). (8) When polygamy is referred to, the conditional, not the imperative, is used. "*If* he takes another wife to himself, he shall not diminish her food, her clothing, or her marital rights" (Ex. 21:10). Polygamy is not the moral ideal, but the polygamist must be moral. (9) The New Testament sets down monogamy as a precondition for church leaders. "Now a bishop must be above reproach, the husband of one wife . . ." (1 Tim. 3:2), wrote the apostle. (10) Monogamy was not only required for church leaders but it was recommended for all men. Paul wrote, "But because of the temptation to immorality, each man should have his own wife and each woman her own husband" (1 Cor. 7:2).

There are other arguments against polygamy, such as the relatively equal number of males and females in the world, which would seem to imply that one woman is made for one man. However, it must be conceded that polygamy is better than immorality, even though it is not as good as monogamy. At least, polygamy is a closed system; it is not free love. It is better to take a woman as a second wife than to use her as a harlot, even though both fall short of God's ideal. Polygamy is at least a relationship where the other can be treated as a person and not merely used as a thing. Nonetheless, polygamy is inferior to monogamy because one cannot have a unique (one-of-a-kind) relationship with more than one wife. The other wives will never be more than second best and not part of that most intimate union which God designed for marriage. Jealousy and hatred will be natural outcomes of the polygamous relation.

II. HIERARCHICAL BASIS FOR A CHRISTIAN VIEW OF SEX

Does not the special case of polygamy provide an exception to the moral principle that sex is to be a unique and abiding personal relation between a man and a woman? Furthermore, does not the justifiable case of divorce (viz., when one's partner has been unfaithful) mentioned by Jesus (Matt. 19:9) provide an exception to the morality of the marital bond? From a biblical and hierarchical point of view the answer to both questions is no. There are no *exceptions* to the singularity of the marital relation (i.e., one man for one woman); there are only some *exemptions* in view of higher obligations. Likewise, there are no legitimate exceptions to the permanence of the marriage bond (divorce as such is wrong); there are only some transcendent obligations which may intervene. That is, some duties are higher than others. There are some circumstances where even the monogamous marital relation is overshadowed by a higher responsibility.

A. Polygamy and a Hierarchy of Duty

Moses commanded that the surviving brother should raise up seed for his brother by his brother's widow. This law of the kinsman was performed by Boaz to Ruth (Ruth 4). However, there are several factors which make this a very limited and exceptional form of polygamy. (1) It was tied into the system of inheritance of the land as God's chosen people (cf. Ruth 4:3). (2) It was connected to God's blessing through children; it being a curse not to have children in their situation (Deut. 25:5). (3) It was to be performed only for one's deceased brother. (4) One was not forced to do it (Deut. 25:7), even though it was considered an act of love to one's brother to perpetuate his name in the land (v. 7).

With all of these qualifying factors, there is no way to use this special situation as normative for men in general. It was not even normative within Israel. Indeed polygamy as such was not designed for God's people or any people. It was permitted by God, like divorce, as a concession to men's hardness of heart (cf. Matt. 19:8), and it was commanded by God only for a very special circumstance, viz., so that one would not go utterly heirless in a culture where heirs were an essential part of the blessing of God. [8]

In terms of a hierarchy of responsibility, it may be said that polygamy *as such* is never right. It is less than the best. It is not the best possible relation between husband and wife (or wives). However, when there is a transcending moral obligation, then monogamy may be suspended for this greater good. That is, if (and only if) polygamy is the relation which will be a greater good to a greater number of persons (as was the case in the law of the kinsman), ought one to engage in it. In brief, if God commands that a special use of polygamy is justified, then it is morally right to so transcend the moral monogamous relation. But the suspension of the moral duty of monogamy in some cases in no way negates the universality of the ideal of monogamy. Monogamy is *always* the right marriage relation, providing it is not transcended by a higher obligation ordained by God under special circumstances.

Under what conditions, then, can the monogamous relation be transcended by polygamy? There are several such higher duties which might justify special cases of polygamy. (1) When it is a

---

[8] It was of special significance to an Israelite not to go heirless because of allocation of the promised land and because of the promised Messiah who was to come possibly by way of one's offspring.

direct command of God for reasons perhaps fully known only to Him. (2) When one could do what is best for most people via polygamy. For example, it would have been selfish for a man in the Old Testament not to continue his brother's inheritance by raising up offspring for his brother's wife. (3) If a man were the only male in the world and his wife was unable to have children, then polygamy would be justifiable in order to propagate the species. [9] But all of these are special cases; they are not normative. Monogamy is the norm. [10] But even a good norm should not be followed so legalistically as to destroy more persons than it saves. In brief, polygamy is justified only if there is an overriding moral principle such as obedience to God or the preservation of life (or more lives) which demands it.

B. *Divorce and a Hierarachy of Duty*

Divorce is not an exceptioin to the biblical ethic, "What therefore God has joined together, let no man put asunder" (Matt. 19:6). However, the biblical rule is not: "Divorce is always wrong." The rule is this: "A permanent, abiding, and unique relation is always right." In other words, the Scriptures are concerned with the *permanence* of marriage. The rule is to keep a unique love relation going at all costs as long as it does not mean the perpetuation of of an evil or lesser good in favor of a greater good.

The question, then, is not really of "divorce" (separation) but one of whether there really is still a "marriage" (union) of two persons. That is, of course, man should not divide what God has united; the question is: Has God united this couple? If God has not united them in a unique and abiding love, then it can be just as wrong to try to unite what God has not united. Jesus' reference to fornication or unchastity as a ground for separation is a case in point. If one partner has broken the unique marital relation by sexually joining himself (or herself) to another, then both the permanence and uniqueness of the bond has been broken. In such a

[9] Abraham was wrong in taking Hagar to bear children when Sarah was barren because God had unconditionally *promised* Abraham children; God had not conditioned His promise on a command that Abraham *do* anything to help fulfill the promise. Whereas God did command the race to do something to propagate itself. Therefore, any circumstance which threatens the race and can be best overcome by polygamy (say, the only man in the world had an unfruitful wife) would justify using polygamy. Adam faced no such circumstance. His *one* wife was fruitful.

[10] Polygamy is not justifiable simply on the ground that the command of God to fill the earth can be fulfilled *faster*. God placed no time limit on His command. If there was ever a time the world needed filling it was at the very beginning, and God gave Adam only one wife. This is a clear indication that God was not in a hurry and that He did not desire polygamy.

case, where there is no chance of restoring and perpetuating a permanently meaningful relation, then separation is better.

In 1 Corinthians 7 Paul seems to develop further the legitimate grounds for terminating a marriage to include the unwillingness of the unbelieving partner to keep the contract going after the other has become a Christian. "But if the unbelieving partner desires to separate, let it be so; in such a case the brother or sister is not bound [to their marriage vows]" (v. 15).[11] If this is the correct interpretation of the passage, then Paul is supporting the point that God is primarily concerned with making permanent those relations where there is a willingness or consent among the partners. Of course, this does not mean that mere incompatibility is a ground for divorce. Love demands effort to overcome differences. But if there cannot be a unique and abiding union, there is no reason to force a permanent impersonalism out of it. God is interested in permanently joining persons in a personal relationship. If this is not possible between persons A and B, then we may assume that separating them will be more helpful to more persons (children included) than solidifying this bad relationship.

Under what higher responsibilities, then, are divorce or separation justified? (1) When God never joined them in a unique love relation to begin with and when there is no hope that it will occur in the future (Matt. 19:6). (2) When the unique relation is irreparably broken by unfaithfulness (Matt. 19:9). (3) When one partner "dies," i.e., when a permanent physical separation occurs. This may be an actual physical death or its equivalent. A soldier "lost in action" may in time be pronounced legally "dead" and his wife released to remarry. Even a spaceman's being lost in space could qualify his wife to remarry. These are not exceptions to the permanence of marriage. For a permanent marriage partnership depends on there being two persons willing to carry on this unique relation.

C. *Fornication and a Hierarchy of Duty*

If polygamy and divorce or separation may sometimes be justified in view of a higher responsibility, can fornication or sexual intercourse outside of marriage ever be morally right? Again the answer is no, not as such. However, there may be some overriding responsibilities which could exempt one from his normal responsibilities. For example, one may be obliged to engage in sexual intercourse outside of his own marriage in order to save a life. Such would be the greatest good in that situation. Surely the refusal to save a life (or lives) by way of sex would not be right. Of course, one would

---

[11] Others interpret this to mean that they are not bound to continue to live together. That is, the verse is approving separation but not divorce.

want to explore all other possible alternatives before he assumed there was really no other way to save the life.

Sexual encounters for purely therapeutic reasons would be morally unjustifiable. There are other ways to release tension and to heal. Besides, sexual fidelity is a higher value than the achievement of one's psychic balance. Indeed, sexual infidelity may very well contribute to psychic imbalance. Fletcher is wrong in implying that the harlot was right in teaching the young sailor self-confidence. [12] There are other ways of teaching self-confidence without sinning sexually. Lower ethic responsibilities like sexual fidelity are to be suspended only in view of higher ones like saving a life and then only if there is no other way to save the life.

There may be times when the lives of many people depend on the information that can be obtained only by the sacrifice of one's sexual purity. If so, then the patriotic "prostitute" is a moral possibility. Esther put her sex as well as her life on the line for her people, being urged that she was called to the kingdom for such a purpose as this (Esth. 4:14). In a similar manner it is conceivable that sex could be used to save lives if that was the *only* way to get the needed information or whatever.

D. Summary and Conclusion

Sexual fidelity is based in the highly personal, unique, and abiding relationship which sexual intercourse establishes between two persons of the opposite sex. God made sex good and gave the good channel through which it is to be exercised, viz., the life-long commitment called marriage. Only the monogamous relation perfectly exemplifies this unique (one-of-a-kind) relation. No man can have two one-of-a-kind marital relations at once. Polygamy is thus eliminated from the morally normative. Only if there is some higher, transcending duty can one be morally exempt from his monogamous relation.

In like manner, the marriage commitment is life-long. Marriage is not only a unique relationship but a permanent one. What God has joined men should not separate. This does not mean that God has joined everyone who have joined themselves. [13] Then, too, there

---

[12] Joseph Fletcher, *Situation Ethics*, pp. 126-127.

[13] The question as to whether one is right in "unjoining" a marriage (whether it is called divorce or annulment matters not) on the grounds that God never joined it to begin with is a difficult one. Nehemiah (13:25f.) commanded the Israelites to put away their unbelieving wives. Paul, on the other hand, advises the Corinthians to remain married to their non-Christian spouses, unless the non-believer departs (1 Cor. 7:10-15). Of course, there is no contradiction here for the situations differ. First, the Christians at Corinth were urged to maintain the relationship only if the unbeliever was willing and also on the assumption they could be a sanctifying influence on them (vv. 12 - 14). Second, in the case of the

are cases when the lower duty to one's wife is transcended by a higher duty to human life. On such occasions intercourse outside marriage might possibly be morally justified. However, the higher obligation does not break the lower one; it merely suspends it temporarily. There are no exceptions to the rule of sexual fidelity; there are only some exemptions in view of higher values. Sexual fidelity is a high moral value, but human life and direct duty to God are even higher. The Christian ought always to do the highest good possible.

SELECT READINGS FOR CHAPTER ELEVEN: SEX

Bainton, Roland, *What Christianity Says About Sex, Love, & Marriage*, New York: Association Press, 1957.

Begeman, Helmut, "Christian Ethics in the Face of the Changes in Marriage and Sexual Behavior," *Lutheran World*, 13, No. 4, 1966.

Cole, W. G., *Sex and Love in the Bible*, New York: Association Press, 1959.

Miles, Herbert J., *Sexual Understanding Before Marriage*, Grand Rapids, Michigan: Zondervan Publishing House, 1971.

Piper, Otto, *The Biblical View of Sex and Marriage*, New York: Charles Scribner's Sons, 1960.

Thielicke, Helmut, *The Ethics of Sex*, New York: Hawthorn Books, 1960.

Israelites it was their extra wives which they were to put away (i.e., polygamy was their sin and not a bad monogamous relationship) and the religious influence seemed to be going the wrong way, viz., away from God. The only resolution we can suggest here is that one ought never break up a monogamous relation unless it is involving him in a greater sin to maintain it. In brief, the greatest good principle would demand that one "unjoin" himself from a marriage which God never intended to begin with or which would engage him in worse sins by continuing.

12 / The Christian and Birth Control and Abortion

There are numerous areas of moral complexity facing the Christian. While the basic Christian ethic is rather simple (viz., love), it is often very difficult to apply. The subjects of birth control and abortion are prime examples of the difficulties. At first glance these topics might appear to have little in common. Actually, they both bear on the question of preventing life or taking a human life. Is either ever right? If so, under what conditions?

I. AN ETHIC OF BIRTH CONTROL

Is it morally wrong to use artificial devices which prevent human life from occuring naturally? Is one disobeying God's command to propagate the species by using contraceptives? These are important questions for which an ethical answer must be sought.

A. The Arguments Against Birth Control

Those who oppose birth control from a Christian point of view usually appeal to one or more of the following kinds of arguments: (1) to practice birth control is to disobey God's command to propagate the race (Gen. 1:28); (2) to prevent life from occuring naturally is a kind of incipient murder of intent; (3) the purpose of sex is exclusively procreational; (4) the Scriptures clearly condemn a man who practiced a form of birth control (Gen. 38:9).

1. *Birth Control Is Disobedience to God's Command to Propagate*
The first command God gave to the race was to "be fruitful and multiply, and fill the earth and subdue it" (Gen. 1:28). God made humans male and female and ordered them to reproduce after their

211

kind. It is often implied by those opposed to birth control that God
wants men to share His goodness by multiplying their offspring. To
refuse to do this is selfish, they say. The obligation of life is to pass
it on. The numerous references in Scripture to the blessings of
children — even large families — are used to support this position.
"Like arrows in the hand of a warrior are the sons of one's youth.
Happy is the man who has his quiver full of them!" (Ps. 127:5).
Further, "Lo, sons are a heritage from the Lord, the fruit of the
womb a reward" (v. 3). Indeed, barrenness was considered a curse
(Gen. 20:18; Deut. 17:14). Therefore, those who deliberately delimit
life thereby disobey God's plan to share it with as many as possible.

2. *Birth Control Is an Incipient Murder of Intent* — To deliberately
limit the number of lives which come to be is one step before nipping
life in the bud; it is refusing to let life bud at all. It is like a farmer
refusing to plant seed. If the field is barren and there is no produce
to keep life going, then one is just as guilty for not sowing it as he
would be for spraying poison on it after the seeds germinate or
begin to grow. Likewise, birth control is a kind of killing in advance.
Only God has the right over life to determine how much shall be
and which shall be. God opens and closes the womb (Gen. 20:18;
29:31). God alone has the power over life. "See now that I, even
I, am he, and there is no god beside me; I kill and I make alive,"
said the Lord (Deut. 32:39). The Lord gives life and the Lord
takes it away; the prerogative is His (cf. Job 1:21). No man has
the right (except as God delegates it) to assume the power as
to which men shall live and which shall not. Birth control is an
attempt to play God (i.e., to control life) and, hence, is morally
wrong.

3. *The Purpose of Sex Is Procreation* — Another argument advanced by those who oppose artificial birth control methods is that
the basic purpose of sex, viz., that of procreation is thwarted by
contraceptives. [1] God ordained sex in order to reproduce the species.
The pleasure of sex is concomitant to the procreative purpose, but
sexual pleasure should not be an end in itself. Seeking the pleasures
of sex apart from the responsibilities involved in raising a family is
contrary to the natural order established by God. Sex is not recreational but procreational, and to seek the former without the latter
is a distortion of sex. Hence, birth control devices used to maintain
the delights of sex while evading the duty to have children are
morally wrong. The use of contraceptives is an expression of selfish
desire — a passion for pleasure without the plan to propagate. Sex
is not to be a selfish end in itself but a means to an unselfish end —

[1] Traditional Roman Catholic natural law ethics has been a strong force behind
this argument. See R. A. Armstrong, *Primary and Secondary Precepts in Thomistic Natural Law Teaching,* Hague: Guilders, 1966.

sharing one's life with others. Birth control is a selfish way of working against the law of nature.

4. *The Bible Specifically Condemned an Attempt at Birth Control* In a very clear example, the Scriptures condemn a man who deliberately refused to propagate. We read, "But Onan knew that the offspring would not be his; so when he went in to his brother's wife he spilled the semen on the ground, lest he should give offspring to his brother" (Gen. 38:9). "And what he did," the Bible adds, "was displeasing in the sight of the Lord" (v. 10). Here is a clear instance of a man who engaged in sexual intercourse but refused to propagate with it — a distinctive contraceptive measure. God commanded him to raise up seed and he refused. Since this is the only reference in Scripture to a contraceptive maneuver and it is clearly condemned of God, it would seem that the burden of proof rests on those who would defend the use of birth control methods. So go the arguments against birth control.

B. *Answering the Arguments Against Birth Control*

Whatever merit the foregoing arguments against birth control possess, they certainly do not prove that birth control is *always* wrong. At *best* these arguments show that in general it is natural to have children and that in some specific cases it is definitely wrong to use devices to hinder conception. [2] The arguments will be examined in the order given above.

1. *God's Command to Propagate Is General Not Specific* — The command to propagate is to the race in general and not to each specific individual in it. God desires the species to reproduce and not necessarily every individual in it to multiply If the command to propagate were more than general, then everyone who refused marriage would be sinning as much as those who married and refused to have children. Voluntary bachelorhood would be as great a sin as the use of contraceptives by married people. But the Scriptures are unmistakable on this point. Jesus said, "there are eunuchs who have made themselves eunuchs for the sake of the kingdom of heaven. He who is able to receive this, let him receive it" (Matt. 19:12). Likewise, Paul added, "Only, let every one lead the life which the Lord has assigned to him, and in which God has called

[2] Sometimes "natural" birth control methods like the rhythm method are considered right and "artificial" methods are held to be wrong. This would certainly be the case if the artificial devices were harmful to human lives. Short of this, however, none of the arguments permitting natural methods are inapplicable to safe artificial methods. What is the essential difference between planting seeds on top of a rock (where one knows they will not grow) and treating the seed or soil or putting a protector between seed and soil so that it cannot take root? Likewise, all of the safe methods of preventing human conception are essentially the same, viz., an attempt to prevent life from multiplying naturally.

him [whether married or not]" (1 Cor. 7:17). [3] A person does not necessarily sin by celibacy. God calls some not to marry as well as some to marry.

Further, if one were sinning by not propagating, then even voluntary sexual abstention of married couples would be sinful. But the Scriptures permit sexual abstinence "by agreement for a season" (I Cor. 7:5). That is, there is no ethical reason why partners cannot mutually agree not to have intercourse. Likewise, there is no reason why couples should not voluntarily refrain from sexual activity at the fertile periods of a woman's monthly cycle. Even those who argue against artificial contraceptives usually permit this voluntary method of birth control known as the rhythm method. So the question is not really *whether* birth control is morally permissible but *which* kind and *how much*.

This leads to another point. The command to propagate the species does not say *how many* offspring there should be nor how soon propagation should be done. Obviously, time was not of the essence in the command to multiply the species. For if it were, then polygamy would have been a far more effective method, but God gave the first man only *one* wife. Indeed, God opposed polygamy and judged the polygamists. [4] Granted, then, that having as many children as one can as soon as one can is not of the essence of the command of Genesis 1:28, then the door is open for some form of birth control. A man does not necessarily sin simply by limiting or spacing his offspring.

2. *Birth Control Is Not Incipient Murder* — If limiting the number of children one brings into this world is not in itself sinful, then it cannot be called murder in any meaningful sense of the word. There is a great difference between *preventing* some life from giving birth to more life and *taking* a life after it has been born. The latter can be murder; the former is not murder. Voluntary selectivity with regard to the amount of offspring is no more sinful as such than choosing to limit the amount of trees one plants in his yard or the number of grains of corn one plants in a row.

In fact, indiscriminate seeding (whether among plants or humans)

[3] Throughout this chapter Paul's teaching on marriage in 1 Corinthians 7 is taken to be of God. Paul's statements that ". . . I say, not the Lord . . ." (v. 12) and "I say this by way of concession, not of commandment" (v. 6) do not imply that what he taught the Corinthians was not of God. He means that: (1) some of the subjects Christ had not specifically spoken on, so Paul gave his convictions on the subject; (2) later in Corinthians Paul said, ". . . what I am writing to you is a command of the Lord" (14:37). That is, even though Jesus had no occasion to speak directly on the subject, Paul's teaching comes with the same divine authority as if Jesus had spoken on it. That apostolic teaching was authoritative is clear from other Scriptures (Acts 2:42; 15:22ff; Eph. 2:20).

[4] See chapter eleven where polygamy is discussed.

can be more harmful than selective planting. A well-placed life (human or otherwise) is a beautiful thing. And a poorly-planned planting can have very ugly results. Overcrowded conditions can stifle and even stultify life rather than enhance it. In other words, the failure to control the amount of living things which are to be born can be murderous. If one is not careful to *prevent* too many living things from coming to be, then his indiscriminate action may precipitate conditions which will actually *take* the lives of some. And taking innocent human lives is murder. Hence, the failure to control births, although not being murder, could lead to a kind of murder.

At any rate, one who limits the amount of human life does not necessarily sin. If one limited *all* life from multiplying, then this would be contrary to God's command to multiply man's kind, but limiting *some* life, particularly with a view to making life more livable for the lives which are already here, is not wrong.

In this whole discussion, pro and con, one important factor has been omitted thus far, viz., the *quality* of life. [5] If limiting the quantity of people born can enhance the quality of persons living, then certainly it is not morally wrong to do so. Who would vote for a magnitude of mankind which severely limits the personhood of individual men? Sheer quantity over quality is a distortion of values. Hence, if the quality of personhood can be furthered by preventing an undue quantity of persons in a given family (or world), then birth control for this purpose is justifiable.

3. *Procreation Is Not the Only Purpose for Sex* — Procreation is obviously a (perhaps even *the*) basic purpose of sex. However, it is not the *only* purpose of sex. Sex has also unificational and recreational purposes. [6] A human marriage is more than mating. It is a unique union of two persons to share mutually in the experiences of life. Sex is one of the means of encouraging and enriching that union. Also, sex is a pleasure which enhances the union in a kind of re-creational re-enactment of the bliss of the marital first love. Hence, sex serves at least two purposes other than having children. And if sex is intended by God to unify and to satisfy as well as to multiply, then there is no reason why some form of birth control could not be exercised so as to promote these other purposes of marriage without producing offspring.

If sex were intended only for procreation, then it would be strange that nature has it that women can procreate less than half of their married life (i.e., only until menopause) and then only at a very

[5] Whether the quality of life over the quantity of life would justify *taking* lives of the inferior to enhance the lives of the suprior will be discussed in chapter thirteen under "mercy-killing."

[6] These other aspects of sex were discussed in chapter eleven.

limited time each month. A woman who is married at the age of 20 will have, say, 25 years of fertility on only, say, three days a month, or 1/10 of the time. This means that the actual time of her ability to conceive will be less than three years (i.e., c. 1,000 days) of her married life. Now it would seem strange that God designed sex with its drives for several decades of one's life, if it was intended only for these brief procreative periods. It is much more in accord with the wisdom of God, the facts of nature, and human experience to assume that the role of sex is broader than the procreative purpose. And if sex is not merely for propagation, then there is no reason why one cannot enjoy the other purposes of sex without producing children.

4. *The Bible Does Not Condemn Birth Control in General* — The specific case of Onan's refusal to raise up seed for his brother cannot be used to establish a general rule against contraceptives for several reasons. First, his disobedience was not to the *general* command (of Gen. 1:28) to have offspring but to the *specific* responsibility of a surviving brother to raise up offspring for his kin (cf. Deut. 25:5). Second, the data of this single case is not sufficient to establish a pattern for all situations. Further, the context clearly indicates that Onan's motives were selfish (Gen. 38:9). The *most* that could be proved from this passage is that birth control is wrong when it is used for selfish reasons. It leaves the door open for unselfish use of contraceptives. For example, what if one were using birth controls for hygienic reasons or even for the psychological and emotional welfare of a wife who already is over-burdened with children and/or other duties?

In summary, there is nothing in nature which necessarily limits sex to procreation and nothing in Scripture to forbid the use of contraceptives when there is a proper (unselfish) motivation. The question is not *whether* but *when* contraceptives are morally permissible.

C. *A Christian View of Birth Control*

From the foregoing discussion we may deduce several conclusions. It is wrong for everyone to use birth control *all* of the time. God commands the race to reproduce itself. If everyone had no children, the race would die out after one generation failed to reproduce. Neither is it always wrong for *all* men to use birth control methods. For in some cases not to have any (or many) children may be the more loving and unselfish thing to do. Perhaps it will be more clear if we outlined some of the occasions when birth control would be wrong and some when it would be right.

1. *When Birth Control Is Wrong* — There are several situations in which birth control would be wrong. (1) It would be wrong

if one were using it outside of marriage for illicit sexual activity. Contraceptives are not to be used to avoid the consequences of one's lust. Marriage is the proper channel for the sexual drive. Avoiding the responsibilities of marriage while indulging in its pleasures is morally wrong. The joys of sexual union are planned by God only for those who are willing to make the life-long commitment which is demanded by this unique relation.

(2) Birth control would also be wrong for those who refuse to help propagate the race when its existence is threatened. For example, it would have been wrong for Adam to use complete birth control to the point of having no children. And in the event of a nuclear war with only a few survivors it would be morally wrong for them to refuse to keep the race going. Such would be tantamount to committing suicide for the race. Suicide of an individual is evil, and suicide of the race is a greater evil. [7]

(3) In fact, it is wrong in general for men not to have children when the population of the race is not increasing toward its maximum. God's command is to increase and fill the earth. Each individual directly or indirectly bears some responsibility to help fulfill this command. Of course, this command holds only until the world is full (unless new worlds open up). It would be disobedience to God for the race not to reproduce with increase, for it is God's command to the race to increase.

(4) Finally, it can be wrong to refuse to have children *solely* because one does not want to assume the responsibility of them. If this selfish reason were willed to be a universal law (*a la* Kant), then there would be no race. Indeed, if the individuals who feel this way had parents who felt that way, these individuals would have never come to be. There is a general duty to pass life on.

2. *When Birth Control Is Right* — One must not conclude that because some usages of birth control are selfish that all are selfish. Indeed, there are several situations in which birth control may be the unselfish or right thing to do. (1) For example, to *delay* one's family until he is better able to care for them can be a very wise and unselfish action. If psychological, economic, or educational reasons should indicate a better future time for a family, then it is not morally wrong to wait. For most couples who marry at the usual age, some program of artificial family limitation is an emotional and economic necessity.

(2) Further, if birth control can be used to *limit* the size of one's family to fit his ability to provide for them, then he does not sin. The Scriptures urge a man to provide for his own (1 Tim. 5:8) and to plan for the future. "For which of you," said Jesus, "desiring

[7] See discussion on suicide in chapter thirteen.

to build a tower, does not first sit down and count the cost, whether he has enough to complete it?" (Luke 14:28). And who would argue that a family is not more important than a tower?

(3) Also, to refrain from having children for reason of *health* (physical or mental) is not wrong as such. In fact, it would be wrong to bring children into the world if it would be destructive of their parents and/or if the conditions would be destructive of the children.

(4) Finally, it is not wrong to avoid having children for some *higher moral purpose* such as Jesus referred to in Matthew 19:12. Men can voluntarily dedicate themselves to be celibate or to go childless for the kingdom of God. As long as the species is not being threatened by their abstention and as long as their dedication is to the good of others, it is not wrong to use birth control to avoid having their own children. In fact, there are some legitimate and needful vocations and callings in life for which a family is a handicap but a wife would be a help.

In summary, a Christian ethic of birth control is built on the intrinsic value of persons. The basic obligation is to multiply persons. But complete persons are better than incomplete ones. Hence, whatever advance planning can place persons so that they can better develop their personhood is preferable. Further, many persons are better than few. Therefore, one ought to do what he can to maximize personhood but not to propagate too many persons. Birth control can be a useful means of helping to follow the higher ethical value in these cases.

II. An Ethic of Abortion

Birth control is essentially an attempt to *prevent* more life from occurring. Abortion is an attempt to *take* life after it has begun to develop, which is a much more serious affair. Birth control is not murder (i.e., the *taking* of a human life), but what about abortion? Is it murder? What does the Bible have to say on the subject?

A. *Abortion Is Not Necessarily Murder*

The one clear thing which the Scriptures indicate about abortion is that it is not the same as murder. For when a natural abortion was precipitated by fighting, the guilty was not charged with murder.

1. *An Unborn Baby Is Not Fully Human* — According to the law of Moses, the killing of an unborn baby was not considered a capital offense. "When men strive together, and hurt a woman with child, so that there is a miscarriage, and yet no harm follows, the one who hurt her shall be *fined* . . ." (Ex. 21:22). In the case of killing a

baby, child, [8] or adult there was more than a fine exacted — the *life* of the murderer was demanded (Ex. 21:12). Apparently, the unborn baby was not considered fully human and, therefore, causing its death was not considered murder (i.e., the *taking* of an innocent human life).

2. *An Unborn Baby Is Not Sub-Human* — If an embryo is not fully human, then what is it? Is it sub-human? Can it be treated like an appendix — an expendable extension of the mother's body? The answer to this is no. An unborn baby is a work of God which He is building into His own likeness. It is a being with an ever increasing value as it develops. The Psalmist wrote, "For thou didst form my inward parts, thou didst knit me together in my mother's womb. . . . Thou knowest me right well; my frame was not hidden from thee, when I was being made in secret, intricately wrought in the depths of the earth" (Ps. 139:13-15). Perhaps too much should not be made of this poetical description of an embryo, but it seems reasonable to conclude that there is a big difference between an unborn baby and an appendix. The former can become a fully human being; the latter cannot. [9] A human embryo is a *potentially* human being, and an appendix is not. There is a vast difference between that which can develop into an Einstein or a Beethoven and an appendage of the human anatomy. The former has immortality in the image and likeness of God before it; the latter is merely an expendable tissue of a human body.

B. *Abortion Is a Very Serious Activity*

Abortion is not murder, but it is a very serious activity. Artificial abortion is a man-initiated process by which one *takes* a potential human life. Abortion is a much more serious question than birth control, which merely *prevents* a human life from happening.

1. *Abortion Is Less Serious Than Murder* — Murder is a man-initiated activity of taking an *actual* human life. Artificial abortion is a humanly initiated process which results in the taking of a *potential* human life. Such abortion is not murder, because the embryo is not fully human — it is an undeveloped person. By aborting, the human life is nipped before it buds (assuming birth begins the budding). If a life must be stopped, it is obviously better to stop it before it ever really gets started. But the question is

---

[8] The Hebrew midwives were commanded by God not to kill the Hebrew babies as they were born (Exod. 1:16f). Herod's slaughter of the children around Bethlehem is held out as a great evil in Scripture (Matt. 2:16f).

[9] If scientists ever discover a way to grow a human being from some organ(s) or cell(s) of the human body, then at the stage the cell gains this potential to develop into a fully human being, it too must be treated like a human embryo.

this: should a human life ever be stopped before it really has a chance to get started?

2. *Abortion Is More Serious Than Birth Control* — Birth control is not essentially wrong, for it merely *prevents* some life from occurring. Abortion, on the other hand, *takes* an undeveloped life after it has occurred. Since God is the Author of life, it is a serious thing to stamp out a life which He has permitted to come to pass. One must have a good reason for extinguishing what God has kindled. The human embryo will develop (all things being equal) into an immortal, never-dying person. To snuff out what could become a human being is not an amoral act. There are serious implications to an act of man which strikes at an act of God in initiating a life.

In begetting children parents are serving as a channel through which God can create life. It is wrong, of course, to block the channel completely so that no life can get through (as in complete birth control of the whole race). But it is not necessarily evil to limit the amount or kind of flow through the channel (as in proper birth control). However, once the flow of life has begun it can be definitely wrong to snuff it out without ever giving it a chance to develop. Conception is a prima facie case in favor of giving the undeveloped person a chance to develop. One must have some higher moral duty which demands abortion before he initiates it.

C. *When Abortion Is Justified*

Abortion is neither the murder of a human person nor a mere operation on or ejection of an appendage of the female body. It is a sober responsibility to take the life of a would-be human being. The only morally justifiable circumstances for abortion are those in which there is a higher moral principle which can be served.

1. *Abortion for Therapeutic Reasons* — When it is a clear-cut case of either taking the life of the unborn baby or letting the mother die, then abortion is called for. An *actual* life (the mother) is of more intrinsic value than a *potential* life (the unborn). [10] The mother is a fully developed human; the baby is an undeveloped human. [11] And an actually developed human is better than one which has the potential for full humanity but has not yet developed. *Being* fully human is a higher value than the mere possibility of *becoming* fully human. For what *is* has more value than what *may* be. Just as the flower has more value than the germinating seed

[10] See the discussion of this moral principle in chapter seven.

[11] This assumes, of course, that the mother is healthy and will live. If there is clear evidence the mother will die shortly of an incurable disease or for some other reason, then one would not really be saving an actual life by saving her but destroying a potential one (i.e., the baby). In such cases, saving a potential life would be of greater value than letting both lives die.

(a potential flower), so the mother is of more value than the embryo. She *is* a mature, free, autonomous subject, whereas the unborn has only the potential to become such.

The question may be raised here as to whether some potential humans are more valuable than some actual humans. What if the unborn will turn out to be an Albert Schweitzer and the mother is a derelict? What if the mother is a harlot and the unborn will turn out to be a missionary? One might be tempted to agree that a potentially good human life is better than an actually bad human life, if he could be sure in advance that the baby would turn out to be good. But this would require a kind of omniscience which only God has. Hence, only God could make a decision based on a complete knowledge of the end or results. That is, only God could effectively use a utilitarian calculus.[12] Finite men must be content with the immediate consequences based on intrinsic values as they see them. On this basis an actual life (evil or not) is of more intrinsic value than a potential life.

Furthermore, God does not judge the value of an individual life by what a man *does* with it (evil or good) but by what it *is*. Jesus loved Judas even though He knew Judas would become infamously evil by his betrayal. A human life has value as such because it is made in the image of God — it has perfections and powers as God has, whether these are used to glorify God or not. Hence, when the choice is being made between the bad mother and a potentially good embryo, one must prefer the former to the latter on the grounds of intrinsic value, not pragmatic value.

If one were to carry through the logic that good men are better than evil ones, one could justify a host of inhumanities to criminals and so-called "lesser elements" of the race. Men who perform evil acts are not thereby intrinsically evil. Their intrinsic value as humans must not be judged by what extrinsic acts they have performed. They are not to be judged simply on the basis of what good they *do* for others but for the good that they *are* as God's creatures. Hence, the higher intrinsic value of a mother must not be determined by what she *does* but by what she *is*. And the mother's actual humanity is of more value than the unborn's potential for it.

2. *Abortion for Eugenic Reasons* — What about abortions for eugenic reasons? Is it ever right to take a life of an embryo because it will be born deformed, retarded, or sub-human? Here again one must proceed with care. It is always a serious thing to take the life of a potential human being. There must always be a higher moral reason for nipping a life before it buds.

There are several eugenic grounds on which abortions have been

[12] See the end of chapter one for a further critique of utilitarian ethics.

recommended by some, such as mongolism, others for deformation due to thalidomide or similar drugs, and some for retardation or other deformities due to measles or other causes. Are these legitimate grounds for an abortion? Christians differ in their responses to these situations. However, from the standpoint of hierarchical ethics the basic principle is this: eugenic abortion is called for only when the clear indications are that the life will be sub-human and not simply because it may be a deformed human. Specifically, mongolism is a justifiable grounds for abortion but thalidomide is not. Deformed humans and even retarded humans are still *human*. Handicaps do not destroy one's humanity. In fact, they often enhance the truly human characteristics in both the handicapped and those who work with them.

Another factor sometimes overlooked in the matter of whether an embryo should be allowed to live is the right of the unborn. Does not a potentially human fetus have a moral right to life, even if the life will be somehow handicapped? How do maimed and retarded children and adults feel about whether someone else should decide their fate before they were born? The answer seems clear: a human life, handicapped or not, is worth living and anyone who takes it upon himself to decide in advance for another that his life should not be given the opportunity to develop is engaged in a serious ethical act.

3. *Abortion in Conception Without Consent* — Should a mother be forced to give birth to a child conceived by rape? Is there a moral obligation to generate a child without consent? This raises the whole question of the moral duty of motherhood. Can one be forced to be a mother against her will? Is her womb a mere tool for the tyranny of outside forces of life? This is a delicate question but it seems to involve a negative answer. Birth is not morally necessitated without consent. No woman should be forced to carry a child if she did not consent to intercourse. [13] A violent intrusion into a woman's womb does not bring with it a moral birthright for the embryo. The mother has a right to refuse that her body be used as an object of sexual intrusion. The violation of her honor and personhood was enough evil without compounding her plight by forcing an unwanted child on her besides.

But what about the right of the child to be born despite the evil way in which it was conceived? In this case the right of the potential life (the embryo) is overshadowed by the right of the actual life of the mother. The rights to life, health, and self-determination — i.e., the rights to personhood — of the fully human mother

[13] The Bible considers every conception to be the result of wedlock whether it was legalized by the state or not (1 Cor. 6:16).

take precedence over that of the potentially human embryo. A potentially human person is not granted a birthright by violation of a fully human person unless her consent is subsequently given.

4. _Abortion in Conception by Incest_ — Incestuous conception may involve rape and eugenic consequences and, hence, may provide an even firmer basis for a justifiable abortion. On either grounds alone there seems to be no moral obligation placed upon a girl to carry through with her incestuous pregnancy. Her personhood has been violated and the potential personhood of the unborn may be seriously marred by eugenic defects as well.

Some evils should be nipped in the bud. Allowing an evil to blossom in the name of a potential good (the embryo) seems to be a poor way of handling evil, especially when the potential good (the embryo) may itself turn out to be another form of evil. It is better to prevent the evil from coming to fruition than to perpetuate it. Incest can be wrong on both ends, conception and consequences of it.

D. _When Abortion Is Not Justifiable_

Now that some of the circumstances under which an abortion may be called for have been discussed, the situations under which it is not right should be discussed. As a rule abortion is not justified. Only under pressure of an overriding ethic responsibility, such as those just discussed above, is it ever justifiable. As a rule abortion is wrong and the following list gives some specific examples to illustrate the rule that abortion as such is wrong unless done for a higher ethical principle.

1. _Abortion Is Not Justifiable After Viability_ — The first and most basic point to make is that no abortion is justifiable as such after the fetus has become viable, i.e., after birth is possible. At this point it would not even be a question of abortion (i.e., the taking of a potentially human life) but the killing of an actual human life. To take the life of a viable fetus without higher ethical justification would be murder.

From conception through the first eight weeks the unborn is called an embryo. From this time on it is called a fetus. Somewhere around six months and after it is possible to give birth to a baby who can live and breathe on its own and who can develop into a mature human being. Any justifiable abortion which is to be performed must take place before this point of viability to qualify as an abortion. From this point on any allegedly justifiable life-taking would have to fall under the class of mercy-killing which is an even more serious ethical question. [14]

In point of fact, from conception on the unborn has emerging value

---

[14] See chapter thirteen for a discussion of mercy-killing.

as it develops. It is now known that the unborn receives its entire RNA and DNA genetic potential at conception. By the end of four weeks a budding cardiovascular system begins to function. At eight weeks the electrical activity of the brain is readable and most essential organ formations are present. And by ten weeks the fetus is capable of spontaneous motion. [15] In many states the law requires a birth certificate for a twenty-week-old fetus. From this it appears evident that every point of progress realizes an increased value until finally the full human value is attained.

2. *Abortion Because of Unwanted Children Is Not Justifiable* — The simple fact that a mother does not want the baby is not sufficient grounds for snuffing out a potential human life. Personal whims or desires of a mother do not take precedence over the value of the embryo or its right to live. The principle articulated by Fletcher in his situational ethic that no unplanned nor unwanted baby should ever be born is surely wrong. For one thing, if it were so then probably much (if not most) of the human race should never have been born. The unborn has a right to life whether or not its life were humanly planned or desired at that time. Furthermore, many children who were not wanted initially have come to be wanted subsequently by either their parents or someone else. Why should not the "unplanned" child be given an opportunity to be born and to be loved by someone?

Furthermore, the basic moral question does not have to do with whether or not the baby was *wanted* but with whether or not it was *willed*. Men do not necessarily want many things which they do will. Therefore, they are responsible for these acts. The drunk does not *want* a hangover even though he did *will* to get drunk. The unwillingness to accept the moral responsibility of one's choices does not lessen the responsibility for them. In other words, if one consents to intercourse then he must accept the consequences which are known to come from intercourse, viz., the generation of offspring. When there is no consent to intercourse, as in rape, then it is a different matter as was pointed out above. But when one chooses or consents to have intercourse he is thereby implicitly consenting to have children.

Since marriage is automatic consent to intercourse (1 Cor. 7:3ff), then it follows that the children conceived are automatically *willed* whether they are *wanted* of not. And since even harlotry is a marriage in God's eyes (1 Cor. 6:16), then children born out of fornication are also *willed* whether they are *wanted* or not. In brief, any child born of intercourse by consenting parties is implicitly willed and as such has the right to live. Abortion does not solve the problem of unwanted

[15] Cf. "Abortion: Can an Evangelical Consensus Be Found?" *Eternity* (February, 1971), p. 21.

children; rather, it compounds the problem. Two wrongs do not make a right.

3. *Abortion for Population Control Is Not Justifiable* — Another contemporary abuse of abortion is a kind of "after-the-fact" birth control method. Bluntly put, once conception has occurred it is too late to decide that it should not have been done. There are some morally one-directional decisions in life and intercourse leading to conception is one of them. When a man decides to jump off a cliff it is too late to change his mind when he is in the air on the way down. Likewise, when a man chooses to have intercourse which may result in procreation, it is too late to decide he does not want the child after conception has occurred. The point of morality was in the consent to intercourse. Taking a potential life is not morally justifiable simply because one does not want to suffer the social or physical discomforts which come from their own free choices.

There are effective means of birth control short of abortion. Contraceptive devices have been perfected to virtually guarantee that conception will not occur. Voluntary sterilization is fool-proof as a method of population control. Actually in view of these there is no need to engage in the morally unjustifiable use of abortion to control the population.

4. *Abortion for Anticipated Deformation Is Not Justifiable* — The argument for abortion on the grounds of anticipated deformity is insufficient. First of all, the percent of chance for deformity is not as high as is sometimes estimated. For example, nearly half of all babies born with defects have only minor ones which need no medical attention. Of those which are serious half do not become apparent until after birth which is too late for an abortion. Furthermore, in about half of the cases where children are born with serious defects the defect can be satisfactorily corrected or compensated for by operations or by artificial aids. Even in the case of German measles there is an 80-85 percent chance for a normal child if the mother contracted the disease after the first month. [16]

The second and most basic reason against abortion on the grounds of mere deformity is that a deformed child is fully human and capable of interpersonal relations. Deformity does not normally destroy one's humanity. Hence, artificial abortion of a deformed fetus, even in the few cases where this can be known with assurance in advance, is the taking of what can become a fully human life. The handicapped are human and have the right to live. Abortion thwarts this right in advance.

E. *Some Problem Areas*

The above examples of justifiable and unjustifiable abortions do not

[16] *Eternity, op. cit.,* p. 27.

exhaust the possible problem cases. What about the mother whose very mental health, and consequently her ability to care for her other children, is seriously threatened by another pregnancy? Without spelling out the specifics of a given case of this kind it will suffice to say that the decision should be based on the highest value which can be reasonably expected to be achieved by a given course of action. What must be guarded against is rashly undertaking abortion on alleged but uncertain possibilities of physical and psychological consequences which may never materialize.

Another problem area is whether abortion would be called for in a young girl who became pregnant by experimentation in sex without really understanding what could happen. If the girl was forced by an older male who knew what he was doing, then it is conception by rape and abortion is legitimate. If there was consent but in ignorance of the consequences, then it is an open question which will have to be decided in view of the higher values of the total situation. Abortion is conceivable in such a case. All the facts must be weighed and the higher value pursued. The problem is not basically a moral one — i.e., one of knowing what is the higher value — but a factual one, i.e., determining as a matter of fact which course of action will realize this higher value.

F. *Can Abortion Be Justified on the Quality of Life Principle?*

It is sometimes argued that abortion of imperfect and deformed humans can be justified on the grounds that the Bible stresses the quality of life and not the mere quantity. Hence, whatever pruning is necessary to improve the race is actually in accord with God's intent. Why have a deformed child when a healthy one could be produced the next time? And in view of the population crisis, why bring imperfect children into the world when there is scarcely room for the complete ones? Nature itself aborts imperfect embryos. Hence, when men know that an embryo will be imperfect should they not carry through the pattern which nature has established?

There are at least three premises in the quality of life argument which bear examination. *First*, granted that the Bible is committed to a quality of life principle, is it the quality of the race which is to take precedence over the individual or is the value of the individual more important than that of the race? The answer seems evident: God values the individual. The individual was created in His image and likeness (Gen. 1:27). It is wrong to kill the individual because he is in God's image (Gen. 9:6). It is the individual whom God loves (Matt. 6:25f) and so on. Pruning out imperfect individuals to improve the race is scarcely justifiable by Scripture. Improving the individual is of course biblical, but abortion is no way to improve an individual. Helping the handicapped, not taking their life in advance, is the way to improve the quality of their life. [17]

The *second* premise of the argument for abortion based on the quality of life principle which needs examination is the implication or assertion that artificial abortions can be carrying through the very pattern which God has ordained in natural abortions. There are some serious problems with this argument. First, it assumes that God is not causing enough abortions, i.e., that nature is not really carrying through on God's intent. Second, that God has no purpose for allowing some imperfect beings to be born. That is clearly contrary to Scripture (cf. John 9:1f). Third, it implies that man is capable of playing the role of God in that he can do a better job than nature and even out-guess the providential purposes of God. To say the least, the whole premise rests on some large assumptions. Actually, there is no indication in Scripture that man's dominion over the earth includes the authority to decide which human beings should be born and which should not. God alone holds sovereign power over life and death and He has not relinquished it to man. [18]

This leads to the *third* problem in the argument for abortion based on the quality of life and the pattern of nature which is this: how much authority does a man have to play God? Man was made in God's image but he is not God. He is limited in knowledge and foresight. But the argument for abortion according to the plan of nature assumes that man's knowledge is more than finite. Can a human being know better than nature what is the plan of God for an individual life, especially in view of the fact that God has a plan and purpose for even imperfect lives? It seems not. It is a difficult enough role to apply the hierarchical principles which God has revealed let alone attempt to determine values which God alone can establish. Applying God's values is one thing; playing with God's values is another. God has placed His value on the individual human life, perfect or not. It is a serious moral operation to tamper with an individual life. When the life is sub-human or when it will destroy another fully human life then that is another question. But when the question is merely should this imperfect potentially human life be taken by artificial abortion without such a higher ethical justification, then abortion has been carried beyond the bounds of morality.

[17] The only sense in which an individual should be sacrificed for the race is when the lives of more individuals can be saved by the loss of such an individual. But to perform abortion on the grounds that it will be more convenient to individuals in the race and/or that percentage-wise the race will be better (i.e., it will have fewer imperfect individuals in it) is not to value the life of the individual as highly as the Scripture indicates God values it.

[18] God may sometimes *delegate* the authority of life and death when more lives are at stake as in capital punishment or a just war but He never *relinquishes* His sovereign control.

III. WHAT ABOUT ARTIFICIAL INSEMINATION?

In line with the question of what makes a birth moral or legitimate is the problem of artificial insemination. Is the process of spermatic transplantation really adultery by proxy? Is it immoral for a woman to be artificially impregnated by the sperm from one other than her husband? Does this not involve two sins — masturbation and adultery by proxy? This is a complex question, but one on which the Scriptures shed some light.

A. *When Artificial Insemination Would Be Wrong*

In view of the foregoing discussion on abortion, one general conclusion may be drawn, viz., artificial insemination would be wrong if it were done *without consent* of all three parties involved. No woman should unwillingly conceive, nor should she be impregnated by another man's seed without her husband's consent. And, further, no man's sperm should be used to conceive a child without his consent (unless the survival of the race depended on it).

Of course, it does not automatically follow that artificial insemination is morally right if done with the consent of all three parties any more than wife-swapping with consent is morally right. That is, artificial insemination would definitely be wrong *without* consent but is not thereby right *with* consent. Under what conditions, if any, would artificial insemination be right?

B. *When Artificial Insemination Would Be Right*

Before one can specify any conditions under which artificial insemination would be right, there are two charges to be answered, viz., that it involves two sins — adultery and masturbation.

1. *Artificial Insemination Is Not Necessarily Adultery* — There is a distinct difference between adultery and artificial insemination. Adultery involves a sexual act of a woman with one other than her husband, whereas artificial insemination does not. Scripture definitely condemns adultery on the ground that it is a *union* of two persons who are not properly married (1 Cor. 6:16). This leaves open the possibility that impregnation without the adulterous union *could be* morally right.

2. *Artificial Insemination Is Not Necessarily an Auto-Sexual Sin* — In order to rule out artificial insemination on the grounds that it involves masturbation one would have to show that no such autosexual act can possibly be good. We argued above that autosexuality is wrong only *if* it leads to sin such as lust or an enslaving habit. If, on the other hand, such an act would not lead to sin, then it would not thereby be morally wrong. In fact, if the act were performed for unselfish reasons, then it could be considered, on that ground, right to do so.

3. *The Biblical Example of "Artificial" Insemination* — Is there any example in Scripture of artificial insemination? The direct answer is, "No, not exactly." However, there is a close equivalent to it. The Old Testament law of the kinsman redeemer's responsibility to impregnate the wife of his deceased brother is an example of natural insemination of one who was another's wife (cf. Deut. 25:5). This kind of natural insemination has two moral problems the artificial kind does not. First, it involved the act of sexual intercourse. Second, it sometimes involved a special kind of polygamy; i.e., taking a second wife. On this ground, the artificial route is more moral than the natural insemination.

Furthermore, if there was a justifiable ground for natural insemination of another (dead) man's wife, then why could there not be occasion when God would approve of conception by the artificial method? The essence of the Old Testament command to raise up seed to one's deceased brother had to do with the curse of being childless and heirless. In fact, artificial insemination has the advantage of evading the adulterous and polygamous problems of the kinsman-redeemer way of raising up seed to the barren. [19]

If artificial insemination is justifiable on biblical grounds, why did they not use it in biblical times? There are two possible reasons. First, they may have been ignorant as to how to perform it effectively. Second, even if they could have performed it medically without intercourse, the Scriptures hold high the value of one's having a father. (Compare God's special concern for the orphans or fatherless.) [20] Modern psychological studies support this value the Scriptures place on the role of the father in rearing healthy children. So in order that the childless mother would not have fatherless children, a special form of polygamy was instituted. From this we may conclude that bachelor motherhood by way of artificial insemination would not be approved by God. It is a great enough evil that some children (of widows, unwed mothers, etc.) are reared fatherless, without intentionally bringing more fatherless children into the world.

There is another advantage which artificial insemination has over the Old Testament system. There was no way in the biblical system for sterile married couples to have children of their own. That is, there was no way to do it except by their committing adultery, of which God obviously does not approve. But with artificial insemination a sterile couple can avoid both adultery and being childless. Hence, artificial insemination by mutual consent of married couples does not

[19] Even non-sterile couples whose genetic potential is not likely to produce a completely sound child might consent to artificial insemination for having a healthier child.

[20] See discussion of orphans in chapter ten.

appear to be a moral evil. Indeed, it could in some cases be a great good.

By way of summary, it should be emphasized again that the basic principle involved in deciding the ethical issues on which the Scriptures do not speak directly is that of the intrinsic value of persons — whole and complete persons. Whatever one can do to promote and preserve complete and whole human personhood should be done even if it sometimes involves abortion or artificial insemination. On the other hand, when either of these violate personal consent and/or the intrinsic value of personhood, it will be wrong.

SELECT READINGS FOR CHAPTER TWELVE: ABORTION, BIRTH CONTROL

Callahan, Daniel, *Abortion: Law, Choice and Morality,* New York: The Macmillan Company, 1970.

Grisez, Germain, *Abortion: The Myths, the Realities, and the Arguments.*

Noonan, John T. Jr., *The Morality of Abortion,* Cambridge, Mass.: Harvard University Press, 1970.

Ramsey, Paul, article in *Religion in Life* (Summer, 1970).

Ransil, Bernard J., *Abortion,* New York: Paulist Press, 1969.

Rosen, H., (ed), *Therapeutic Abortion: Medical, Psychiatric, Legal, Anthropological and Religious Considerations,* New York: Julian Press, 1954.

Runia, Klaas (ed.), *Eternity* Vol. 22, No. 2 (February, 1971) has articles by Nancy Hardesty, Carl Henry, Klaas Runia, and a symposium of opinion.

Spitzer, Walter O. and Carlyle L. Saylor, (ed.),*Birth Control and the Christian,* Wheaton, Ill.: Tyndale House Publishers, 1969.

Thielicke, Helmut, *The Ethics of Sex,* New York: Hawthorn Books, 1960.

Valsecchi, Ambregio, *Controversy: The Birth Control Debate, 1958-1968,* New York: Corpus, 1968.

13 / The Christian and Mercy-Killing, Suicide, and Capital Punishment

This chapter continues the discussion of when, if ever, it is right to take a human life. Previously (in chapter eight), it was argued that it is right to take another human life in a justifiable war. Chapter twelve discussed when it is right to take a potential human life (as in therapeutic abortion). In the present chapter we return to the question of when, if ever, excluding war, it is justifiable to take a human life. For example, are "mercy-killings" morally right? Is capital punishment ever justified? Can suicide be performed in sacrificial love?

I. A CHRISTIAN ETHIC OF MERCY-KILLING

What should the Christian do to a man hopelessly caught in a burning airplane who begs to be shot? Most humane persons would shoot a horse trapped in a burning barn. Why should a man not be treated as humanely as an animal? Or, when a monstrously deformed baby is born, and suddenly stops breathing, is the doctor morally obligated to resuscitate it? Would it not be more merciful to let it die? Again, say a man with an uncurable disease is being kept alive only by a machine. If the plug is pulled out he will die; if he lives it will only be artificially in a kind of "vegetable" existence. What is the moral obligation of the doctor? These and many like situations focus the ethical problem of life-taking. When, if ever, is life-taking morally justifiable?

A. Not All Life-Taking Is Murder

Before these cases are examined in particular, it will be well to establish a general principle which lies at the basis of our conclusion.

It is this: not all life-taking is murder. The biblical command means (as the New English Bible reads), "You shall not commit murder" (Ex. 20:13). There are several cases in Scripture where life-taking is not considered morally wrong. For example, life-taking in a just war against an evil aggressor (Gen. 14:14f). Also, there was the accidental killing of one's neighbor (Deut. 19:4, 5) for which a man was not held guilty. Finally, there was capital punishment instituted by God through Noah (Gen. 9:6) and repeated by Moses (Deut. 19:21).

From these illustrations we may deduce two differences between murder and justifiable life-taking. First, to qualify as a murder (i.e., a morally wrong act) the life-taking must be intentional. For if by accident a man killed a neighbor whom he did not hate, he was not held guilty by the law. Second, not even all intentional life-taking was murder, unless it was done without just cause. Taking the lives of innocent babies is not a just cause (cf. Ex. 1:16ff), nor is killing one's brother in anger (Gen. 4:8, 10). However, killing a man in self-defense or in defense of one's country can be a just cause. In other words, the prohibition against taking the lives of innocent persons does not thereby rule out the rightness of taking the life of a guilty murderer. Nor does the command not to kill one's peaceful neighbor necessarily prohibit shooting at one's warring neighbor. There are times when taking the life of another human is justified in order to protect the innocent. It is both unbiblical and unrealistic to categorize all life-taking as morally wrong. On the contrary, sometimes it is morally necessary. Tyrannicide, or the assassination of a dictator who has assumed the role of God may be a merciful act for masses of oppressed men. [1] In fact, it could be better than a war against that dictator in which more lives were lost.

B. *Mercy-Dying Is Not the Same as Mercy-Killing*

Another distinction which should be made is between *taking* a life and *letting* one die. The former may be wrong; whereas the latter in the same situation need not be wrong. For example, to withdraw the medication from a terminal patient and allow him to die naturally need not be a moral wrong. In some cases — where the individual and/or loved ones consent — this may be the most merciful thing to do. Indeed, if an illness is incurable and the individual is being kept alive only by a machine, then pulling the plug may be an act of mercy.

This is not to say that a doctor should give medicine or perform an operation to speed death — that could very well be murder. But this position does imply that mercifully *permitting* the sufferer to

---

[1] The contemporary theologian, Karl Barth, discusses the circumstances of a justifiable tyrannicide in *Church Dogmatics* III, 4, pp. 445f, eds. G. W. Bromiley and T. F. Torrance, Edinburgh: T. and T. Clark, 1936-62.

die is morally right, whereas *precipitating* his death is not. Medicine should be given to relieve suffering but not to hasten death. If, however, the lack of medicine or machine can lessen suffering by allowing death to occur sooner, then why should one be morally bound to perpetuate the patient's suffering by artificial means? In brief, killing involves *taking* the life of another whereas natural dying does not; it is merely *letting* one die. A man is responsible for the former, but God is responsible for the latter.

But is there not a moral responsibility to preserve a life if at all possible by whatever means (natural or artificial)? As was argued in the case of falsifying to a would-be murderer, it is wrong not to prevent a murder if possible as well as it is wrong to commit murder. Why, then, should one not prevent a death by medicine or machine if he can? How can it be morally right to allow someone to die when it could have been prevented, if it is not considered morally right to allow someone to be killed without preventing it? The answer is that the cases are very different. In fact, despite their apparent similarity, the two cases are almost opposite. Preventing a murder is preventing the suffering of an innocent victim. But preventing a death of someone already suffering is actually perpetuating the suffering. Further, permitting a murder is preventing the continuance of one who has the desire and possibility of living a meaningful human life. This is not so for some sufferers whose humanity has been diminished to terminal or nearly "vegetable" status.

C. *The Obligation Is to Perpetuate Life That Is Human*

The objection that miracles do happen even in supposedly "incurable cases" is sometimes leveled against allowing mercy-dyings. Why not keep the person alive and pray for a miracle? Or, maybe a cure will be discovered by scientists if the individual can be kept alive long enough. In attempting to answer this question it is necessary to point out that one should be kept alive as long as there is any reason for hope (medically or supernaturally) that he can recover to a meaningful human life. However, when both God and medical science have been given ample opportunity to cure the disease and yet it appears beyond all reasonable doubt that this patient will have little more than a "vegetable" type of existence, then one may conclude that God wants him to die a natural death. The basic moral principle behind this conclusion is that one ought not perpetuate an inhumanity while futilely waiting for a miracle. Hoping for a cure without any assurance it will come while one delays an act of natural mercy does not seem morally justifiable. Waiting without reasonable expectation for grace is not a justifiable basis for refusing to allow mercy to do its work.

There is another overall moral principle at work here. The obligation of humans to perpetuate life does not mean that one should be obligated to perpetuate it if it is no longer a *human* life in any significant sense of that word. As a matter of fact, it is morally wrong to perpetuate an inhumanity. If a monstrously deformed baby dies naturally, it should be considered an act of divine mercy. A doctor should not feel morally obligated to resuscitate a monster or human "vegetable." Just as the moral command is not to take a *human* life, so one's duty is only to perpetuate a *human* life. Perhaps at this point the Hippocratic oath needs reinterpretation. The medical profession should not be duty-bound to perpetuate every life but only a truly *human* life. In other words, it is no more evil to flip the switch on a machine which is artificially propping up life that is sub-human or post-human and has no chance to be truly human than it is to abort a pre-human which will not become human. The moral duty is twofold: to perpetuate the human and to prohibit the inhuman.

D. *Is Mercy-Killing Ever Justifiable?*

So far it has been argued that allowing mercy-*dying* is justifiable. But what about mercy-*killing?* Are there any occasions when it is right to take artificially a human life which is not dying naturally? Taking the life of a *pre-human* (i.e., potential human) is justifiable if one can save a human, e.g., abortion to save a mother. [2] Also, letting the life of a *subhuman* pass away (though not taking that life) can be justified as an act of mercy (as in mercy-dying). But can taking the actual life of another *human* be justified as an act of mercy? It is not difficult to see that (1) taking a life is a much more serious matter than letting one die naturally, and that (2) taking a pre-human or subhuman (or post-human) life is less serious than taking a fully human life. It is a most serious thing to take a fully human life. However, it is not merely a question of the seriousness but of the justification of life-taking. When, if ever, is a mercy-killing justified? To whom would it be merciful?

1. *Killing as an Act of Mercy to Others* — It is always wrong to kill another human being *as such.* However, there are overriding circumstances which may exempt one from this duty. There are times when it is necessary to take one life in order to save many lives. In such cases it is an act of mercy to the many to sacrifice the one. How many fathers would stand by and permit a murderer to strangle their children without resisting him if they could? In a society which is concerned about mercy for the guilty murderer, one wonders what has happened to mercy for the innocent multitude. It is a distorted view of mercy to be more concerned about protecting the life of the one who had no regard for the lives of others

[2] See chapter twelve.

than about protecting the masses who do have a proper regard for life. In the name of mercy for the masses surely there is justification in killing a sniper who is gunning down innocent citizens. A just war is mercy-killing on a larger scale. For what makes a war just is that it is a protection of the innocent against the bloody aggression of the guilty.[3] It is an attempt to preserve the many good lives from destruction at the direction of a few evil men.

2. *Killing as an Act of Mercy to the Individual* — What about the man helplessly trapped in a burning airplane? Or patients who plead for the doctor to put them out of their misery? Is it ever right to accede to the wishes of the sufferers to snuff out their suffering? Perhaps a "no" answer will seem too categorical, but this is the kind of answer indicated by Scripture. Of course, one is morally obligated to do everything possible to relieve suffering short of life-taking as far as an individual human life is concerned. However, it is never an act of mercy to the individual as such to take away his life when it is truly human. Human life has intrinsic value and should not be taken by another human even if the victim requests it. God alone holds the right to give and take life. He is the only One who is sovereign over all existence. To take the life of another human is to be a henchman at that man's own request. It is to be an accomplice to the crime of assisting one in his own suicide.[4] Where there is human life there is hope for that human life. It is a far more serious ethical issue to take a human life (as in mercy-killing) than to allow a subhuman life to depart (as in justifiable mercy-dying).

But is it right to watch a man suffer without attempting to relieve his agony? No, of course not. But there are means short of death to relieve suffering. The Bible recommends drugs for this purpose. "Give strong drink to him who is perishing, and wine to those in bitter distress" (Prov. 31:6). A man trapped in a burning airplane might be shot with a tranquilizer, but he should not be shot with a bullet. Even where drugs are not available one should use every method short of life-taking to relieve the suffering. The body has a natural threshold of pain. Men lapse into unconsciousness before they suffer unduly. In case of fire men usually die of the fumes before the flames consume them. Knocking one out or precipitating unconsciousness to alleviate his suffering would be justifiable but

---

[3] See chapter nine.

[4] There are cases of assisted suicide in the Bible, and it was not approved by God. Abimelech's armor-bearer responded to his mortally wounded master's request to kill him, but the act is not *approved* by Scripture but only *recorded* there as the vain way Abimelech desired to die lest it be said, "A woman killed him" (Judges 9:54). King Saul's armor-bearer refused his wounded master's request to kill him, "for he feared greatly" (1 Samuel 31:4). See discussion on suicide below.

taking his life simply because he is suffering and/or simply because he requests it is not.

There is no valid comparison between life-taking on demand and abortion on demand. For in abortion there is only a potential human life whereas mercy-killing involves a fully human life. Only if other human lives can be saved by it should a human life be taken. Neither is it right to *initiate* death simply because one *anticipates* it. Committing suicide or assisting one to do it are not justified simply because one welcomes death. The Christian's desire for death (cf. Phil. 1:23) may lead him fearlessly to face death but should never lead him carelessly or selfishly to take his own life. Nor should it lead him to ask another to help him. The Christian should welcome death from God's hand but not force the hand that brings it.

II. AN ETHIC OF SUICIDE

According to some contemporary existential philosophers, suicide is the number one philosophical problem. Life is absurd, an empty bubble on the sea of nothingness, and it is a serious question as to whether or not it should continue. [5] Long before the philosophy of the absurd, Cebes asked Socrates why, if death was so blessed, a man could not be his own benefactor. [6] The Roman materialist, Lucretius argued that death was nothing and following him some concluded that suicide is a viable option to bring on the bliss of this nothingness. [7]

Other philosophers of note like Schopenhauer have struck pessimistic notes which more than flirt with suicide. And gathering from the increased number of suicides and attempted suicides by contemporary men, suicide is a live option for a sizeable number of people.

Of course, the ethical question is not what men *are* doing but what they *ought* to be doing. Hence, the question here is not *why* men commit suicide but *whether* they should do so and *when* (if ever).

A. Suicide for Oneself

There are two dominant reasons for suicide or taking one's own life: it could be done for oneself or it could be done for others. The first will be called selfish suicide. Is it ever morally right to take one's own life in self-interest? Or, even more basically, is taking one's life ever really in the interest of oneself?

1. *Suicide for Oneself Cannot be Justified Philosophically* — De-

[5] Cf. Jean-Paul Sartre, *Being and Nothingness*, New York: Washington Square Press, Inc., 1966, pp. 762, 766, esp. pp. 479, 556.

[6] Plato, *Phaedo* 62 a.

[7] Cf. George Santayana's *Three Philosophical Poets*, Harvard University Press, 1927. Pertinent section is reprinted in Melvin Rader's, *The Enduring Questions*.

spite the Stoic's [8] futile attempt to justify suicide and despite Schopenauer's pessimistic propensity to it, suicide lacks sound philosophical grounds. Perhaps the best evidence for this conclusion comes from contemporary existential philosophers who consider the suicide question the most basic one — and whose philosophy gives them most reason for doing so. For among these atheistic existentialists there is a strong rejection of suicide. Suicide, says Sartre, is wrong because it is an act of freedom which destroys all future acts of freedom. It is an affirmation of being by which one finally negates one's being. Or, in everyday words, suicide is an act of the living which destroys one's life.

Defining suicide this way points up precisely how irrational the act really is. It is a reasoned act which would destroy one's reasoning. As such suicide is an absurd piece of reasoning, for it is the "reason" which destroys itself in affirming itself. Actually, there is no real reason for suicide. It is an anti-rational act which lacks a true rationale.

2. *Suicide for Oneself Cannot Be Justified Ethically* — The immorality of suicide can be seen from an analysis of its alleged motive. According to those who have been tempted by suicide and/or who have attempted it, suicide seems the best way out of their situation for themselves. Yet how paradoxical it is that one should conclude for himself that the best thing he can do for himself is to destroy himself. How can the best thing *for* oneself be the ultimate act *against* oneself? Surely it is a perverse use of reason which would destroy one's reason. Can one ever be acting in self-interest when his plan is to destroy himself? Suicide is not self-interest. It cannot be! It is a lack of proper interest in oneself. The only way one can show interest in himself is to preserve himself. Suicide is just the opposite. It is really self-hate. And self-hate is irrational, absurd. For it is an affirmation of the self in an attempt to negate itself; it is the choice to eliminate all choice.

From this analysis of the irrationality of suicide it can be deduced that no one ever really *wills* suicide, even though some *wish* it. That is, when a man commits suicide he does so against his basic will to live. Suicide is based on a man's *wish* to be relieved of the (miserable) kind of existence he has, despite the fact that he *wills* existence itself. As Augustine said, suicide is a failure of courage. It is contrary to one's basic *drive* for being; suicide is a desire for non-being. It is existential "copoutism." Briefly put, suicide is not

---

[8] The Stoics gave several reasons for suicide (*Stoicorum Veterum Fragmenta* III, 768). According to A. H. Armstrong, Plotinus agreed with at least three of the Stoics' arguments, viz. suicide is justifiable in long and extremely painful illness, in the case of madness, and probably when there is coercion to immoral behavior. See *Enneads* of Plotinus I, 9 in Loeb classics edited by Armstrong.

a philosophical problem at all; rather, it is a moral and/or psychological problem. That is to say, men do not attempt suicide because it is the most reasonable thing to do but because it is the "easy" way out of their problem. And when someone thinks that the easiest way out of his situation is to attack himself fatally rather than attacking the problem, then he has a moral, if not a psychological, problem.

In brief, there is no way to commit suicide *for* oneself, since suicide is the most basic act *against* oneself that can be committed. Hence, suicide on the alleged moral ground of self-interest is ruled out. Selfish suicide, as other forms of selfishness, is not really in one's own best interest. True self-love will never desire to eliminate the self it loves.

Still one might argue that suicide, like mercy-killing, might be justified if one has reached a subhuman or "vegetable" stage of existence. Why not pull the trigger on oneself to prevent the continuation of one's own inhumanity? If it is morally right to be the benefactor of mercy for another human "vegetable," then why not for oneself? The reason is quite simple: no one who is capable of reasoning himself to the conclusion that he should end his life has yet lost his humanity. He may have lost his sanity (or part of it), but he is still human. And if he is still human enough to reason (albeit, wrongly) that the best thing he can do for his life is to end it, then he is not yet subhuman. From this it follows that because he is not subhuman, there is no justification for performing a mercy-killing on himself, for mercy-killing is justified only when more human lives can be saved by it. Self-mercy-killing is a contradiction in terms, for the final act against oneself cannot at the same time be an act for oneself.

As far as Scriptures are concerned, suicide comes under the prohibition of murder. It is at least as wrong illicitly to take one's own life as it is to take the life of another. One should love himself as well as loving others, as is implied in the command to love others *as oneself* (Matt. 22:39; cf. Eph. 5:29). [9] And if loving another person implies that one should not murder him, then loving oneself surely implies the same in regard to suicide. Suicide is wrong because it is the murder of a human being made in the image and likeness of God, even if the individual happens to be oneself. [10]

B. *Suicide for Others*

Since selfish suicide is wrong it remains to ask if sacrificial suicide is ever right. That is, is it ever right to take one's own life for the

---

[9] See chapter eight above on self-love.

[10] In fact, killing oneself may be a worse sin than killing another. Suicide is a greater evil than homicide — because self-love is basic to loving others. The command is to love others *as ourselves*. If love of oneself is basic to loving others, the improper love of oneself (i.e., suicide) is a more basic sin.

sake of preserving other lives? The answer will depend on whether or not it is really done to save other lives.

1. *Not Every So-Called "Sacrificial" Suicide Is Justifiable* — There are cases where sacrificing one's life for other men is not really morally right. Paul implied that it is possible to deliver one's body to be burned and yet lack real love (1 Cor. 13:3). In other words, not every death "for others" is really for others. It may be an attempt to draw attention to oneself or to gratify some other selfish need. Sacrificial suicide may be a test of one's sincerity, but sincerity -is no proof of morality. Men can hate sincerely as well as love sincerely. Men can sincerely do what they *want* to do rather than what they *ought* to do. What futility for a man to prove his sincerity for his own selfish cause by suicide! It may be admirable to sacrifice one's life for a cause it is not necessarily moral. For if one's cause is vain, his sacrifice is also vain, whether it is the supreme sacrifice or not.

Furthermore, to sacrifice one's life intentionally for an animal or for non-personal objects (wealth or whatever) is not morally right. Persons are more valuable than things. People are of intrinsic value; things have instrumental value for persons. Man is an end, but animals and things are means to human ends. Hence, sacrificial suicide for a nonhuman object would be wrong because it gives up the higher value (a human life) for the lower life (a subhuman life). [11]

2. *Some Sacrificial Suicide Is Justifiable* — Not all suicide is wrong. As the Bible notes, some even dare to die for good men (Rom. 5:7). History, especially military history, contains many examples of men willing to die for others. The story of Samson's death seems to be one of a divinely-approved suicide (Judg. 16:30). There are other intimations in the New Testament of sacrificial suicide (cf. Rom. 5:7). Paul indicated his willingness to sacrifice his life for Christ (Phil. 1:23). However, the real proof for the Christian that sacrificial suicide is morally right is the death of Jesus Christ who came ". . . to give his life a ransom for many" (Mark 10:45). Jesus said, "I lay down my life, that I may take it again. No one takes it from me, but I lay it down of my own accord" (John 10:18). Surely this is the supreme example of the supreme sacrifice. It was in view of this that John wrote, "By this we know love, that he laid down his life for us; and we ought to lay down our lives for the brethren" (1 John 3:16). Indeed, it is in the light of the cross of Christ that the highest form of love is revealed.

---

[11] It no doubt is possible to conceive of a situation where giving one's life for an animal (say, a rescue dog) may help save more human lives. If so, the purpose of giving one's life is for the other humans and not for the dog as such.

"Greater love has no man than this," said Jesus, "that a man lay down his life for his friends" (John 15:13). This kind of sacrificial "suicide" is not only *not* immoral; it is the highest moral act possible. It goes beyond the demands of the moral law, which requires one to love his neighbor only *as* himself. True sacrificial "suicide" is more than that; it is to love others *more* than oneself. There is no greater love.

Perhaps some may object to the use of the word "suicide" in this connection. They may argue that a sacrifice of one's life for others is not suicide. The soldier who falls on a hand grenade to save his buddies is not committing suicide, it may be argued. He is protecting other lives with his own. This is true. There is a difference between selfish suicide and what we have called sacrificial suicide, and only the latter is morally justifiable. Whether or not one wishes to use the word "suicide" of such a sacrifice is a matter of word choice. Whatever it is called, it is a self-initiated act to save other lives by sacrificing one's own life. It is an intentional but justifiable relinquishing of one's life. In view of this it seems appropriate to call it a "sacrificial suicide."

III. A Christian Ethic of Capital Punishment

Much controversy has raged around the question of capital punishment. On the one hand it has been hailed as divinely instituted and socially necessary. On the other hand it has been labeled as barbaric and unchristian. [12] Is it ever morally right to take the life of another human being for social reasons? Should life-taking ever be used penally? What do the Scriptures say on the subject?

A. *The Biblical Basis for Capital Punishment*

There are several distinct passages of Scripture which teach that God ordained capital punishment for certain heinous social crimes. These passages are found in both testaments.

1. *The Old Testament on Capital Punishment* — The first reference to capital punishment is found in Genesis 9:6. Noah and his family survived the great flood which was precipitated by the evil and violence of that pre-deluvian civilization (cf. Gen. 6:11). When Noah emerged from the ark God gave the following injunction: "Whoever sheds the blood of man, by man shall his blood be shed; for God made man in his own image." Murder is wrong because it is killing God in effigy, and the taker of other men's lives is to have his life taken at the hands of men. The predeluvians had filled the world with violence and bloodshed. By the use of capital punishment men were to quell the violence and restore the order of justice.

---

[12] Much of the emotional sentiment against capital punishment is expressed in John Laurence's *A History of Capital Punishment*, New York: Citadel Press, 1960.

God ordained social order and peace and gave government the authority over life to ensure mankind these benefits.

Under the Mosaic law capital punishment was continued and even broadened. The basic principle was "life for life, eye for eye, tooth for tooth" (Ex. 21:25). Capital punishment was used for other crimes besides murder. Both the adulterer and adulteress were to be stoned to death (Lev. 20:10). In fact, even a stubborn and rebellious son who would not receive correction was to be killed by the same method at the hands of the citizens (Deut. 21:18ff). At the direction of God, Achan and his family were stoned for disobeying God's command not to keep spoils from the battle of Jericho (Josh. 7:1, 26).

There are indications that God delegated authority over life to nations outside Israel in the Old Testament. Human governors in general are said to be set up by God. Both Nebuchadnezzar (Dan. 4:17) and Cyrus (Isa. 44:28) were given authority by God over human lives. Indeed, there is indication elsewhere in the Old Testament that human government in general is given such authority by God to resist evil in the world, as was stated in Genesis 9:6.

2. *The New Testament on Capital Punishment* — The New Testament presupposes the same basic view on capital punishment as the Old Testament. Rulers are ordained by God; they are given the sword as well as the crown by divine authority (cf. Rom. 13:1f). Paul noted that the ruler ". . . does not bear the sword in vain; he is the servant of God to execute his wrath on the wrongdoer" (v. 4).

It is sometimes overlooked that Jesus reaffirmed the principle of capital punishment in His Sermon on the Mount. "Think not that I have come to abolish the law and the prophets; I have come not to abolish them but to fulfill them." Continuing, Jesus added, "You have heard that it was said to the men of old, 'You shall not kill; and whoever kills shall be liable to judgment [by capital punishment]. But I say to you that everyone who is angry with his brother shall be liable to judgment" (Matt. 5:21, 22). According to Josephus (*Antiquities* IV, 8, 6 and 14) the Sanhedrin or Council of Seventy had the power to pronounce the death sentence, and sometimes exercised it as is manifest in the martyrdom of Stephen (Acts 7:59) and the execution of James (Acts 12:1, 2). It is no doubt so, as John 18:31 says that Rome had taken away the Jews' legal right to capital punishment. This does not mean, however, that the Jews had given up their belief that God had given them this authority and, hence, that they should exercise it when they thought they could get away with it. [13]

---

[13] See article by Edwin Yamauchi on "Historical Notes on the Trial and Crucifixion of Jesus Christ," *Christianity Today* (April 9, 1971), pp. 6-11 [634-639].

Within the New Testament apostolic church there seemed to be a kind of capital punishment in effect. Ananias and Sapphira were condemned to death by the apostle Peter for telling ". . . a lie to the Holy Spirit. . ." (Acts 5:3). Although there is no indication that this particular application of the death sentence is not limited to the original apostles, nevertheless, it is clear proof that the God of the New Testament executed a death sentence on guilty men through other men.

In another passage Jesus recognized the God-given authority over life which human governors possessed. Pilate said to Jesus, "Do you not know that I have power to release you, and power to crucify you?" Jesus answered, "You would have no power over me unless it had been given you from above" (John 19:11). The implication here is that Pilate did possess divinely-derived authority over human life. As a matter of fact, he used it (Jesus was sentenced to death), and Jesus submitted to it.

In summary, there is ample biblical data from both testaments that God ordained and men exercised capital punishment for specific offenses. The death sentence for certain crimes is enjoined by God through men upon the guilty. Hence, the question from a strictly biblical perspective is not *whether* capital punishment was and is authorized by God for men but *when* and *why*. But before the application and rationale of capital punishment are discussed a word is in order on some objections to the death sentence.

B. *Some Objections to Capital Punishment*

A number of objections to capital punishment have been offered by those who oppose it. Three of these are worthy of comment from a biblical standpoint.

1. *The Case of Cain* — It is sometimes argued that capital punishment was not the intention of God from the beginning as may be deduced from God's intervention to spare Cain from it. When Cain killed his brother Abel, God explicitly forbade anyone to slay Cain in return. "If anyone slays Cain," He said, "vengeance shall be taken on him sevenfold" (Gen. 4:15).

What is easily overlooked in this obvious exemption from capital punishment is that the passage clearly implies the validity of capital punishment. Cain's was a special case. [14] Who would have executed the sentence? His brother was dead. Surely God was not to call

---

[14] At the beginning of the race there were bound to be situations differing from later, more developed society. For example, Cain no doubt married his sister (cf. Genesis 4:17 and 5:4), a practice later forbidden by God (Leviticus 20:17). But in the very beginning there was no one else to marry but a close relative.

on the father to execute his only remaining son! In this situation God Himself personally commuted the death sentence.

However, in God's suspending the death sentence on Cain, the Bible clearly indicates that this was not to be the rule. Several factors support this conclusion. First, the Lord Himself said, "The voice of your brother's blood is crying to me from the ground" (Gen. 4:10). Crying for what? For justice, no doubt. The biblical principle is that only another life can satisfy the justice of a lost life (cf. Lev. 17:11; Heb. 9:22). Second, Cain's fear that someone in the future would slay him shows that capital punishment was his own natural expectation. "Whoever finds me will slay me," he cried (Gen. 4:14). One naturally anticipates the loss of his own life as a consequence of taking another's life. Third, God's answer to Cain implies capital punishment. "If anyone slays Cain, vengeance shall be taken on him sevenfold." This no doubt means capital punishment would be used on anyone killing Cain. So, contrary to what may appear on the surface, Cain's case is the "exception" which proves the rule. From the beginning God's intentions were that capital crimes should receive capital sentences.

2. *Jesus and the Adulterous Woman* — Did not Jesus show His disdain for capital punishment by refusing to apply the Old Testament death sentence to the woman taken in adultery? Did not Christ say to her, "Go, and do not sin again" (John 8:11)? Moses commanded capital punishment for adulterers; Jesus forgave them. Is it not, then, more Christian to do away with capital punishment and to exercise forgiving love?

The first thing to note in attempting to answer this objection is that the passage under consideration (John 7:53-8:11) is textually suspect. It is found in different places in ancient manuscripts. [15] It definitely interrupts the narration here (read John 8:12 immediately after 7:52). Even though there is sound textual evidence for questioning the authority of this story we will, for the sake of discussion, assume its authenticity. [16]

In point of fact, there is nothing in this passage against capital punishment. Jesus claimed never to have broken Moses' law (Matt. 5:17) and there is no proof here that He did. Moses had commanded death *only* if there were two or three eyewitnesses (Num. 35:30). There were none here who claimed (in the end) to be eyewitnesses nor who pressed charges. After they all left, Jesus explicitly asked her, "Woman, where are they? Has no one condemned you? She said, No one, Lord" (vv. 10-11). On the basis of "no witnesses,"

[15] Sometimes it is found at the end of John's gospel and sometimes after Luke 21:38.

[16] See the discussion on this point in *General Introduction to the Bible*, Chicago: Moody Press, 1968, pp. 371-372.

no sentence was called for. The woman had been given due process by the Savior.

3. *The Cross of Christ and Forgiving Grace* — There is another and more sophisticated argument against capital punishment which claims that in view of the cross of Christ and forgiving grace it is *now* (in New Testament times) unchristian to mete out justice as though God has not given pardon to all men. This objection maintains that capital punishment is based on a sub-Christian or pre-Christian concept of justice which is transcended by a New Testament morality of grace. God does not desire to punish men, least of all with capital punishment; rather, God wants to pardon men through Christ. All our crimes were nailed to His cross (Eph. 2:15, 16). The law was fulfilled by Christ in precept and penalty (Matt. 5:17; Gal. 3:13). Since God's justice has been satisfied by Christ's sacrifice, there is no need for men to pay the penalty for their sins. God offers pardon to everyone and for everything.

Basically, this objection to capital punishment is built on a misunderstanding of grace. Forgiving a sin does not automatically rescind the results of that sin. A drunk who confesses his sin has no right to expect God to take away his hangover. A reckless driver who harms his own body should not expect pre-crash health and wholeness immediately upon confesssion. The grace of God takes care of the *penalty* of a man's sin but not always the immediate *consequences*. "Do not be deceived," wrote Paul, "God is not mocked, for whatever a man sows, that he will also reap" (Gal. 6:7). This applies to the Christian. When the Corinthian saints abused the Lord's Supper, God visited them with sickness and even death (1 Cor. 11:30).

If forgiveness of sin meant also the elimination of all its consequences, surely men would sin more that grace would abound. It is part of God's grace that He teaches us not to sin again. Indeed, the clearest evidence that God does not automatically eliminate the results of sins which He forgives is the fact that even Christians die. Death has spread to all men because all men have sinned (Rom. 5:12). And becoming a Christian does not cancel this consequence of sin. Even the best of Christians die as a result of sin — forgiven sin.

If the cross does not automatically eliminate the immediate and social consequences of one's sin, then the objection to capital punishment built on this premise fails. In fact, there is a more serious implication to this whole objection which needs to be examined. There is a radical kind of dispensationalism implied in the contention that God's system of moral justice is not the same in both testaments. Christ did not abolish the moral law of the Old Testament. Each of the Ten Commandments is reaffirmed in the New

Testament. [17] Even under grace it is wrong to murder, to lie, to steal, and to commit adultery. When the New Testament declares that the Christian is "not under the law but under grace," it means that the particular Mosaic codification and application of God's unchanging moral principles to the nation of Israel have been fulfilled by Christ. However, this does not mean that the ethical norms embodied in the Ten Commandments are abolished by the cross. The same basic moral law of God's divine justice is in effect in both Old and New Testaments. Neither God nor the moral law which reflects His nature have changed. And, for that matter, neither has God's plan of grace changed from one testament to the other. In the Old Testament men were saved by grace through faith in the Gospel just as in the New Testament (cf. Rom. 4:6f; Heb. 11:6). Paul declared emphatically that there is only one Gospel, pronouncing anathama even an angel who would preach another one (Gal. 1:6-9). Yet in that same epistle he wrote that this Gospel was preached to Abraham (3:8). There is only one moral law for both testaments and there is only one plan of saving grace. Any objection to capital punishment built on a dispensational change in either God's justice or grace is on very specious grounds biblically.

C. The Rationale for Capital Punishment

Some of the social objections to capital punishment are based not so much on *use* as on the possible *abuse* of the power of capital punishment. But the fact that mistakes will be made by fallible humans in applying this punishment is not a good argument for doing away with it completely. Doctors make fatal mistakes and so do politicians, but these mistakes are not good reasons for doing away with the practice of medicine or government. The abuse of marriage by unjustified divorce does not mean that the institution of marriage is not divinely established. Many individuals make fatal mistakes, but their fallible judgment does not thereby eliminate the need for men to exercise good judgment in applying moral and social justice. Of course, capital punishment should not be executed on anyone who has not been given due process of law and whose guilt is not beyond all reasonable doubt. On the other hand, one whose crime is so heinous as to demand capital punishment should not be spared on the fallacious allegation that it is unjust or contrary to grace. It is unjust not to mete out justice when it is called for by injustice.

The *administration* of justice is another question. What is of con-

[17] Even the principle of the commandment about keeping one day in seven as a day of rest and worship is reaffirmed in the Christian Lord's Day, although the particular day was changed from Saturday to Sunday (cf. Acts 20:7) in view of the resurrection and appearances of Christ (cf. John 20:1, 26).

cern in normative ethics is not the application (or misapplication) of justice but the very principle of justice itself which sometimes demands capital punishment. One of the implications behind some social objection to capital punishment is that it is inhuman or unjust to so punish men for their wrong. Social action for criminals should not be penal but reformative, it is argued. The concept of punishment is sub-Christian or barbaric. Civilized men should try to reconcile men not destroy them. There is no place for such gross punishment among civilized men, it is said.

Granting the truth that wherever possible men should be reformed, there are some strange inconsistencies in the above arguments against capital punishment. First, it assumes a biblical kind of justice in order to say that the biblical concept of capital punishment is unjust. The standard of justice which demands capital punishment cannot be used to deny what that standard demands. Second, there is a strange twist in logic to call capital punishment inhuman. The inhumanity was the crime which called for the capital consequences. The inhuman act was performed *by* the criminal in murder, not *on* the criminal in capital punishment.

The fact of the matter is that capital punishment itself can be a very human act. It can be a kind of mercy-killing, that is, a kind of mercy to society to guarantee that this criminal will not repeat the crime he committed. The social relief to know that men are free from the bloodthirsty is a gift of mercy to the rest of mankind. What kind of perverted humaneness is it that concerns itself with the single life of a guilty man more than with the many lives of innocent men? In the name of mercy for men in general, one could offer a strong plea for capital punishment for certain crimes which are likely to be repeated.

Further, it may be argued that the unreformability of certain criminals is one reason for capital punishment. The Old Testament, on this ground, demanded that a rebellious and incorrigible son be put to death (Deut. 21:18). When one calculates the untold sorrow and death which can be brought on innocent men by one incorrigible human, perhaps there is more sense in Moses' law than an indulgent contemporary social justice is willing to admit.

However, unreformability is not the only reason for capital punishment. Indeed, it is probably not the basic reason. *Justice* is the prime reason for capital punishment. Capital punishment is obviously not intended to be reformatory on the criminal; it is a punishment. Of course, a by-product of capital punishment may be the detering of evil in others. However, this is moot. Since, for all practical purposes, a contemporary American criminal about to commit murder has no real reason to expect that he will ever be punished by death, it is probably not possible to make a real social test of whether the real threat of capital punishment would deter the criminal. The Bible does seem to imply, however, that punishment is intended to deter evil doers (cf. Rom. 13:3). The prime reason for capital punishment, however, is that justice demands it. A just order is disturbed by murder and only the death of the murderer can restore that justice. Restitution is not possible for murder, and reformation can at best only guarantee that the same act by the same man will not occur again. But nothing has satisfied justice in regard to the first murder. God can *forgive* it, but even God cannot *justify* sin. In fact, nothing ever really justifies sin. Sin is always unjustifiable. This does not mean it is unforgivable. It is forgivable through Christ. Nor does it mean that justice sinned-against is unsatisfiable. There is only one thing that satisfies an offended justice and that is payment of the debt to justice. And the biblical payment for murder is one's life. Life for life, blood for blood, is the rule. The penalty for taking another man's life is giving one's own life.

The reason why this rationale may sound strange to the modern ear is that the true sense of justice has been obscured. When men no longer believe in God nor in an unchangeable moral law, it follows that no penalty should be incurred for transgressing a law which is not there. Along with this contemporary distortion of justice is an anemic concept of love. A loving God would not punish anyone, it is vainly thought. Hence, it is concluded that a loving parent should not discipline his child. It is little wonder that men do not understand the need for capital punishment; they do not see the need for any kind of punishment. They fail to see that loving parents punish their children (Prov. 13:24) and that a loving God chastises His sons (Heb. 12:5, 6). [18] Indeed, almost the converse of the modern mentality is true. The Bible teaches that proper punishment is proof of love. The love is *in* the discipline. The lack of correction is an indication of the lack of true concern for the wayward.

One final point should be made in response to the alleged inhumanity of capital punishment. Capital punishment, contrary to what some so-called humanists would lead us to believe, actually implies a higher regard for the individual. Individual man is in the image of God, and that is why it is wrong to kill him (Gen. 9:6). Man is so valuable as an individual that anyone who tampers with his sacred right to live must face the consequences of losing his own

[18] Overcorrection is also wrong (cf. Colossians 3:21) because justice demands only the appropriate amount or kind of punishment for the offense.

life. The worth of the individual is so great that the highest penalty is attached to those who tamper with the life of even one man.

IV. HIERARCHICALISM AND TAKING OTHER LIVES

The problem of when and why it is right to take other lives is not an easy one. The tension is resolvable, however, when a hierarchical ethic is applied. Killing is justifiable when many lives can be saved while fewer are sacrificed, or when complete lives are preserved in favor of the incomplete, or when an actual life is preferred to a potential one. Even suicide to save more lives is justifiable. The basic principles behind these conclusions are: (1) persons are more valuable than things; (2) many lives are more valuable than fewer lives; (3) actual persons are more valuable than potential persons; (4) complete persons are more valuable than incomplete persons. [19]

It is because of the intrinsic value of persons that murder is wrong. And it is because murder is a great offense against the intrinsic value of the other person, and to the Person of God whom they reflect, that the penalty is so great. Capital punishment is not impersonal or anti-human. It is pro-human. By putting away the anti-human, one is vindicating the value of the individual person. At this point it is easier to see the applicability of another principle of hierarchicalism, viz., (5) what promotes the interpersonal is more valuable than what does not. This is why capital punishment for Eichmann was a very personal act. The death sentence on a man who masterminded the plan to annihilate a race is an eminently appropriate way to bring this anti-personal career to a just end. Punishing the impersonal and anti-personal is not itself impersonal. On the contrary it is a vindication of the intrinsic value of every person. Not to punish the anti-personal is an impersonal act. To refuse to intervene with justice when the intrinsic value of innocent persons is violated is a highly impersonal ethic. Capital punishment justly applied can be an expression of a very person-centered ethic.

In brief, capital punishment is called for in capital crimes to protect the intrinsic value of an individual person's right to live. Further, the death sentence may be justified on less than capital crimes when the lives of more innocent people are at stake if the wicked man lives. Outside of capital crimes or activity which would surely lead to the death of innocent men the state has no divine right to exercise the death sentence. It is a serious responsibility for a government to bear the sword and it should take care not to do it in vain.

[19] See chapter seven for an elaboration of these and other ethical principles involved in hierarchical ethics.

SELECT READINGS FOR CHAPTER THIRTEEN:
SUICIDE

Aquinas, Thomas, *Summa Theologica*, Part 2, Question 64, A5.
Augustine, *City of God*, Book I, Chs. 17-28; Book IX, Ch. 4.
Camus, Albert, *The Myth of Sisyphus and Other Essays*, trans. by Justin O'Brian, New York: Alfred A. Knopf, Inc., 1955.
Plotinus, *Enneads* I,9 trans. by Arthur H. Armstrong, Loeb Classical Library, Cambridge, Mass.: Harvard University Press, Vol. I.
Seneca, *Epistulae Morales*, Vol. II Cambridge, Mass., Harvard University Press, trans. by R. M. Gumere.

CAPITAL PUNISHMENT

Ressig, Herman F., *Social Action*, April, 1970, has several articles against capital punishment.
Taylor, E. L. H., *The Death Penalty*, Houston, Texas: St. Thomas Press.

MERCY-KILLING

More, Sir Thomas, *Utopia* (1516) was one of the first Christian writers to allow mercy-killing.
Williams, G. L., *The Sanctity of Life and the Criminal Law*, Ch. 8, New York: Alfred A. Knopf, Inc., 1957.

14 / The Christian and Ecology

A brief treatment of ecology, a subject of great contemporary interest, seems called for on several grounds. First, ecology does have moral implications and, hence, does fall within the limits of this work. Second, it is not clear on the surface how an ethic built on the intrinsic value of *persons* is compatible with an all-out attempt to rescue inanimate *things* like air, land, and sea. Finally, some ecological ethics allege that Christianity is incompatible with stress on man's natural environment.

I. A Biblical Basis for Ecology

Of all the great religious and philosophical systems none gives greater dignity to the material world than does the Judeo-Christian tradition. Both testaments of Scripture support the contention that matter is good and that the natural world is god-like. In view of this it is strange to hear the charge from contemporary writers that the biblical view of the world is responsible for the present ecological crisis. As one writer put it, "On the subject of man-nature . . . the Biblical creation story of the first chapter of Genesis . . . not only fails to correspond to reality as we observe it, but in its insistence upon dominion and subjugation of nature, encourages the most exploitive and destructive instincts in man rather than those that are deferential and creative."[1] How far this criticism misses the mark can only be revealed by an examination of the biblical data itself.

[1] Ian I. McHarg, *Design With Nature* (Garden City, New York: The Natural History Press, 1969), p. 26.

A. *The Value of Creation*

Contrary to the Greek mind, the Old Testament affirms the essential good of the material creation. The physical world is not an evil to be rejected; it is a good to be enjoyed. The material world is not a manifestation of evil but a reflection of the glory of God.

1. *Material Creation is Good* — After nearly every day of creation the record says that "God saw that it was *good*" (cf. Gen. 1:4, 10, 12, 18, 20, 25). On the final day "God saw everything that he had made, and behold, it was *very good*" (1:31). [2] Man is said to be the very best of the material creation, made in the "image of God."

Not only are matter and the human body esssentially good but the latter is the blessed instrument of propagating more of the like material good in the world. God ordained sex as the means of making more men. He blessed the first pair and commanded them to fill the earth with their kind. This is indeed a great dignity given to matter, that it should both be pronounced good and also be the instrument for producing more good of its kind.

According to the Greeks, [3] matter is eternal and formless, an irrational surd which is both necessary and evil. It is chaotic and formless, having no content of goodness in itself but only the sheer capacity to receive good forms from without. In its corporeal manifestations in man matter becomes a prison for the soul, a hindrance to man's spiritual development. To be delivered from the clutches of the material is the heart of salvation. It is little wonder that the Athenian philosophers laughed when they heard Paul speak of the resurrection of the body (Acts 17:32).

2. *Material Creation Reflects God's Glory* — Not only is the natural world called essentially good, but it is also said to reflect the glory of God. The Psalmist wrote, "The heavens are telling the glory of God, and the firmament proclaims his handiwork" (Ps. 19:1). Again, "When I look at thy heavens, the work of thy fingers, the moon and the stars which thou hast established; what is man that thou art mindful of him" (Ps. 8:34). Creation reflects the glory of the Creator, according to the Old Testament. Nature is a kind of theophany or appearance of God. God is everywhere manifest; He is in the light and darkness, on the land and in the sea, in the height and in the deep (cf. Ps. 139:7-12).

The observing eye can see evidences of God everywhere. According to the New Testament, "ever since the creation of the world his invisible nature, namely, his eternal power and deity, has been clearly perceived in the things that have been made" (Rom. 1:20).

---

[2] Throughout this chapter the emphasis on biblical quotation is our own.

[3] Plato may be taken as the chief representative of a sophisticated Greek view of matter. See his *Timaeus* in particular.

The growing seasons and their produce are a testimony to God's faithfulness (Acts 14:17), said Paul to the heathen at Lystra. So close is God in nature that "in him we live and move and have our being," as the apostle declared to the Athenian philosophers (Acts 17:28). God is evident in the storm, in the thunder, and in virtually every fact and event of nature, according to Job (cf. ch. 38). In brief, the whole natural world is a reflection of the glory of its Creator.

B. *The Value of the Incarnation*

Without a doubt, the greatest dignity ever given matter was not its good as a creation of God, nor its glory as a reflection of God. The greatest honor bestowed on material creation was God's becoming part of it in the incarnation of Christ. "The Word became flesh and dwelt among us, full of grace and truth," wrote John (1:14). Deity entered the bloodstream of humanity. God asssumed a material body. To create matter is one thing for God, but to make it a permanent part of the resurrected and glorified Son of God is another (cf. 1 Cor. 15).

No non-Christian system has given a more exalted position to the material world. Matter is both good as a creation of God and the vehicle of the incarnation of God. "For in him [Christ] the whole fulness of deity dwells bodily" (Col. 2:9). With such a high view of the natural world and the material and corporeal creation, it is not difficult to base a solid ethic for ecology. Why should man preserve his world? Because it is good, because it is like God, and because God likes it and has made it like Himself. Furthermore, one day God will redeem even nature (Rom. 8:18ff), purify it (2 Pet. 3:10ff), and perpetuate it forever (Rev. 21:1). Hence, in polluting the world men are destroying what is good and defacing the mirror that reflects God. Likewise, disregard for the human body — polluting it with drugs — is abusing the vessel which God adorned in His image and honored with the incarnation of His Son. Surely no higher and no better reason can be given against pollution.

II. Ecology and the Intrinsic Value of Persons

It seems evident from Scripture that polluting man's world (really, God's world) is morally wrong. What may not be as clear is just how this is compatible with the hierarchical personalism defended in this book. This is, if persons are more valuable than things, i.e., if persons are the central value, then how can marring material creation be considered a sin? If one's sins are really against a person (whether human or divine), then how can abusing the natural things which surround man be evil? The basic rule is that persons are to be loved (as ends) and things are to be used as means to personal ends. Why then is it wrong for persons to do anything they wish to their resources and environment? Isn't that what things are for, to be subservient to persons?

A. *Evil Is Always Personal*

Before attempting to reconcile a biblical morality of ecology with the view that persons have more value than things, it may be well to state again the rationale for personalism.

1. *Persons Have Intrinsic Value* — Three reasons were given as to why persons have intrinsic value, things having instrumental value as they are used for persons. First, only persons have self-awareness. That is, only persons can know themselves as objects. Objects cannot be aware that they are objects; only subjects can be aware of objects. Second, only persons have the power of self-determination. Only subjects are free. Objects are determined by other subjects but do not determine themselves. Third, only persons can interrelate with others. Subjects can relate by the web of intersubjectivity; objects cannot. That is to say, only persons can have an I-thou relation. Objects as such are things ("Its") and cannot *relate*; they can only *be related* to others. In brief, persons have intrinsic value because they are subjects and subjectivity is more basic than objectivity, for only subjects are self-aware, free, and intra-personal. Persons have intrinsic value, for persons transcend objects which can be manipulated, used, and completely determined by what as such defies being used as an object; it is a free subject. Others can treat it as an object, but they do not thereby *make* it an object; it *is* a free subject as such.

2. *All Evil Is a Misuse of Persons* — If persons are the most basic value, then does it follow that all sin must somehow be related to persons? Are there any sins against things as such? Can one sin only *with* things but not *against* things? Specifically, can man sin against his environment as such?

There are several prima facie cases of allegedly "impersonal" sin which upon closer scrutiny support our answer that all sin is really personal. For example, so-called private sins, by which one secretly hates or lusts after another, are really against persons, even though these persons may never feel the effect. Hate is a sin because it *intends* to do something against a person. Lust is evil because by it one shows one's *desire* to have another person improperly. But could not one hate a tree or lust after an animal? The Bible explicitly condemns the latter (Lev. 18:23). Admittedly, these are unusual forms of sin but they are not nonpersonal. In both cases they could be said to involve "persons," for they are treating things as though they were "persons." Of course, the tree or the animal is not really a person but the sin consists precisely in the fact that it considers them to be such. Hate and lust are reactions to persons not things. When they are vented on things it is usually because persons are not available or because the sinner is demented into personalizing the non-personal.

How about the miser who hoards his money but hurts no one; does he sin? Saving money for a better use of it is one thing; selfishly hoarding it is another. [4] The latter can be morally wrong in several ways. First, it may be a form of idolatry, viz., treating money (thing) as a god (a person). Second, it may be a neglect of persons, viz., oneself, his family, or his fellow man for whom he could be using the money. Jesus made it very clear that money was not to be hoarded but to be invested in other persons (Luke 12:16ff; 16:1-13).

What about swearing or blasphemy or other "private" sins? These, too, involve the personal. They are sins against the Person of God. Indeed, according to Scripture even David's sins of murder and adultery were really against God. David confessed to God, "Against thee, thee only, have I sinned . . ." (Ps. 51:4). Since God is the Source of all value and the One who determines value, then it would follow naturally that all sin — even sin against nature — would ultimately be against Him personally.

Even the hermit who abuses his dog or the sadist who privately torments animals sins when these acts are deleterious to himself or others. It is difficult to see how cruelty (even to animals) does not in some way affect the person who performs the cruelty. *Doing* wrong tends to solidify that predisposition in the person and make him a worse person. In brief, even "solo" sins are sins against a a person, viz., the one performing them. Immediately they are sins against one's own person, and ultimately they are sins against God.

B. *Polluting the Environment Is Morally Wrong*

There are a number of ways in which pollution of man's physical environment is morally wrong. But basically pollution is wrong insofar as it affects persons who are the highest value in the world. Pollution need not be a sin against the earth *as such*. It is an evil performed against the people of earth and the One who made the earth for people, and who made the earth as a revelation of Himself. [5]

1. *Pollution Is Basically Selfish* — At the basis of pollution is selfishness. Man wants much out of nature but he is willing to put little back into it. He wants to use it for gain whether it is usable

---

[4] Jesus rebuked the man who buried his talent of gold in the earth (Matthew 25:26f).

[5] Carl H. Reidel, "Christianity and the Environmental Crisis," *Christianity Today* Vol. XV, No. 15, April 23, 1971, p. 5 [685].

again or not. Men cut down forests but often leave wasteland behind them. They use natural resources but do not put the waste products in a reusable form. It is nearsighted and selfish to want the use and gain of nature for oneself without due regard for other men today or future generations. Most forms of pollution are directly traceable to man's exuberance in the greed for gain. According to the Bible, "the love of money is the root of all evil" (1 Tim. 6:10). The destruction of man's environment is a sad but striking support of this truth. As one Christian put it, "Pollution is an inevitable consequence of an affluent society that values material progress above all else." [6]

2. *Pollution Affects People* — Further, pollution is wrong because it affects people adversely. Garbage influences sanitation and sanitation affects the health of *persons*. Sewage affects rivers and lakes, and polluted water affects the health and enjoyment of *people*. Bad air is breathed by good *men* and it tends to make them less complete.

The physical world was made for man but it is not to be abused by man, because there are other men yet to use it. As Francis Bacon noted, man can subdue nature only by submitting to it. [7] The world, like a park, would be an enjoyable place in which to live if each man left it at least as clean and usable as he found it. When the earth is polluted there is no sin against it as such; there is, however, a sin against other men whose lives it affects adversely, and against God who made it good. Pollution is wrong on this ground, even if there were no other reason.

This reasoning applies to public pollution, but what about private pollution? What about the garbage at the country cottage or the debris in the basement? That is, is it morally wrong to pollute where it does not affect other men? In a crowded world this question is somewhat easier to answer. Are there any truly private places where pollution will not affect someone somehow someday? If there are such places, then by definition they are not pollutable. For if the waste material is being disposed of in a way which neither affects others badly in the process nor refuses to be absorbed in the environment in due time, then by definition it is not pollution. Dumps or incinerators of some kind will be necessary somewhere for this kind of world. [8]

It is instructive to note in this connection that the Mosaic law had rather strict anti-pollution laws. Sanitation was stressed, including washing, separation, and other preventive measures. At the time when flush toilets were not available, human waste products were

---

[6] Reidel, *Ibid.*
[7] Francis Bacon, *Novum Organum* I, 3 in *Great Books of the Western World*, Chicago: Published by William Benton for Encyclopedia Britannica, 1952.
[8] Reidel, *Ibid.*

to be buried in the earth (Deut. 23:13). Contamination of all kinds was to be avoided. Only certain kinds of animals were to be eaten (Lev. 11) and the blood of animals (a noted carrier of disease) was to be avoided at all cost (Lev. 7:26; cf. Acts 15:20). Intercourse was forbidden during the time of a woman's impurity (Lev. 15:19-24). Any contact with a bodily discharge or emission rendered the person unclean. Separation and the washing of body and clothes were demanded for those who were "contaminated" (Lev. 15:25ff). In the case of contagious disease, quarantines were enforced; polluted houses were torn down (Lev. 14:43ff). In brief, there were both preventive and curative pollution procedures in the Old Testament. If men would live by the laws of God, there would be no pollution of the world. This leads to the next point.

3. *Pollution Violates God's Laws* — The reason that pollution affects other people is that God has set up certain relationships between things and persons. In order to maximize one's personal existence he must know what his proper relationship should be to the other persons and things around him. When any person or thing gets out of its proper God-ordained relationship to others, evil results. In fact, that is precisely what evil is, viz., a misarrangement of God's world. Things are not evil as such; things in themselves are morally neutral and metaphysically good. They are good as creatures, i.e., as beings which reflect the good and glory of God. But when one good thing (say alcohol) is put in too great a quantity into another good thing (a man), then there is an evil relationship set up. That is to say, evil results when persons and things do not relate as God intended them to relate.

The God-intended relationship among persons and things is what the Bible calls "laws." A law is a structure of relationship designed to maximize the intrinsic value of persons. A true law is not an arbitrary injunction intended to curb the fulfillment of human desires. On the contrary, the heart of law is a very personal thing. Laws are made by God and for persons. Jesus pointed this out in reference to the law of the Sabbath. "The sabbath was made for man, not man for the sabbath," Jesus said (Mark 2:27). Laws are made for persons: persons are not made for laws. Laws are God's way of pointing persons to their intrinsic value as persons so that this value may be most fully realized. Ultimately, of course, the value of finite persons is based on and related to the infinite value of the Person of God. The source of all personhood and value is the most valuable of all.

When a man pollutes the world, then, he is violating a law which God has ordained to help persons. Pollution is an offense to God because He is the One who ordained the laws of purity for the good of persons. When men transgress any law decreed by God they are performing a personal act, for it is an act which is ultimately an offense to the Person of God who ordained it. No man sins unto himself, even when he seems to be sinning only against himself or against his private world. In fact, no sins are really private. All sins are before God. And few sins are really private with respect to other men — fewer as the world shrinks. Pollution is one of the greatest public sins, because, if allowed to continue, it will make it impossible for men to be persons.

Pollution, most scientists agree, is the world's number one problem, for the problems of race and war are a *threat* to mankind, whereas extermination of human life will occur unless the course is reversed. [9] Persons have intrinsic value as persons, for as such they are the creatures of God made in His image and likeness. Therefore, to diminish or destroy this intrinsic value of persons is of the greatest moral consequence. Pollution is not an act directed merely against things. It is an act by persons which affects persons. It is a public sin against the public. It is an evil against persons and the One who made them and made a good world for them.

III. ECOLOGY AND THE MORAL DUTY TO CONTROL MAN'S ENVIRON-
MENT

There is a basic point of Christian responsibility that should not be overlooked in the discussion of pollution or of any other relation which man has with his world. The point is this: God commissioned man to be in *control* of his world. The first man was told to "subdue it; and have dominion over [it]" (Gen. 1:28). Surely this implies that whatever environmental controls are necessary to preserve man's life without destroying its humanity are not only morally permitted but also divinely commanded. [10]

A. *Controlling the Physical Environment*

Pollution control is man's moral responsibility. God commanded that man should subdue and master his environment. The world should not conquer man; rather, man should conquer the world. If man does not control the physical world, then the physical world will control man. And this is the inverse of God's order to creation. Man is to be king or victor over all the earth, not the slave or victim of it.

If man is morally responsible for controlling his physical environment, then it may be necessary for him to legislate the use of the elements. That is, there must be controls on the unwise and selfish use of the earth at the expense of other persons who live here. Men

[9] Carl H. Reidel, *op. cit.*, p. 4 [684].
[10] See chapter twelve above.

must not be permitted to destroy the physical environment of other men.

B. *Controlling the Human Environment*

The moral duty of men to legislate the use of the physical world raises an interesting question discussed in an earlier context. What about people pollution? That is, what about polluting the world with too many people? Do men have the moral right to limit the size of the population? If so, by what means? Birth control? Abortion? These have already been discussed apart from the question of over-population. [11] But what about human controls on the number of people permitted to live in this world?

1. *The Basic Alternatives Calamity or Control?* — Fundamentally, there are two ways of solving the over-population problem. One method is to institute some kind of human controls of it such as birth control, abortion, and/or euthanasia. The other is to let nature take care of over-population in terms of starvation, plagues, natural disasters, and wars (insofar as war is brought on by over-crowding, etc.). That is, the fate of the race can be left to the physical fortunes of the world *or* it can be rationally and morally determined by men in control of their total environment. Men can either plan their future *or* they may submit it to the fates of the world. Pollution can be left to random selection or controlled by rational planning. Which does God intend?

Disaster is not as good as design. God is the Author of the cosmos and not of chaos. The divine command to man is to *control* the world, and man is an essential ingredient in that world which needs to be held in check. True, men were commanded to multiply and fill the earth, but they were not told to over-fill it. The world is of a limited size. [12] It can support only a given, finite number of men. And if men fail in their duty to control their own number, then there is only one alternative to their negligence — nature will level its numbers.

2. *The Morality of Preventing Population Pollution* — The crucial moral question is not *whether* man should control the population but *how* he should do it. The best answer to this is *education*. First, men should be informed of the evils of over-population and of their responsibility to control the numbers of births. This can be accomplished by some form of voluntary birth control. Second, if education does not accomplish the task, then it may be necessary

[11] If and when other planets were to open up for some cosmic pilgrims, then of course, it would take the pressure off the overpopulation of the planet earth.

[12] According to scientists the fossil fuels of the world may run out in the foreseeable future and the world is using up 10 percent more energy than photosynthesis is returning. See Reidel, *op. cit.*, p. 4 [684].

for some *legislation*. Appropriate means of penalizing the over-popu-
lators should be devised. As an extreme measure, *sterilization* of
those who over-produce is to be preferred to the fortuitous disasters
of starvation, plague, and war. The divine imperative is for man to
control his environment and not for the environment to control him.
Abortion is *not* a morally justifiable method of population control.
That is, abortion is not morally justifiable for population control
unless all else fails. And it is difficult to see how abortion could be
any more successful than sterilization. Theoretically, an abortion
would be called for as a means of population control *only if* it could
be demonstrated beyond doubt that this *potential* human life (the
unborn baby), if allowed to live, would actually crowd out or destroy
some *actual* human life. Such instances are surely not abundant.
Birth control is a much better way of population control because by this
means one is controlling the race by *preventing* life from occurring
and not by *taking* a life after it has already occurred. Taking a
potential human life is always a very serious business and it should
never be done unless an actual human life can be saved by so
doing. And it goes without saying that taking an actual human life
(i.e., mercy-killing) as a means of population control is even worse.

There is a strange irony about man's pollution of his world. It is
simply this: if man pollutes his environment long enough he will
destroy himself but the environment will remain. Ultimately the sin
is not really against the environment; it is against the persons who
would live in it and against God who made the world both as a
revelation of Himself and for the good of man. If man destroys
himself from the environment, the environment will remain in one
form or another. Men were made to be keepers of the earth. If they
do not keep the earth, then the earth will not keep them. The question
men should ask themselves today is this: *am I my earth's keeper?*
For if I am not the earth's keeper, then it is becoming increasingly
evident that neither am I my brother's keeper. For this is my brother's
earth. And if I do not keep it, then it will keep neither him nor me.

260 / ethics: alternatives and issues

SELECT READINGS FOR CHAPTER FOURTEEN: POLLUTION

Feenstra, E. S., "The Spiritual Versus Material Heresy," *Journal of American Scientific Affiliation* 29 (1966).

Heiss, Richard L. and Noel F. McInnis eds., *Can Man Care for the Earth*, Nashville, Tenn.: Abingdon Press, 1971.

McHarg, Ian I., *Design with Nature*. Garden City, New York: The Natural History Press, 1969.

Reidel, Carl H., "Christianity and the Environmental Crisis," *Christianity Today* Vol. XV, No. 15 (April 23, 1971).

Schaeffer, Francis A., *Pollution and the Death of Man: The Christian View of Ecology*, Wheaton, Illinois: Tyndale House Publishers, 1970.

White, Lynn, Essay in *Science* (March 10, 1967) reprinted in *The Environmental Handbook*. Published by Friends of the Earth, 1970.

Bibliography

Altizer, Thomas J. J. *The Gospel of Christian Atheism.* Philadelphia: The Westminster Press, 1966.

Altizer, Thomas J. J. and Hamilton, William (ed.) *Radical Theology and the Death of God.* The Bobbs-Merrill Company, Inc., 1966.

Anderson, John B. *Between Two Worlds: A Congressman's Choice.* Grand Rapids, Michigan: Zondervan Publishing House, 1970.

Aquinas, Thomas. *Summa Theologica.*

Armstrong, R. A. *Primary and Secondary Precepts in Thomistic Natural Law Teaching.* The Hague: Guilders, 1966.

Augustine. *Against the Epistle of the Manicheans, The Nicene and Post-Nicene Fathers.* Ed. by Philip Schoff. Grand Rapids: Wm. B. Eerdmans Publishing Company, 1956.

————. *City of God.* Book XIV. Garden City, New York: Image Books a division of Doubleday & Company, Inc., 1958.

Austin, John. *The Province of Jurisprudence Determined.* (1832) London: Weindenfeld and Nicolson, Ltd., 1954.

Ayer, A. J. *Language, Truth, and Logic.* New York: Dover Publications, Inc., 1946.

Bacon, Francis, *Novum Organum.* Chicago: Encyclopedia Britannica, Inc., 1952. William Benton, Publisher.

Bainton, Roland H. *Christian Attitude Toward War and Peace.* New York: Abingdon Press, 1960.

————. *What Christianity Says About Sex, Love and Marriage.* New York: Association Press, 1957.

Barth, Karl. *Church Dogmatics.* Ed. G. W. Bromiley and T. F. Torrance, Edinburgh: T. and T. Clark, 1936-62.

Begeman, Helmut, "Christian Ethics in the Face of the Changes in Marriage and Sexual Behavior," *Lutheran World,* 13, No. 4, 1966.

Bennett, John C. *Christian Ethics and Social Policy.* New York: Charles Scribner's Sons, 1946.

————. *Foreign Policy as a Problem for Christian Ethics.* New York: Charles Scribner's Sons, 1966.

Bentham, Jeremy. *Introduction to the Principles of Morals and Legislation.*

Bonhoeffer, Dietrich. *The Cost of Discipleship,* trans. by R. H. Fuller. New York: The Macmillan Company, 1963.

————. *Ethics.* New York: The Macmillan Company, 1955.

Brunner, Emil. *The Divine Imperative.* Philadelphia: The Westminster Press, 1947.

261

Burnet, John. *Greek Philosophy*. Cleveland, Ohio: The World Publishing Company, 1957.

Camus, Albert, *The Myth of Sisyphus and Other Essays*. trans. by Justin O'Brien. New York: Alfred A. Knopf, Inc., 1955.

Carnell, Edward J. *Christian Commitment*. New York: The Macmillan Company, 1957.

Clouse, R. G., et. al. (eds.) *Protest and Politics: Christianity and Contemporary Affairs*. Greenwood, S. C.: Attic Press, 1968.

Cole, W. G. *Sex and Love in the Bible*. New York: Association Press, 1959.

Collins, Gary, Ed. *Our Society in Turmoil*. Carol Stream, Illinois: Creation House, 1970.

Collins, James, *The Existentialists*. Chicago: Henry Regnery Co., 1952.

Cowan, Marianne. "Introduction," *Beyond Good and Evil*. Chicago: Henry Regnery Company, 1966.

Cullmann, Oscar. *Immortality of the Soul or Resurrection of the Dead?* The Epworth Press and the Macmillan Company, 1958.

Curran, Charles E. (ed.) *Absolutes in Moral Theology?* Washington, D.C.: Corpus Books, 1968.

de Beauvoir, Simone. *The Ethics of Ambiguity*. trans. by Bernard Frechtman. New York: Philosophical Library, 1948.

Epicurus. On Nature. Fragments in Diogenes Laertius' *Lives and Opinions of Eminent Philosophers*. trans. by R. D. Hick. Cambridge: Harvard University Press, 1950.

Eslick, Leonard J. "The Platonic Dialectic of Non-being," *The New Scholasticism*. XXIX, No. 1, January, 1955.

Finn, James (eds.) *A Conflict of Loyalties: The Case for Selective Conscientious Objection*. New York: Pegasus, 1969.

Fletcher, Joseph. "What is a Rule?: A Situationist's View," *Norm and Context in Christian Ethics*. Gene H. Outka and Paul Ramsey, eds. New York: Charles Scribner's Sons, 1968.

————. *Situation Ethics: The New Morality*. Philadelphia: Westminster Press, 1966.

Frankena, William K. *Ethics*. Englewood Cliffs, N. J.: Prentice-Hall, Inc., 1963.

Fromm, Erich, *Man for Himself*. New York: Premier Book, 1968.

————. *Psychoanalysis and Religion*. New Haven: Yale University Press, 1967.

Geisler, Norman L. and Nix, William E. *A General Introduction to the Bible*. Chicago: Moody Press, 1968.

Greene, Norman N. and Sartre, Jean-Paul. *The Existentialist Ethic*. Ann Arbor: University of Michigan Press, 1960.

Grounds, Vernon C. *Evangelicalism and Social Responsibility*. Scottdale, Penn.: Herald Press, 1969.

Gustafson, James M. "Context Versus Principles: A Misplaced Debate in Christian Ethics," in *Harvard Theological Review*. Vol. 58, No. 2, April, 1965.

Heiss, Richard L. and McInnis, Noel F., eds. *Can Man Care for the Earth?* Nashville, Tennessee: Abingdon Press, 1971.

Henry, Carl. *Aspects of Christian Social Ethics.* Grand Rapids: William B. Eerdmans Publishing Company, 1964.

————. *The Christian's Personal Ethic.* Grand Rapids: William B. Eerdmans Publishing Company, 1957.

Hodge, Charles. *Systematic Theology.* Grand Rapids: William B. Eerdmans Publishing Company, 1952.

Hutchison, John A., ed. *Christian Faith and Social Action.* New York: Charles Scribner's Sons, 1953.

Kant, Immanuel. *Critique of Practical Reason.* trans. by Lewis W. Beck. New York: Bobbs-Merrill Company, Inc., 1956.

————. *Kant's Critique of Practical Reason and Other Works.* Trans. Thomas K. Abbott. London: Longmans, Green and Co., Ltd., 1909.

Kierkegaard, Sören. *Fear and Trembling.* New York: Doubleday and Company, Inc., 1954.

————. *The Works of Love.* trans. by Lillian and Marvin Swenson. Princeton University Press, 1946.

Laurence, John. *A History of Capital Punishment.* New York: Citadel Press, 1960.

Lewis, C. S. *The Abolition of Man.* New York: The Macmillan Company, 1947.

————. *Four Loves.* New York: Harcourt Brace Jovanovitch, 1960.

————. *Mere Christianity.* New York: The Macmillan Company.

————. *The Problem of Pain.* New York: The Macmillan Company, 1962.

Luther, Martin. *What Luther Says.* Compiled by Ewald M. Plass. St. Louis, Missouri: Concordia Publishing House, 1959.

McHarg, Ian I. *Design with Nature.* Garden City, New York: The Natural History Press, 1969.

MacGregor, G. H. C. *The New Testament Basis of Pacifism.* New York: The Fellowship of Reconciliation, 1942.

Miles, Herbert J. *Sexual Understanding Before Marriage.* Grand Rapids: Zondervan Publishing House, 1971.

Mill, John Stuart. *Utilitarianism.* (1863) New York: Meridian Books, 1962.

Moberg, David. *Inasmuch: Christian Social Responsibility in the Twentieth Century.* Grand Rapids: William B. Eerdmans Publishing Company, 1965.

Moore, G. E. *Principia Ethica.* Cambridge University Press, 1959.

More, Sir Thomas. *Utopia.* (1516) New York: W. J. Black, 1947.

Nagel, William J., ed. *Morality and Modern Warfare: The State of the Question.* Baltimore: Helicon Press, Inc., 1960.

Niebuhr, Reinholdt. *Moral Man and Immoral Society.* New York: Charles Scribner's Sons, 1932.

————. *The Reasonable Self.* New York: Harper & Row, Publishers, Inc., 1963.

Nietzsche, Friedrich. *Anti-Christ.* New York: Alfred A. Knopf, Inc.

————. *The Basic Writings of Nietzsche.* trans. by Walter Kaufmann. New York: Meridian Books, Inc., 1960.

————. *Beyond Good and Evil.* Chicago: Henry Regnery Company, 1966.

263

————. *Joyful Wisdom.* trans. by Thomas Common. Frederick Unger Publishing Co., 1960.

————. *Thus Spoke Zarathustra.* trans. by Walter Kaufmann.

————. *Will to Power.* trans. by Walter Kaufmann. New York: Random House, 1967.

Nix, William E. "The Evangelical and War," *Journal of the Evangelical Theological Society.* Vol. XIII, Part III, Summer, 1970.

Piper, Otto. *The Biblical View of Sex and Marriage.* New York: Charles Scribner's Sons, 1960.

Plato. *The Collected Dialogues of Plato.* Edith Hamilton and Huntington Cairns, eds. New York: Pantheon Books, 1964.

Plotinus. *Enneads* I, 9. trans. by Arthur H. Armstrong, Loeb Classical Library. Cambridge, Mass.: Harvard University Press, Vol. I.

————. *Enneads.* trans. by Stephen MacKenna. London: Faber and Faber Ltd., 1956.

Rader, Melvin. *The Enduring Questions.* Second edition. New York: Holt, Rinehart and Winston, 1969.

Ramsey, Paul. "The Case of the Curious Exception," in *Norm and Context in Christian Ethics.* Gene H. Outka and Paul Ramsey, eds. New York: Charles Scribner's Sons, 1968.

————. *Deeds and Rules in Christian Ethics.* New York: Charles Scribner's Sons, 1967.

————. *Fabricated Man: The Ethics of Genetic Control.* Yale University Press, 1970.

————. *The Just War: Force and Political Responsibility.* New York: Charles Scribner's Sons, 1968.

————. *War and the Christian Conscience.* Durham, N. C.: Duke University Press, 1961.

Rand, Ayn. *For the New Intellectual.* New York: New American Library, 1961.

————. *The Virtue of Selfishness.* New York: A Signet Book, 1961.

Regan, James. T. "Being and Non-Being in Plato's Sophist," *Modern Schoolman,* XLII, March, 1965.

Ressig, Herman F. *Social Action*

Robinson, John A. T. *Christian Morals Today.* Philadelphia: The Westminster Press, 1964.

Russell, Bertrand. *Human Society in Ethics and Politics.* New York: Mentor Books, 1962.

Santayana, George. *Three Philosophical Poets.* Harvard University Press, 1927.

Sartre, Jean-Paul. *Being and Nothingness.* trans. by Hazel Barnes. New York: Philosophical Library, Inc., 1956.

————. *No Exit and Three Other Plays.* New York: Vintage Books, 1946.

Saunders, Jason L. ed. *On the Nature of Things in Greek and Roman Philosophy After Aristotle.* New York: Collier-Macmillan Limited, 1966.

Seneca. *Epistulae Morales.* Vol. II. trans. by R. M. Gumere. New York: Oxford University Press, 1965.

Simon, Yves. *The Tradition of Natural Law; A Philosopher's Reflections.* New York: Fordham University Press, 1965.

Singer, Marcus G. *Generalization in Ethics.* New York: Alfred A. Knopf, 1961.

Sittler, Joseph. *The Structure of Christian Ethics.* Louisiana University Press, 1958.

Stegall, Carrol R. "God and the USA in Vietnam," *Eternity,* March, 1968.

Stevenson, Charles L. *Ethics and Language.* New Haven, Conn.: Yale University Press, 1945.

Taylor, A. E. *Plato: The Man and His Works.* New York: Meridian Books, Inc., 1960.

Taylor, E. L. H. *The Death Penalty.* Houston, Texas: St. Thomas Press, n.d.

Thielicke, Helmut. *The Ethics of Sex.* New York: Hawthorn Books, 1960.

Tillich, Paul. *The Courage to Be.* New Haven, Conn.: Yale University Press, 1952.

————. *Dynamics of Faith.* New York: Harper & Row, Publishers, 1957.

————. *Morality and Beyond.* New York: Harper & Row, Publishers, 1963.

————. *Ultimate Concern.* London: SCM Press Ltd., 1965.

White, Lynn. *Essay in Science* (March 10, 1967) reprinted in *The Environmental Handbook.* Published by Friends of the Earth, 1970.

White, Lynn, Jr. "The Historical Roots of our Ecological Crisis" *Science* 155, 1967.

Williams, G. L. *The Sanctity of Life and the Criminal Law.* New York: Alfred A. Knopf, Inc., 1957.

Wirt, Sherwood E. *The Social Conscience of the Evangelical.* New York: Harper & Row, Publishers, 1968.

Yamauchi, Edwin. "Historical Notes on the Trial and Crucifixion of Jesus Christ" *Christianity Today.* April 9, 1971.

Index

267

Scripture Index

269

270